A MAN OF HIS TIME

Secrets from a Halfway World

A Memoir

STEVE ROCHINSKI

www.mascotbooks.com

A Man of His Time

The author has recreated events, locales, and conversations from his memories of them. In order to maintain anonymity, in some instances the author has changed the name of some individuals.

For more information, please contact:
Mascot Books
620 Herndon Parkway, Suite 320
Herndon, VA 20170
info@mascotbooks.com

Library of Congress Control Number: 2019915412

CPSIA Code: PRV1119A
ISBN-13: 978-1-64543-020-9

Printed in the United States

To Kathy, my wife and best friend; Anna and Alex, my children; Laurie, the mother of my children; Ronnie, my brother, the Flame Warrior; and Barrie, my teacher, chairman, and friend.

Contents

Prelude

THERE IS A FAMOUS VERBAL exam designed to measure how well someone can think on their feet and outside the box to solve a problem. It goes like this:

A frog is sitting on a railroad track that spans a small pond. A train comes down the right-of-way and startles the frog. At the last second, the frog jumps into the air and lands in the water.

Question: where was the frog when it jumped?

A typical answer is, "That's easy—the frog was on the track."

To which the inquisitor answers, "Actually, the frog was on the track before it jumped."

Confused and a little flustered, the first responds, "Okay then—the frog was in the air."

To which the inquisitor answers, "No, the frog was in the air after it jumped."

On rare occasion, someone offers this as the most accurate answer to the question: "The frog was neither here nor there—you know, it was in-between. In an old, and seemingly dead language, the frog was *in medias res.*"

From the time I was very young, I was clear on where I was going and what I had to become. The outcome of my conviction is that my entire life, professional and otherwise, has been driven and defined by music. This, in turn, informs everything else within the sphere of my perception of life's realities.

I also happen to live with the constant presence of an annoying hyper-awareness of details, because I possess what I refer to as selective total recall (and please, remember to chew that irony at least 32 times before you send it down and around). A tangential characteristic to my selective total recall is that I was born without sonic filters, possibly as a result of some form of synesthesia. Imagine hearing every random sound in your waking hours as having value in the context of a musical thought or idea, where every sound is in the foreground, demanding your constant attention; or, when the slightest flaws in musical intonation, noisy eaters, and close-miking on beverage commercials come across as amplified irritants which can drive you to the edge. It's a handicap I have learned to use to my advantage, but it also makes me quite difficult to live with.

By the age of three, I awakened and answered to a singular awareness of how I perceived and processed the world around me. It all came down to sound. I never questioned it or asked anyone about it, because I simply believed that what I heard, everyone could hear. The simplest way to describe it is an acute awareness of the simultaneous interactions between the musical whole and its parts.

During my earliest years, outside forces imposed a long destructive impact on my life, against which I possessed no power to control or eliminate: the Annihilators. Among them was Myr, a force of evil I had to face, literally running and hiding for my life under the threat of death, and entirely alone in my struggle to survive such terror, all before the tender age of eight. The indelible, tattooed stains of this dark, destructive central experience still linger—faded, but never gone or forgotten.

On the bright side, there are and have been people in my life, whereby if they hadn't been present, life would be awfully boring and dull. There's also a very good chance I would be alone and dying from high blood pressure, diabetes, and prostate cancer while going blind from glaucoma, as a vicuna-covered hermit with only a guitar, living in a leaky geodesic dome on the side of a small mountain, 45 years in the making.

The central narrative of this book is my lifelong fight to survive the effects of childhood sexual abuse: my resurrection and reclamation by tracking through the wreckage of my values—to salvaging what was toppled, but never destroyed; my transformations—moments not only as fixed accents to events in time and space, but in the aggregate outcome of those moments, beginning with the child-man, to the man-child, to the father, to the man. There are disturbing accounts of events, especially for those closest to me hearing them for the first time. Music is the central reason and force for my lifelong survival.

Throughout my life, the equilibrium I have worked to establish and maintain between the good, indifferent, and evil forces has been precarious, to say the least—much like an emotional mobile-type sculpture, in which the heaviest, single static object is my fight for my recovery, with everything else struggling to hold its own against such overwhelming weight and energy.

I'm confident you'll enjoy this book. Once you're finished, consider donating it to your local library and take the write-off. If you don't need the write-off and the library shows no interest, use it to level out an uneven table leg. (There is always an uneven table leg somewhere.) I consider this book to be a full-service endeavor with many useful purposes, so by all means, be creative. You'll cry, you'll laugh, you'll think, you'll call for take-out.

POEM FOR NUMBER 15
— Steve Kuhn

Now and then, I think of when
His teeth were so small and white
He laughed when he heard
The sounds in the distant night

Later on, his smile was gone
His lips spoke of silent things
The least he could do was more
Than his life would bring

Oh, what a shame,
What a terrible shame

To be lost and found below the ground
Beneath every child at play
His life was so short,
It's hard to believe today.

1ˢᵗ PARTIAL

In Medias Res

"Man is a being of volitional consciousness."
–Alice V. Rosenbaum

…I AWOKE ALONE IN A strange single bed, in a strange room, in a strange building, dressed in strange clothes, among strange smells and unfamiliar sounds. My first thought was, *I'm dead, and this is the room where a soul waits to have a knee-to-knee meeting with God—to interview for a rare opportunity to fill a limited number of passenger seat openings for performing crash tests in the after-life; a coveted position despite so few souls are ever qualified to fill such a burdensome responsibility.*

I envisioned a door in red button-tufted leather with a small porthole window—one of several doors lining a long and well-lit hallway. In a goading and mocking manner, on the other side of the door, waiting for the Applicant, stands a wooden, one-legged stool with mandatory footrests. Inside and above each door reads a sign: *"Spe Aeterni Fontis,"* which I hear as, "Pan-One Testifiers." Under the Latin, in smaller letters reads, "Hope Springs Eternal."

A nurse named Dolores entered my room and asked how I was feeling. The best bedside manner she could afford was rote and clinical, as if she had done this countless times with a hard-won understanding of one universal and irrefutable constant: that everyone in this place was fucked up and down on every point of the compass. Regardless of how and why one arrived, we all shared the same place: the Awful and God-damned Bottom. After 10 minutes of cool persuasion, she convinced me I wasn't dead in a waiting room, anticipating the word on whether I would get an interview for God's most impossible day job.

In reality, I was in a locked room on the A-Ward, also known as the psych ward, of Elkhart County General Hospital, on the flat, barren, upper-most northern border of Indiana. It was the coldest time of the year—January of 1984. The nurse checked my vital signs and asked if I was feeling any after-effects from the shot of chlorpromazine she administered the night before. I was too groggy and hungover to respond, however, landing in Freud's compost shed had a fast sobering effect on me. My name was now Number 15, which corresponded to my room assignment. Replacing a name with a number was a way for the staff to communicate with us; it also provided them with some emotional detachment from our human identities and lives and histories. Our reduction in identity brought with it the expected de-humanizing effect. Women were housed in the even-numbered rooms.

I was able to retrieve some memory of my actions from the previous night. My concern was not how much property damage I created, but more importantly, what kind of harm came to Lisa. As it turned out, she was physically fine. The only harm came to my guitar.

The magnetics and weight of living so many lives in my first 30 years finally reached a convergent interaction between repulsion and implosion—a "re-plosion" of sorts. No matter who I thought I was, or believed I should be, this was a crash landing on the bottom of an emotional underworld from which many never return.

Like some poor bastard in a Kesey novel, I could leave anytime or stay for the two-week minimum. I chose to stay and take time to sift and probe my first 30 years—to figure out how so much unresolved pain and sorrow influenced my sense of life and worldview. This was my chance to understand where it all went so terribly wrong, if, in fact, such a conclusion was possible to impound. For the first time ever, I would have to do a stripped-down examination of the good, the bad, and every chromatic variation between those polarities—all in the belief that somewhere in my past may lie answers to many questions. At the very least, I would trip on a clue or two pointing to how this current chokehold became my reality. I was hopeful that the process of healing to set me back on the rails could begin; to continue my journey in fulfilling a life in sound, which

I knew from a young age would be the central reality of my life: to examine if clear and objective value judgments are the only worthy consideration for making choices in life. A course of change wasn't going to be easy to track, but rarely is anything worth doing.

During my first full day of wandering through the day room among the Shuffling Wall Kissers—the blanked-out, silent, slow-moving, chain smoking shades-in-motion, forced to light up with only an open electric coil embedded in the wall—my mind spun in neutral in a state of utter incredulity. Instead of dwelling on this setting of sur-reality, I focused on ways to occupy my thoughts before going deeper into an inevitable mental slice-and-dice in my first appointment with Rutt, the Head Shrinker. Above all else, I really missed having my guitar.

In this place, you were either an alcoholic or a candidate for occupational therapy, otherwise known as basket weaving. The alcoholic assessment was a fascinating piece of oblong reasoning. If I was adamant in my denial of the addiction diagnosis, the experts countered with unshakable conviction claiming I possessed an alcoholic personality—by their reasoning, simply having the alcoholic personality was the minimum requirement for being an alcoholic. Denial was a sure sign, and that made you a prime supplicant for A.A., attended by a healthy dose of God and Jesus.

Early on, a random thought banged against my shuttered fontanel: maybe I was born in the wrong decade, the wrong generation—at least 20 years later than my sensibilities and tastes. Women often described me as an old soul—someone who seemed to have lived many lives—insinuating I was living beyond my years. The old soul description never made much sense. Fortunately, my head-first dive into this romanticized bullshit didn't last. Such a distraction from getting to the heart of my matters wasn't going to work; there was no point in starting from an abstraction. I first had to face this caustic truth: I was in an existential state of being neither here nor there, and that was unacceptable. In the light and shadows cast upon me in my lower 30, my story begins in a place called Cheverly…

For The Time Being

AFTER MY PARENTS WERE MARRIED in 1952, in an inauspicious and unceremonious fashion—a starter pistol wedding replete with blanks—their first apartment was at 3551 55th Avenue, in the town of Cheverly, Maryland. The historic significance of the town's name is unknown, but Cavalier or Chivalry are as plausible an explanation as any. We lived on the blue collar side of town on the edge of historic Bladensburg, nestled up the hill behind the venerable Cheverly Theatre. This old movie house was a major destination for cinematic and adolescent hormonal entertainment for many towns over many years. Built in 1947, in the Art Deco/Streamline Moderne style, it always looked out of place. It resembled a giant, misshapen birthday cake plopped down in the middle of an unpaved parking lot, fringed by non-descript, low-slung commercial buildings.

The Cheverly was a poignant landmark and reminder of happier times throughout the 1960s. It also represented a provincial boundary for me—the beginning of a direct eastbound path to Kentland on Route 202. Directly in front of the theatre, Route 202 split off to Route 450, which also headed east, and took me to a parallel world of pass-through neighborhoods, contiguous to Kentland, so distant and strange. Breeching this landmark, heading in the opposite direction, took me to evermore distant roll-away places like Bladensburg and Mount Rainier, and eventually across Eastern Avenue into the District.

Our apartment was in a tiny project of three story, dark red brick buildings, built with a Third Little Pig level of solidness, like those seeded around the Prince George's County landscape. Entire villages in the area contained these gulag-lite structures, built sometime between the First and Second World Wars, to ease overcrowded inner-city District housing—oppressively hot in the summer and meat locker cold in the winter. Dark and dingy cramped hallways smelled like a medley of diluted Lysol, oil soap, and unidentifiable stovetop fumes. I remember all of these apartment buildings throughout my life had some such smell, and those old crank-handle casement windows with loud, drippy, Freon-sucking air conditioners running nonstop from late May to mid-September.

The casements always contained wavy, distorted panes proving beyond a doubt that glass, when in a frame long enough, is not the solid it appears to be, but an extremely slow flowing liquid. The pooling of the amorphous solid creates the distortion as it loses its fight against gravity; a perfect metaphor for the human lifecycle. The short 10-inch journey from top to bottom, trapped by small, immutable forces of nature, takes around 30 years.

Such wavy panels of fun house mirror distortion surely created spellbinding images of life on the outside for inhabitants on the inside. If I had been born 20 years earlier, I could have been one of the robed and weary stoic souls, gazing out at a glazed, mid-twentieth century world in post-war recovery, lighting my next cigarette from the final embers of the one before and the one before, before dousing it into the bitter remains of a cup of Sanka gone cold—one simple soul as the desiccated optic nerve behind the corneal languor of a lonely and tired window, both waiting with great dispassion for replacement.

So much lay ahead for my Caesarian-born new life. Although this apartment was my first home, it was more like a home away from home, because I was a month overdue—crossing over from my original due date in December of '53 into January of '54. I'm sure it would have been fine with me to stay put in the home I grew into and loved over 10 long months of gestational nirvana. However, at risk to both my mother and me, Dr. O'Donnell performed the cut-and-tug at three minutes past nine-o'clock on a cold, late January morning—and, much against my will. This harsh, unsettling resettlement foreknew nothing worthwhile in life would come easy. The roof top eviction from my mother's womb began my micro-nomadic life, living my first 16 years in only 10 square miles. My transient footprints eventually covered a mere one-half of a square mile for most of the 1960s. Yet, many different lifetimes can unfold within the ambit of short acreage.

The stage was set for the beginning of chaos and dysfunction that would tear at my soul and rip apart my family, setting all of us on separate right-of-ways for survival. Some of the tracks were set for travel, some were built ad hoc along the way, and others led to nowhere, in spite of well-laid rails and ties.

———

I CAN'T IMAGINE HOW TWO adults, a 10-year-old boy, and a baby lived in that cramped walk-up and kept their sanity; maybe they didn't. My brother and I were in one bedroom, our parents in the other. I'm sure my unpredictable nocturnal stirrings did little to contribute to some sense of early brotherly love.

Dad's sole possession was a black 1949 Plymouth given to him by his father, bought new with the first royalty check Granddaddy received from a hit song he wrote in collaboration with Guy Lombardo's brother, Carmen. This little tune played an important role throughout my life.

When my parents met, she was working at the local county hospital, which wore a scathing reputation for being one big collective waiting room for the morgue located in the basement. Mom always recalled her time in the job with considerable fondness and pride, in large part by her attraction to her boss. Otherwise, the myriad jobs she held in her long working life were dead-end desk clerk positions. At best, her occupational skills were minimal. She held no aspirations to do anything more than what allowed her to get by, while at the same time harboring a deluded attraction to a life of glamour and flamboyance—and as a consequence of always choosing to depend on a man, she often paid a price far greater than what she bargained for.

Having little money, my parents furnished the apartment with donations from family and friends. One memorable item was a black wrought-iron bookcase. This thing was no ordinary bookcase. Several pointed spires jutted vertically, spaced evenly along the top edge from one end to the other. To my misfortune, I came to have an intimate, but short-lived relationship with this imposing piece of ill-designed scrap metal. As this event unfolded, Ronnie was doing his favorite summer vacation activity: sitting in the front row of the Cheverly with a hundred other screaming kids, waiting for the weekly intermission raffle to start. His eyes fixed on a cowboy cap pistol and holster set, hoping to hear his number called. It turned out to be his lucky day. My day would have a very different outcome.

After losing my balance reaching for a toy on the top of the bookcase, a spire speared me and broke completely through the upper part of a facial neutral zone, where lip and cheek were still trying to decide where one ended and the other began. It protruded upward and out, just below and to the right of my right nostril. So, there I was, initially tearless and silently hanging in the balance, like a diapered Polish sausage in a Scranton deli window, with no empirical frame of reference for much of anything beyond the needs of eating, sleeping, and a diaper change. If the spire had gone straight up, instead of to the right, I would now be the owner of a double philtrum. The purpose of the vestigial single philtrum, that strange little crease between the upper lip and the nose, is already enough of a mystery.

With my first permanent battle scar securely marked, we eventually packed the Roadshow and moved to Greenbelt, a town in Maryland, about 10 miles northeast of the District line, where we lived from 1955 to 1960. This is where my earliest memories, fears, joys, and lifetime motivations sprang to life. Greenbelt enjoys a unique distinction in the history of the United States as the first government-sanctioned Socialist enclave, which I came to know and fully understand only years after we left.

My father Stan, called Sonny on his side of the family, was only 23 when we arrived in Greenbelt. Two years earlier, he was living his dream in the middle of a very promising, long-term career in professional baseball. (Before my father was 20 years old, no fewer than 10 professional football and 10 major league baseball teams were clamoring to sign him.) My birth motivated Dad's decision to leave baseball, with his painful realization that raising a family on a minor league salary would be more of a struggle than it was worth. His prodigious athletic prowess defined him all throughout his formative years. Such talent allowed him to pursue his life ambitions on his terms, as choices he loved, and not as a means to meet obligations and responsibilities to others.

From here on, his role as a husband and father were external impositions, and this was no easy reality for an only child with a strong self-obsessed streak to accept. After pulling the trigger on baseball, it was all Dad could do to prove to us, and especially his father, that he could hold down some shit job for more than three months. My mother, Lorraine, was 28, in her second marriage, and along for the ride with my half-brother Ronnie, carting her own special designer brand of disappointments and distractions. Ronnie had nine years on me. Our sister Karen would not be born for another two years, in 1957.

With a loan from Granddaddy, they put a down payment on the far-right corner unit of a white-shingled quadplex at the top of 53 Court on Ridge Road, unit K. Our new home cost my parents all of $1,800. This move was a major step up in their quality of life, but hidden in this upward turn was a weak emotional foundation built on too much sand. The cracks would come quickly and would be irreparable. All I could do was survive to the next, and the next, and the next period of adjustment. It was during this time that my interior Penrose Spiral began to emerge as the first sign of some form of synesthesia.

IN 1935, GREENBELT WAS THE first of three U.S. government-sanctioned socialist communities in the United States. We lived in what is now called Old Greenbelt, built in 1937, during the New Deal Era. A government bureaucrat named Rexford G. Tugwell hatched the concept behind these planned green communes. Eleanor Roosevelt also played a major part in assisting Tugwell with the design and layout on what were originally acres of tobacco fields adjacent to the Beltsville Agricultural Research Center, a mysterious federal facility with "U.S. Govt. No Trespassing" signs on barbed wire fences. A tour Mrs. Roosevelt took of 19th century English garden cities allegedly inspired her vision for this government-controlled quasi-utopia.

On the plus side, Greenbelt was beautifully laid out. There were endless trees, gardens, and shrubs. All of the commercial and social activity was centrally located—the Center.

At the Center was everything one would need in the way of day-to-day goods, services, town offices, and recreation. At the center of the Center was an iconic stone sculpture called "Mother and Child," created in 1939 by the WPA artist Lenore Thomas Straus. Some of my earliest memories are of standing before this mysterious and overwhelming statue, studying it from all angles. The entire structure measured 15 feet tall to the top of the mother's head, with a male child standing snuggled in front of his mother, just barely between her knees. The boy faced away and to her left with his eyes closed, drinking from a cup she was holding. The seated mother looked down slightly, with her eyes closed, while kissing the head of her child. Their faces projected an image of tranquility which is forever burned in my heart's memory. Even through all of the cold hardness of the stone, both images projected a deep, serene sense of motherly protection and love, as solid and uncompromised as the material from which it was carved. I felt calm and quiet when standing it its shadow. I knew this wasn't an aspirational image of a mother and her child, but simply the way it should always be.

Greenbelt's most innovative infrastructure was the walkway and road system. The road names were a further reflection of the thoughtfulness in its idyllic design. They were pastoral, yet practical names like Northway, Southway, Woodland Road, Parkway, Ridge Road, Plateau Place, and of course, Crescent Road and Centerway. The layout and design insured that no one would ever have to cross a main thoroughfare. An intricate network of pathways connected the backyards of many homes, located along what seemed like disconnected courts and enclaves. Pedestrian underpasses took you into and out of the Center.

I always felt secure walking alone along the pathways. I recall a sensation, a mysterious warm flush radiating from my chest throughout the rest of my body, like being transported to another place and time—maybe a place and time from long ago, or a place and time yet to be? These images and feelings of safety and security would be all too short-lived. Being too young to understand the concept of hope, I believed that Greenbelt was the way life would always be—the watermark of my first conscious expectation in life.

ONE MAJOR ATTRACTION FOR FAMILIES with children was Greenbelt's many playgrounds. Each had only three rides: a squeaky push-and-ride carousel, a huge sliding board, and a swing set with three metallic-voiced swings with wooden seats. This equipment was made of heavy, flat, gray metal made to possibly stand up to at least one nuclear blast.

During my time in the playground, my earliest awareness of how I heard and perceived pitch and sound came to be; it was never abstract. Because of the way my brain was wired, I could hear meaning and context in the most mundane sonic moments. My ears enlivened when the carousel and the swings were all at once in motion. There was a memorable counterpoint between the squeaks and the silences. When the swings were silent for a moment, the carousel would sing, and vice-versa.

When the two rides sang their little metallic songs at the same time, there was a wonderful moment of harmony, where two different pitches converged. The call-and-response between the swings and the carousel sounded like the moment in the song "Over the Rainbow," where Dorothy sings, "Someday I'll wish upon a star..." From this unique musical interval, I referenced a distant home center, as if the interval was calling for a note not yet there, but I knew there was a place waiting for that single note, and for only that note. The sensation was thoroughly captivating. It's no wonder this interval would be at the heart of a song at the heart a story of a little girl lost in a magical land with only one heart's desire: to go back home. There was no one I could tell this to. My awareness of and reaction to this sound was my first secret. Many years later, I learned to identify this sound as the interval of the minor third.

ONE AFTERNOON, RONNIE AND HIS friends invited me to participate in my first gravity-defying event promising far greater thrills than a swing set. They offered me a blanket fling; sailing me high into the air and then caught a moment before hitting the ground. Ronnie sensed my trepidation. He assured me the blanket would work exactly like the small trampoline firemen used when rescuing someone jumping a short distance from a burning building. This was an opportunity to prove I was as much of a man-in-waiting as the rest of them, in spite of the scuffed Buster Browns I was wearing on my little boy's feet and a shock of white-blond hair.

The blanket on the ground welcomed me to assume my place in the center. I laid down with my eyes closed and opened them as they slowly raised the fabric. An endless Marian blue summer sky awaited me. The energy and excitement of anticipation and the rush of adrenaline made me feel almost chilly. I felt like I was close to wetting my pants, which, as a four year old, was easy to inspire. Ronnie set the count-off to three—slow and deliberate. As he got closer to three, I could feel their synchronized energy setting the blanket a little lower. As I lay suspended and cocooned in anticipation of the big fling, the countdown began: "One...two..." I never heard three.

The next instant I was flying—a towhead chrysalis, airborne and far higher than I had ever experienced. The sky awaited and blossomed before my eyes with its clouded, enticing invitation. At the peak of the rise, I seemed to hang there indefinitely. Then, as I turned over in mid-air, I saw the cocoon I left behind stretched out in anticipation of my return. The enveloping embrace of the blanket came far too soon. The feeling of the soft and safe arrival rippled and rolled over all of my other sensations. I believe this was my first time ever experiencing what we have always been told doesn't and can't exist: perfection— oh, but to the contrary. It was also my first significant memory of surrendering to something called trust.

We continued with this game for a while longer, until Ronnie's friends became bored and wanted to go to the Center to hang out at the statue and mark their territory by spitting on the sidewalk, hoping for girls to walk by. To my surprise, their decision to abandon the blanket was made while on my way down from the peak of my rise. Once the stars and twittering birds from inside my head subsided, Ronnie and I headed home.

There were two things I couldn't get out of my mind for the rest of the day: how trust, surrendering any control that I had over my fate over to someone else, was a mysterious feeling that came to me so easily, and would I experience those indescribably wonderful sensations below my waist ever again?

EARLY IN THE PREVIOUS DECADE, my mother, at the in-between age of 18, married a notorious gangster from Newport News. They produced Ronnie, making him my half-brother. To me, he was never anything but my brother. Mom's relationship with Ronnie's father was complex, and one of the darkest chapters of her life that haunted her to her dying day. The advantage for me having a brother nearly 10 years my senior was that I could study life's little growing-up quirks at the feet of a master.

Ronnie had his group of friends and I had mine. I enjoyed my friends, but I liked his more. I identified with them, which, for a little boy, was nothing more than infatuation with their adolescent swagger and bravado. He and they were cool and they had girlfriends. They rode big two wheelers with playing cards clipped to the spokes which made hot sounds. They played baseball and football. They spit whenever the urge would strike, which seemed to be every minute and a half. They could stay out long after dark and—they used cuss words.

It would be an understatement for me to say this was the year my vocabulary would increase exponentially. Not only were my brother and his friends well versed in the ways of profanity, but my parents were also skilled in the ancient art of imprecation. Mom was selective, Dad was a little less so, but the big guys knew and used every possible word with a hard-sounding suffix, attached to a consonant-laden prefix, to ever come out of the king's language. A constant chorus of —ss, —it, —ck, —ard, —ole, and of course, the gold standard measure for having successfully arrived at adulthood, —uk.

Everyone used these words wherever and whenever they liked, but when adults cussed, someone was usually angry, frustrated, or in disbelief about someone or something. It seemed when Ronnie and his friends cussed, they were engaging in a never-ending search for all of the possible places in a sentence where they could deploy their favorite sound. I could rattle off these words with the biggest and best of them. I used profanity as if I was making public service announcements. It was my time to join the choir.

On April 6, 1957, one day after Ronnie's 12th birthday, our sister Karen Lee was born. During Mom's pregnancy, I was very aware of how her body went through a strange transformation. One day, I saw a long vertical scar below her navel. When I asked her about it, she turned to me and said flatly, "You did that to me. That was where you came out." Those were her only words on the subject. I turned away in shame for doing something that seemed to bring harm to my mother.

Karen's birth was difficult for everyone involved. Yellow jaundice was all I heard the adults talking about. Eventually, the subject was dropped. A half-century passed until my father told me the entire dreadful story: Karen's condition was the most severe case on local record. In a private meeting between Dad and the doctors, they told him there were two choices: they could let her die, or they could perform a relatively new, and very risky blood transfusion, with a high probability that Karen would suffer some form of permanent brain damage. At the all-too-young age of 25, Dad made two fateful decisions: first, he would not involve Mom in his decision. Second, he chose the transfusion. Karen lived.

We returned home to our daily routines, with one exception: there was now a newborn girl sleeping in a crib in my parents' bedroom and I wasn't sure how I felt about that. Being upstaged by my baby sister was something I simply had to accept. Fortunately, I had more important things on my mind, such as shadowing Ronnie and his friends whenever I could.

———

MY RIDGE ROAD DAYS STARTED the same as most any three year old's in the 1950s: a bowl of cereal while hanging out in front of the TV with *Romper Room*, waiting to hear my name called, which was never. Then, on to the *Treasure House* with the captain, and ending the day watching *Dobie Gillis* handwringing over a girl or money, or one of the many live TV theatre productions such as *Playhouse 90*: a daily television microcosm of life morphing from childhood into adulthood, compressed for time, and formatted to fit my day with commercial interruption, including the alternate sponsors. In between the extremes of a typical 12 hours, I abstracted and rehearsed everything I saw coming out of the

Magic Light Box throughout the day. And the music—there was always music everywhere I turned.

During this time in the popular culture, we experienced an unusual event of minor, but enduring historical significance: one evening, off in the distance was a mysterious repetitive loop of music. It sounded like something you'd hear in a movie while a boy and his dog are playing in a field. As the sound got closer and louder, another sound emerged, like a casement window air conditioner—an odd mix of two different mechanized sonic sensations. Then, bright lights appeared, moving toward us. A huge white truck with a blue edge around the bottom pulled into the court with its engine competing for prominence with all the other sounds. On the side of the truck was a cartoon picture of someone dressed in a blue jacket with a large sugar cone-shaped head. There was a big sliding window in the middle of the passenger side of the truck and a bright white fluorescent light bathed the inside of the truck. The driver, dressed in white with a cool paper hat, opened the window, looking as clean as the inside of the truck. We were witnessing the first ever Mister Softee ice cream truck in Greenbelt, and one of the first to ever appear anywhere.

In the 1950s, the delivery of milk, bread, butter, and eggs to one's door was commonplace—a tradition of service going back decades into the 19th century. A scissor and knife man also drove into the court from time to time, with a huge sharpening wheel in the back of his small panel truck. Even a diaper service van arrived twice a week to exchange the obvious, but an ice cream truck bigger than any others? And this was no ordinary ice cream—it was soft serve slowly swirling out of a big, shiny, industrial-strength, stainless steel machine with handles and spouts. Unlike its counterpart, the Good Humor truck, this mammoth vehicle was a virtual ice cream factory. The ice cream—chocolate, vanilla, or better yet, mixed swirl—came in light and crunchy cones. It was an entire industry contained on four wheels—only in America!

1957 was also the year I started noticing girls—unusual, perhaps, for a three-year-old boy. I didn't have to go far in my quest for female attention. There was an abundance of girls in the court. In the first unit on the right were the three sisters with a single mother. The youngest of the three was six years my senior. Many decades later, Ronnie confided to me these three girls carried what was, in the parlance of the 1950s, a bad reputation. Ronnie would know because he and Alice, the oldest of the three, carried on with a loose and swinging time.

Two doors away from them was a beautiful little constellation of four girls with Filipino-American parents: Debbie, Donna, Sharon, and Terry—the four sisters. These girls were nice and quite different from the girls on the end. Donna was my favorite. She was my age and had a sweet disposition. I felt much young affection for her.

One final far-reaching major public event I recall during this transformative year happened in the early evening hours of Friday, October 4th, 1957. We received a televised announcement of national urgency. Word of this imminent event spread quickly through the court, and soon everyone was gathered outside. Adults stood in small groups talking with nervous animation, while we kids ran about, stopping from time to time to gaze skyward.

Then, all became quiet. One of the parents pointed upward and shouted, "Look, there it is!" The "it" turned out to be a tiny, but clearly visible light moving rapidly across the night sky. At first, I thought it was an airplane. I was hoping it was Superman, but no such luck. It was Sputnik I, the first artificial satellite launched the previous day by the Union of Soviet Socialist Republics. We, the people, stood there stunned by fear, trembling with fascination. The future, slightly larger than a basketball, traveling at 18,020 miles per hour, was carving a permanent furrow in the fabric of space and time, and the American body politic, before our eyes. The space race was on and it was ours to win.

53 Court: no kings or queens, no barons or baronesses, but plenty of jesters and jousters, and maybe a knave or two. Life, for now, was pretty great.

The Guitar

MUSIC IN OUR HOUSE WAS constant. One luxury of Ronnie's that he taught and trusted me to use was his record player. I loved stacking several records at a time, as everyone did, and listened in succession. Once all of the A sides played, I flipped the stack for the B sides, with nearly 20 minutes of uninterrupted music. Ronnie set specific rules for listening without his supervision: no touching the surface of the records; never stack more than five records at a time; do not bump the needle; and never remove the nickel taped to the edge of the tone arm.

My brother had the recordings of the greats: the Everly Brothers, Buddy Holly, Fats Domino, Little Richard, Elvis, and even Sheb Wooley. Dad was a huge fan of jazz and jazz-inspired popular music—Stan Getz, George Shearing, Charlie Parker, Dinah Washington, and Sarah Vaughn were among his favorites. All of this music swirled about and captivated me. My wiring crackled and set unstoppable synapses in motion. It was always the parts and the whole in a constant, simultaneous musical interaction with one another that moved my mind and massaged my soul.

I began noticing how specific moments in some songs aroused in me a more intense emotional response. It was the same feeling I experienced on the Greenbelt pathways—I felt as though I was taken to another place and time, which could have been in the past, or a time yet to be, awaiting my arrival. Years later, I came to understand the musical element causing this intense feeling was the song momentarily changing from major to minor. Cole Porter had it right... "There's no love song finer, but how strange the change from major to minor, every time we say goodbye."

My conceptual development was breaking the surface like countless blooms of water lilies. My attraction to order, logic, and purpose was overwhelming. I envisioned a matrix in my mind, an immediate, localized form of the greater Penrose Spiral, representing coordinated points of repetition with variation over a longer period of time—a vivid image always in ascension, with specific times, dates, and locations attached to it, like markers or signposts. With each new year, another step or landing in the spiral would assume its rightful place. I came to learn of this as the spatial sequence/number form of synesthesia. Within this mental image, my desire to make music with a guitar was like three-dimensional strands and paths running through all of my interior landscapes and images, sending me to internal retreats.

The oddest abstraction I encountered was my first experience with transitional interface. It's curious how this occurrence happened in such a common-place location: a sidewalk framing a parking lot in a shopping center, joining the cutout that enabled a vehicle to enter:

The shopping area was in College Park, next to the University of Maryland. The curb, a flat, vertical 90 degree angle from the top of the sidewalk to the roadway, gave way to a graceful and gradual rising curvature with a slight gentle edge to greet the front tires of the car. The edge let you know with an ever-so-slight bump that you were about to change from one location to another. The feel of the car changing from the road surface into the shopping area was mesmerizing. All at once there were boundaries ensconced in a sense of concurrent freedom.

This was the beginning of what I came to understand over my professional lifetime as a phenomenon that I term the "artist's contrariety"—self-imposed boundaries that increase freedom of expression. The parking lot event was the physical manifestation of what I was hearing, and what I would later experience as my fingers moved across the frets on the neck of a guitar—a very strange forecast of a life in constant search for the next transitional interface and innersole innerlock.

STANLEY JAMES ROCHINSKI SR., MY granddaddy, never wavered in his belief that I would one day do good and notable things. He was born in 1900 in the coal region of Glen Lyon, Pennsylvania. Granddaddy claimed to have been born with a caul, a membrane that covers the newborn's head, creating a veil-like image on the face of the infant. In Granddaddy's native Polish language, the word for caul translates to "born in a bonnet." Superstition claims that a person born with this facial covering would always have good fortune in life. He understood it to mean that he could see into the future. Granddaddy was also an old-world, devout Roman Catholic who fell to his knees anytime and anywhere the Holy Spirit struck him. The theological contradictions between his claims on the mystical world of the paranormal and the world of Christian Catholic faith eluded him. He never finished the fourth grade and, for a time, he toiled in the Pennsylvania coalmines alongside his older brother Pete, whom he idolized. Eventually, he followed Pete out of town to ride the hobo rails in search of work and adventure.

Despite Granddaddy's lack of formal schooling, he learned to function very well in a world, which at that time, required not much more than a sixth or seventh grade education from most people. He did, however, possess a highly innate understanding of the gullible side of human nature. He made no apologies for exploiting such weakness whenever it served his needs. Simply put, the man loved to fuck with people's minds. From the tales he told me about his rail time, he honed that characteristic to a fine edge. The man could snatch a fly in flight in a flash, and drop it into a mostly finished plate of food in some low-budget beanery, as a way to not only avoid paying for the meal, but also to get a second plate of food on the house. Whatever it took for him to survive and live to enjoy another day, he developed it to a high art form. He was also the most loving man I have ever known.

In 1914, Granddaddy made his way into the U.S. Army at the age of 14 by doing what so many boys did during World War I: he lied about his age. He became a medic and saw brief combat in Belgium. He never discussed the war, but he suffered a serious back injury during combat and would from time to time convalesce in the local veterans, hospital. Following an honorable discharge in 1919, he subsisted on his disabled veteran pension.

Granddaddy wasn't a musician in any tangible instrumental sense, but he did possess a strong musical ear and sonic sensibility. He was also a very accomplished dancer. In fact, he was so good, when word began to spread of his talent during his service time, the officers conscripted him as a dance instructor for their wives and children. While his buddies did the bullshit grunt work, he lived in comfort doing what he loved.

For a short time, he also worked as a terp—a professional dancer—on the Pantages circuit, known as the Pan-time, with the Ziegfeld Follies. He eventually settled in Washington, D.C., where he met my grandmother, Mary. Two years later, in 1932, my father, Stanley Jr., was born. He would be their only child. To them, he was Sonny and he could do no wrong—an expectation my father would time and again spend his best years living down.

The young family started out in the northwest section of the District before moving to a small farm in Warrenton, Virginia. Granddaddy provided support by raising chickens and training dogs, in addition to his modest service pension. The owner of the property eventually gave them notice that he was selling the farm. This was an opportunity for the family to move back into the District, where Dad could start school.

In addition to the pension, Granddaddy's skills at living on his wits and instincts would now become a necessity for his family's survival. One of his talents was the ability to mimic any kind of foreign language dialect, along with modulating his voice several octaves above or below his normal speaking range. His virtuosity would soon be put to skillful use as one of the great lessons of persistence and mendacity unfolded.

Their plan was to find a home in the northeast section of the District. The paper advertised an apartment in a triple-decker located at 1026 Otis Street, Northeast. The owner was asking $30 a month for rent, and said they were the first to inquire about the rental. Granddaddy said he could afford only $25 a month, and asked if the owner would consider bringing the rent down $5. The owner was in no mood or position to negotiate a lower price. It was a seller's market, and he knew the first to arrive would not be the last. Granddaddy told the man he'd think about it and would call back later.

Never one to back away from a challenge, Granddaddy drove around for about an hour finalizing a scheme to convince the owner to lower the price. He found a gas station with a pay phone where he changed a dollar bill into 20 nickels and began calling the owner. In his most penetrating female Yiddish voice, he asked if the apartment was still available. "She" was told yes, for $30 a month. The "lady" on the other end said she could only afford $15 a month and would he consider lowering it. The owner said absolutely not.

For the next several hours, while my grandmother and father sat in scorching heat, Granddaddy called at 10 to 20 minute intervals. Using every possible vocal ruse, he made lowball after lowball offer, with nothing over $18. He could hear the owner wearing down, but not yet ready to crack. Using his last nickel for the final call, and in his normal voice, he told this broken man that after spending several hours talking it over with a priest, his family, and the guy who ran the filling station, he couldn't afford to pay more than $25 a month. The man was so relieved to hear from the first people to inquire about the place, he said if they got there in a half-hour, he would sign a lease for $20 a month.

Once they relocated and settled into this new and exciting city life, Granddaddy worked whatever deals and scams he could to provide for his wife and son. The die was cast for the lives of three people whose paths would diverge in ways no one could imagine. The most devastating catalyst for change was my grandmother abandoning her son and husband after falling in love with Granddaddy's cousin.

———

GREENBELT'S BARBERSHOP, LIKE ANY IN America, was a gathering place for men to discuss any topic—from the latest sports news to the pressing issues of the day. Our shop came with three chairs. Old, white-haired men stood there and clipped and shaved men and boys all day long. The red and white spinning barber pole was mesmerizing, at least until vertigo set in, causing me to lose balance and fall on my ass. The clean, sweet smell in the air penetrated my airways in an instant. The combination of tobacco smoke, talc, cologne, and Barbasol went straight to my young, un-sullied brain. I suppose this was my first time experiencing intoxication, because I never failed to swoon a little from the initial blast. A radio was always on in the summer with a baseball game, or the soft easy-listening sounds of popular instrumental music, accompanied by the soft puffing and gentle whoosh of ceiling fans in constant motion.

One day, Ronnie and I stopped in to get our usual summer cut. While waiting for the next chair, I needed to use the restroom in the back of the shop. When I turned on the light, an entire wall covered with nudie pin-ups and calendar girls greeted me. Real, grown women in various exposed breast poses beckoned and dared me to inch a little closer for a better peek. I stood there in a state of shock and nervous tension. I knew I should not be seeing these naughty, ribald displays, but I didn't have it in me to turn away. Eventually, a barber came looking for me and brusquely snapped me out of my gaze. I never did get to the bathroom. Ronnie greeted me with a funny little smirk, as he watched me return to the waiting chair with a stunned look in my eyes. I have no doubt Ronnie knew that back room many times before I ever landed there.

Soon after my barbershop back room revelations, on a hot and miserable day, I heard a live electric guitar coming out of the three sisters' house. I ran to greet the sound faster than my legs could carry me. A bald man with a large bump above his left eye was sitting on his amplifier, playing and singing like his life depended on it. Adults stood around listening and singing, drinking beer and having a great time. I was dumbstruck by what I was seeing and hearing—the way he moved his left hand up and down the neck, as his right hand strummed and picked the strings was like nothing I ever saw. Yet, it all made some kind of sense to me. Every time he changed the location of his left hand, a new and beautiful sound emerged, as if he was telling a story. It seemed so effortless even though he was using three fingers at once. He too knew the secrets of the transitional interface. I immediately ran home and begged and pleaded for a guitar, and all they could say was, "No, we can't afford it."

Not long after that encounter, something happened that would forever impact and verify the direction I knew my life would take:

The aftermath of the fire was a scary sight. Among the broken windows were black soot and char marks covering the backside of the house. Half of the roof was a huge hole. It looked like violence frozen in time and smelled of burned everything. I made my way closer to what had been the backdoor. Peering into the dark, the burned-out cavity of what once was a living room came into view. With the light shining in from the opposite side, I noticed in the front yard that someone piled all of the belongings destroyed throughout the house—broken and burned furniture, dishes, a bird cage which was likely for the pet who perished, were among unidentifiable scraps of a life gone up in flames. I wanted to see the debris up close, but the only way to do so was to take a chance and risk walking through hell's waiting room.

It took me some time to get up the courage and take the first step into the dangerous gauntlet of soaked cinders. I quickly made my way to the sunlight at the other side. I stood in the shadow of a massive pile of water-soaked, fire-smoked shit, trash, and jetsam. The sickening smell extended beyond the borders of the yard. This was no place for a four year old.

Looking skyward, toward the top of the heap, an object appeared. Moving in closer to the base of the mound, I saw that it was a guitar perched at the very top—a jewel crowning a world in ruin. I scrambled to the top without ever looking down. Grasping the guitar by the neck, I held it tight as I balanced on the mound of trash, feeling the neck in my hand—something was now there to complete me, starting from my fingers, to my hand, to my arm, to my mind, to my heart, and to my soul. This was the physical manifestation of what I heard in the metaphysical world of the minor third—something uprooted was calling for completion, for reciprocity, like when you awake from a vivid dream where the details are missing, and only the complex of feelings remain. For those few stolen moments, I was the minor third. There was no power in existence capable of prying the instrument from my hand. I departed with my Arthurian prize and made my way up the small hill to Ridge Road, never once relaxing my grip, and never once looking back.

I went straight to the couch and strummed nonstop, fascinated by how the strings vibrated, expanding and then returning to their normal size once the sound died down. What I was witnessing was a waveform created when a string is set into motion. The energy traveling between the two end points caused the string to divide itself—first in half, then in thirds, fourths, fifths, and so on, instantly at the speed of sound. It was hypnotic and perfect. I was witnessing the real-time creation of harmonics, or partials—when a self-dividing fundamental tone not only recreates itself, but also gives birth to different tones; a sonic microcosm of the creation of the universe. A simple fact of my life from that fateful day onward was born. There are two kinds of musicians—those who want to do it and those who have to do it.

How Brakemen Break And Live To Tell The Tale

WE CHILDREN IN THIS POST-WORLD War II baby boom world-in-recovery were easily entertained. We climbed 30-foot trees and played in potential polio-laden puddles of water. We ran after DDT fogger trucks as they emitted toxic gas to kill mosquitos. We jumped from swings and shed roofs. We rode in cars and school transports without seatbelts, and we hid in the underbrush near the dump from cycloptic trash men, who enjoyed nothing more than scaring the piss out of a kid who dared to breech their municipal wasteland. We even lurked around secret government agrarian research installations responsible for inventing who in hell knows what—maybe corduroy cows for easy detection, in the event they wander off in the middle of the night? Embracing risks as a way of exposing life's uncertainties and facing them head-on was exciting and important. It gave us the feeling we were alive and living life on the edge. If we paid attention, learning to overcome such perils would play an implacable role in developing our survival skills, especially as a reward for fighting the good fight. It was such a great time to be alive.

On an entirely different order of risk and first-time encounters, there was a girl in my first grade class named Sylvia. One day, after an early dismissal, we walked home together. I invited her into my house for a snack. For some unknown reason, Mom was gone when we arrived. After we ate, we went up to my room to play. There was something about being alone in the house that stirred some biological desire to explore one another—so normal and common with little kids. She was as willing as I was to see where this activity would lead. Before I knew it, she was laying naked on my bed. All I could do was stand there and stare like a deer caught in headlights; frozen in a strange combination of fear and excitement. Neither of us considered that our parents knew this was an early dismissal day. Once Sylvia dressed, she rushed out of there and ran. She was two hours late in returning home.

Later that day, our teacher, Mrs. Pulliam, showed up at my door. A major "oh shit" moment was about to unfold. After some quick reflection on the day's events, it occurred to me that she must have been told Sylvia was late arriving home. I got a major ass whipping for having started this chain of events.

The next day in school, Mrs. Pulliam called me out in front of the entire class for inviting Sylvia into my house without parental supervision. All I can remember is sitting there, with my head down and my chin resting on my folded hands, like a hang dog being admonished for stealing food from the kitchen table. I felt the heat and flush of public embarrassment and humiliation coursing through me. Sylvia was conspicuously absent from class.

Years later in high school, I had several vocational shop pals who were from Old Greenbelt. I asked if they had known Sylvia and someone said he knew her and her reputation. He said that for years, she was the victim of incest by her father and became pregnant with his child. She still lived in the Greenbelt house, which was in serious disrepair from years of neglect. Her mother and two siblings had long since left with their whereabouts unknown. The horror I felt from hearing those words and knowing the hell this sweet, innocent little girl endured for untold years was so intense, it brought me to the verge of tears.

Not long after this event, the true, defining inaugural moment for my burgeoning sexual awareness happened one night when my parents went to a neighbor's house to play canasta: Ronnie was out and Karen was asleep. The only person available to babysit for Karen and me was the youngest of the three sisters. I was five and she was 12; she might as well have been 20. Once my parents left, we settled in to watch television. Like most people did during these early years of primetime entertainment, she turned out the living room light to enhance the viewing experience. Afterward, I got into my pajamas and she asked me if I wanted to play a new game she learned. Of course, any reason to stay up late was fine with me, so I agreed. We went downstairs and took our place under the dining room table. She plugged in a green night light and explained the game was Spin the Bottle. I had never heard of it.

When her spin stopped, it landed on me. She immediately reached over and gave me a kiss on the lips. I felt a combination of many different things: I was scared, worried my parents would walk in and catch us; I was excited and remember feeling the same sensation when Ronnie and his friends were throwing me in the air on the blanket; I didn't want to stop; I felt naughty, like I was doing something wrong, but at the same time it felt okay because maybe I was now a big kid; I felt like I had a girlfriend, just like the big kids. Confusion clouded my mind. We continued under the table and then she led me upstairs to my parents' bed.

I lost all awareness of where and who I was. I wasn't a five year old boy with parents and a brother and a sister. I was someone in the middle of some kind of Never Never Land playtime because of the surreptitious enticement of a 12 year old girl. It was as if Wendy magically came to life in my parents' bed—and all for her sake. She found someone who was safe and would do her bidding. Then, it was over.

One thing she kept repeating was that I was to never say anything to my parents or anyone else; this would be our secret. I promised I wouldn't tell anyone. The few times we saw each other in the court, we acted like nothing ever happened. She ignored me the way a girl of 12 would ignore a boy of five. I felt a little fear and apprehension in her presence, tempered with a pang of affection—another layer of childhood stripped away and discarded.

I never saw girls the same way again. For a five year old boy, what lingered was a double-edged sword of towering dimensions. I had no guidance and no direction to confront such complex feelings, to sort through it all. What we did was no Candy Land game board with markers and a spinner, with a beginning, middle, and end, where the person across from me was playing by the same rules as me. There was a winner and a loser, but no box to store the pieces and set on the shelf of a closet, putting the game out of your mind, only to come back the next day and start all over again, hopefully with a better outcome for the loser than the day before.

My instinct was to keep all of these thoughts and feelings inside, folded over and over and over again, so the layers would hide the deepest feelings of shame and confusion. What was an indelible series of iniquitous moments ended for me in guilt. She had no idea what she unleashed, and I had no idea what I allowed her to do. With no means of resolution, I was left with this experience to form one facet of how I would regard women for most of my adolescent and adult life—as ready and willing playthings for physical pleasure, a temporary emotional escape from pain, with no basis in love as an answer to the shared values that define one's sense of life. I now had a room in my mind for my first dirty secret, and it was a lonely place to visit.

FROM THE START OF 1958 and into 1959, Mom and Dad were arguing about things that only adults create and live by. One of the things they fought about was money. Although Granddaddy was always cash-ready to help tide us over, Dad and Mom grew tired of having to put up with his constant presence as a condition for accepting his generosity. This was particularly troubling for Dad. On one hand, he loved his father, but Granddaddy could be a pain in the ass in his own gregarious and charming way. I loved having him around. Dad's lifelong aversion to speaking on the phone was probably the result of Granddaddy calling the house at all waking hours—a ploy to continue having contact with his son. After my grandparents divorced, when Dad was around 14, Granddaddy became over-protective and smothered him with vigils on his whereabouts, making sure his son stayed focused on his goal of becoming a star athlete.

In Dad's teen years came his attraction to running the streets, chasing girls, gambling, liquor, and worst of all, his brief addiction to heroin. His junk habit came as a complete surprise to me. He revealed it when I was around the age he started using the needle. That was his one and only explicit cautionary tale. He explained that it was something a lot of young guys were doing in those days, because their jazz heroes such as Charlie Parker and Billie Holiday were hooked, so hipster chic required that one follow suit. Granddaddy knew all too well that his influence and control had limits. In the end, he was powerless to redirect his wayward son.

Dad scraped together what work he could, but nothing lasted. He was a talented, restless, free-spirited young man in his twenties who was in over his head, and always looking for something better to come along and offer itself for the taking. Deep down, he was smart enough to know that approach to developing a life with the responsibilities of a family was not going to work. Gambling was always his fallback to such dead-end work, and eventually, that would be his downfall.

The mounting pressures of his responsibilities must have become unbearable. One evening at the dinner table, without warning, Dad stood up and heaved a full plate of food against the wall, shattering everywhere. It was the first violent act I saw come from my father, and it wouldn't be the last. He seemed to be pathologically losing his mind at the age of 27, and all of this tension and fighting was taking a heavy toll on all of us. Ronnie was staying out of the house for long periods of time, and at any opportunity, he would stay overnight at a friend's house. Karen's crying fits became more frequent. I was showing impatience with the smallest things and my incontinence was out of control. The situation in the house grew more and more desperate.

As Dad became more unstable, he was consuming a lot of booze and was content to sit in his chair, staring in silence as he twirled his hair with an index finger. None of this made any sense to me. This was my Dad, the baseball player—my hero and protector. He would never hurt me. I loved and trusted him with all of my heart.

Another major fight between my parents started over Mom's prolonged disappearances and Dad being completely out of work. I never saw or heard it get this loud and violent. At one point, he hit her full-force with his fist, knocking her back on the couch. As I ran from the living room, the only place to hide was the kitchen. As she came around the corner and into my hiding place, she grabbed a long butcher knife and warned him to stay back. He was able to wrest the knife from her hand and then grabbed me and pulled me in close in front of him. Dad held the knife out in front of me and demanded she come clean about where she was. As she stood her distance in the doorway to the kitchen, she pleaded and begged, through more tears than I ever saw, to please let me go. I stood in silent tears waiting to die.

In a flash of clarity and reason, Dad remembered I was his only son, as he was his father's only son—maybe his Catholicism compelled him to walk everything back from his only son, to the point he was taught to believe his God's only son was the living and dying embodiment of all sacrifice to and for the end of time. He didn't have to go off the deep end to realize that all of the long-term damage he would do to himself, the family, and the family name was not worth it. He knew it was simply wrong to hold the child accountable for the choices and sins of the parents. He released the knife and broke into tears as he hugged me and spoke reassuring words of sorrow and regret.

Granddaddy knew the time came to intervene and save his family from disintegrating. He was going to find Dad a job no matter what it took. It was time for him to call on his bravado and his talent for disguising his voice. After some investigating, Granddaddy came up with a plan to contact someone at the main yard of the B&O Railroad in Baltimore. He called the main office and spoke with the foreman asking if there were any open positions. The voice on the other end of the phone said, "Mister, there are no jobs here. We're pink-slipping people at this very moment. All they've left me with is a skeleton crew. I'm sorry. I can't help you."

The old man was never one to take no for an answer.

The next day, in his inimitable fashion, Granddaddy was able to contact by phone the head of the Interstate Commerce Commission. He disguised his voice and told this person that he was U.S. Senator Estes Kefauver from Tennessee. He explained that a constituent, who was relocating into the area, needed a job. The next day, Dad got a phone call from the railroad office asking him to report to the main yard in Baltimore to start work the following day. In this spectacular and unprecedented move, Dad walked through the main gate to begin work as a brakeman as dozens of long-standing railroad employees walked out of the gate on indefinite furlough. "Mister, I don't know how you pulled this off, but in my all of my years on this job, I have never seen anything like it." Those were the first words Dad heard when he reported to work.

The job of the brakeman entails many responsibilities. Besides helping to slow down the train under emergency conditions, the job requires checking all of the couplings, verifying that the signals along the route worked, and overseeing the moment-to-moment safety of the train's exterior operating systems. Once all systems were go, the brakeman signals the conductor, who signals the engineer that it's safe to start rolling. The brakeman spends his remaining time hanging out in the caboose until the train reaches its destination.

As far as jobs went, being a brakeman was as far removed from baseball as one could imagine. It didn't take Dad long to learn the job, and his gratitude to Granddaddy for pulling off such an astonishing magic trick didn't go unnoticed. For the time being, the paychecks helped to bring some needed stability at home. Dad's work schedule sometimes required him to do night work, which meant he left in the morning and wouldn't return until the next afternoon—typical of an interstate run into Ohio or West Virginia. The calm at home between my parents didn't last. Something besides money was tearing at both of them. There were two brutally violent incidents raising serious concern among the authorities, family members, and the neighbors.

The first was during a weekend crab feast at the Tuxedo-Cheverly firehouse: Mom and Dad were excessively spifflicated and something started between them. I was trapped in the backseat of the car while they were having this vicious fight in the front seat, as Dad was attempting to drive. Without warning, he reached over, opened her door, and pushed her out of the moving car. To my shock and horror, my mother went tumbling and rolling onto the ground and across the roadway. Dad stopped the car and several people came running over to help her as they subdued him and calmed me down. After she arrived at the hospital, the police determined she was going to be okay with only scrapes and bruises. She decided not to press charges, although Dad spending a few nights in jail would have done everyone some good.

Another fight started over some kind of accusations he leveled at her. He threw her on the couch, and beat her, full force, with his fists. There was nothing she could do but cover her head and cry out for help. I stood by the front door watching this and something in me snapped. I ran as fast as I could, jumped onto his back, and pounded him repeatedly with my fists as I screamed and cried in white hot anger for him to stop. Time allowed for tempers and feelings to calm and settle, but not without lasting damage.

Dad continued working at the railroad. Ronnie was still in and out, but more out than in. Between my fantasies of being Clark Kent turning into Superman in an instant, and listening to music wherever and whenever I could, I was living on tenterhooks in worried anticipation of the next fight to erupt between my parents.

Speaking of Superman, on June 16th, 1959, the unthinkable happened— Superman died. Ronnie pulled out the morning edition of the *Washington Post*, and there it was: George Reeves allegedly put a gun to his head and pulled the trigger. The concepts I processed were overwhelming, especially the meaning of a new word—suicide. Although I knew from experience my favorite toys and ducks and chickens given as Easter presents didn't always come back after disappearing, I believed people's lives went on forever. But now, Superman, who was Kal-El on Krypton, but on Earth, Clark Kent; who was actually George Reeves, who, before George Reeves, was George Bessolo; who was born George Keefer Brewer 15 days and 40 years before me, died as Superman. I wonder which of these identities he believed he was as the hammer came down on the rim?

DAD CAME OFF OF AN extended night shift and was quite shaken and in tears from a devastating accident that occurred on the shift before his. A young brakeman was in the process of joining a coupling between two boxcars when, without warning, the boxcar moving to the stationary car was upon him and the man became coupled in between the two. When Dad arrived, the poor soul was still alive, only because the intense pressure from the couplings kept his severed torso intact.

Medical and rescue personnel were on the scene when Dad arrived. The brakeman was conscious and aware of what happened to him, although he was in an extreme state of shock. When they asked him for any final requests, all he wanted was to have his wife notified before they uncoupled him. The only reason anyone could figure for making such an unusual request was so they could tell her he was still alive at the time of the phone call. This was in all likelihood so he could give his wife, with the fewest details possible, a few more minutes of hope he would somehow survive this rare, but always fatal accident. He then asked for someone to call a priest to have his last rites administered.

Once the priest arrived, everyone cleared away so only the brakeman and the priest were present. After a few minutes passed, the medical crew and the supervisor, along with the engineer and the conductor, returned to the scene. The brakeman requested the priest stay with him while they released the coupling. The supervisor asked if he had any last words to pass on to his wife. To the best of Dad's recollection, the brakeman said, "Tell her I love her and the kids. There is no one but me to blame for this. Tell her there was never a day when I didn't see her like it was the first time ever. Tell her I'm sorry I won't be able to grow old with her, and please tell her I looked forward in our old age to the quiet moments when we could just sit and talk about our wonderful time and life together."

As the brakeman began to slip into unconsciousness, he did his best to thank his co-workers and rescue team for doing everything they could to help him. He signaled he was ready for release. "Go ahead, let me go," he said. He asked the priest and the conductor to please hold his hands and for the priest to please sing his favorite hymn, "Shepherd Me, Oh God." As the priest sang, the conductor, through his own tears, spoke softly as he stroked this young man's head. He knew him for barely a month. He whispered assurances that everything would be okay; his wife and children would be well taken care of. As the priest continued through choked-back tears to sing the hymn, the conductor intermittently told him he loved him. The man would attempt to mouth the words of the hymn as he drifted in and out of consciousness. A moderate rain started to fall, but the brakeman never shed a single tear.

The next sound to crack through the night was the deafening hiss of air. The hydraulics released multiple tons of torque pressure between the gigantic clasps designed to hold together thousands of tons of raw locomotive power and dead weight freight. Slow and imperceptibly, the two boxcars parted. The priest and the conductor were the only ones remaining, as the rain fell at an ever-steadier rate. They never released their grip on the brakeman, as the lower half of his body remained rested against the inside of the coupling of the stationary boxcar.

In his final moment, and barely conscious, the brakeman had two final requests. His first was for everyone, except the conductor and the priest, to leave the area because he didn't want them to have to witness what condition his body would be in after being freed. His second request was that he wanted everyone to remember him as a whole man, and for the priest and conductor to keep the upper half of his body rested on the lower half until someone arrived to remove him, so he would remain as bodily intact as possible. The brakeman wanted to minimize what the medical personnel would have to see as they removed his body.

Shortly thereafter, the conductor resigned, the priest left his calling, and though no one ever heard from him again, allegedly he began drinking to excess and ended up on Baltimore's skid row. My father took 10 days of sick leave. The calm and quiet in our home was palpable.

DAD EVENTUALLY RETURNED TO THE job. He was re-assigned to the freight yards located in the Ivy City area of the District, off of New York Avenue and Florida Avenue, Northwest; a huge, sprawling facility operating nonstop every day. On the first night back, he worked in an area of side tracks, where a line of recently emptied box and tanker cars were standing to be sent down the line and hooked-up to a waiting locomotive. He had to check that the brakes were off and that the coupling from the engine to the single car was in place. Then, the empties could roll one at a time down the hill to the waiting engine. In light of the recent coupling accident in Baltimore, he was in no hurry to get this job done.

The speed of this procedure was slow and deliberate. After securing the engine and freight car, the engine moved at a crawl. Once the engine got to the hill for the final approach to the waiting main engine, Dad walked the short distance back to the next empty car to prepare for the trip. Other than some standard issue tools and a really cool-looking gold-plated key he used for access to certain kinds of doors, his main piece of equipment was a signal lantern. The night wore on and everything was going smoothly. What happened next would justify his vaunted position as the grand marshal in the poor bastard parade.

The boxcar uncoupled from the engine. This would not have been a major problem, except it occurred prior to the beginning of the downhill portion of the track. He waved his lantern at the engineer with the fervor of Diogenes, but to no avail. The only thing left to do was to run after the boxcar and jump onto the access ladder to the huge brake wheel at the top. Dad caught up to the boxcar just before the slope. Several yard workers also saw what happened and were running behind him. He climbed the ladder and reached the brake wheel as the boxcar started the long slight descent to the line of waiting cars. This situation was not looking good and was about to become quite surreal. He set the lantern aside and turned the wheel as fast as he could. When the wheel reached its terminal point, there was nothing—the brake was broken. As the empty car continued to pick up speed, the men running behind the boxcar screamed for Dad to hang on.

By now, the speed of the boxcar reached about 20 miles per hour and continued gaining speed. In about a quarter of a mile, it was going to make violent contact with the last car in line. There was no line of sight from the back of the boxcar to the point of impending contact. Dad figured if he held tight to the ladder and pressed his body against it, he could end up with a crushed ribcage from the impact. The only way he was going to get out of this alive was to hold on with both hands and time it so he could let go at the point of impact, and hopefully land in an area not littered with railroad track or ties or any other kind of industrial strength shit.

Workers lined up along the last few hundred yards of the track, in a manner reminiscent of the crowds who watched him run in for a touchdown during his Ohio State football career. As he passed the line of men, one of them shouted when to let go and jump off from the side closest to the ladder. An area containing piles of dirt was fast approaching. If Dad timed it just right, he could let go with a good chance of landing in the dirt, and maybe survive with some bruises and a fracture or two. In a few seconds, there would be a violent collision. He got the signal to jump. Unfortunately, it was a second too late. He was standing half on the ladder with his back to it as he held on with his right hand. His other half was hanging off the side, cleared of the ladder. From the vantage point of the men on the ground, the lantern flew in one direction, resembling a shooting star; Dad flew up and away in the opposite direction.

By some estimates, he cleared the roofline by more than half the distance from the ground to the roof. This put him sailing through the air, heels over ass, at about 25 feet. All anyone heard was the Doppler effect on his scream as he sailed to his ultimate landing point, followed by the muffled sound of impact. As his great fortune would have it, he overshot the anticipated dirt pile and landed in a hole containing about four feet of standing industrial effluvium and spillage of a quality found only in a railroad freight yard. As everyone rushed to help, he was already standing in a state of mild shock. Someone handed him a half pint of whisky, which he consumed in record time. Once they determined Dad was okay and didn't need any medical attention, he was sent home for the rest of the night. His supervisor suggested he take a few days off to recover and report to work after the weekend.

Upon returning to work, the first thing he did was look for his lantern. No one saw it anywhere in the vicinity of its descent. Later that day, a call came in from a freight yard in West Virginia asking if anyone at the D.C. yard left a lit lantern on top of a boxcar up near the engine.

───

I WAS SOUND ASLEEP. RONNIE was staying over at a friend's house. Karen was in her crib, also asleep. I awakened to a combination of Mom's screams and the sound of major destruction. The terror I felt put me in a state of immobility. This wasn't the kind of kid terror one imagines as a pretend monster under your bed waits for the room to become completely dark before slowly making its way to crawl in next to you and eat you alive. This was an all-out assault on my amygdala starting with my most acute and responsive sense—the audio pathway. I stayed in bed frozen with fear, too frightened to cry or go see what was causing this violent sound. Eventually, there was an uneasy quiet in the house. I fell back into sleep until the next morning.

When I awoke, getting downstairs took forever in fear of what lay ahead of me. When I turned the corner into the living room, it looked like a good day at the Aberdeen Testing Grounds. Dad was nowhere to be found. Mom was on the telephone with her head and body covered in lumps and bruises. She went upstairs for a while and then returned without saying a word. Eventually, we arrived at Nanny's house and stayed there for several days. We returned to Greenbelt and the coffee table with the hole was still there. The television was sitting there with the remaining picture tube glass removed; now it only was a big empty box standing on four legs. The three-foot golf trophy with the little guy on top, initially embedded where the picture tube once existed, was standing next to the television. Someone patched and painted the hole in the wall. Dad returned and things seemed to be back to normal, but with little said between him and Mom.

Many years later, I learned why Dad took such violent and destructive action: he went to do a night shift and upon arriving was told they had enough of a crew and to return home. When he arrived, he found Mom in bed with the lover he suspected she had for quite some time. The puzzle pieces fell into place. The affair she was having was what he alluded to the night he held the knife to me in the kitchen—the affair was what precipitated the beating on the couch and his pushing her from the moving car. Dad finally reached his breaking point. His mind finally snapped.

No one in any kind of relationship, especially one based on a lifetime commitment of love, ever deserves abuse of any kind. The only thing Granddaddy could do was recede to the shadows as his son—the one with so much potential for doing exceptional things, the darling of the Washington sports press corps, the son of a successful local songwriter—released years of pent-up anger, disappointment, and self-loathing. His emotional rubber-banding probably started at a young age and eventually released a hard and violent snap-back. However, this was not the final act of this tragicomedy. The penultimate blow was Dad being furloughed from the railroad because of massive layoffs. He was now one of those men he passed on the way in, when they were on the way out.

Another fear-filled awakening came again in the middle of the night—this time, not by the sound of shattering glass and wood, but a loud and long series of knocks at the front door. I stayed in bed as Mom answered the door. The next thing I heard was the sound of unfamiliar voices in their bedroom. Dad's voice was among them. The talking stopped followed by the sound of several footsteps going down the stairs. I went to the window looking out onto the court. To my surprise, there were many parents in the court standing around gawking as Dad walked out in handcuffs to one of several waiting police cars. I was too frightened to go downstairs and see firsthand why he was being arrested and carted off to jail. Once everyone was gone, all I could hear was Karen crying for Daddy. Mom was on the phone in tears telling Granddaddy what happened to his son.

As I LAY IN BED, I searched the corner of my pillow for the end of a feather that made its way to this small outlet to freedom. Once I captured an unsuspecting quill, I slowly pulled it out. I never pulled them out quickly. I liked the tension and release I felt in the feather as the pillow slowly set it free—unlike the cut and tug I experienced on the day of my birth. Once it was free, it was mine. There must have been hundreds of feathers under my bed from the hundreds of times I did this. It gave me splendid comfort and consolation to slowly and gently rub the quill across my face and my arms. I imagined how a baby bird must have felt as its mother rubbed her wing against her hatchling. This was my secret way of putting myself to sleep and to escape from this adult world, which seemed to hold so much promise for a kid so eager to love the things that mattered to him. As usual, sleep took its time making its way to my bedroom. As I drifted off, music was the last thing on my mind. During much of the disintegration and breakdown of my family, I had no motivation to listen and pay attention to that which I loved so much—as I so much loved to do.

The feather ever so slowly made its way down to the floor to join countless others and, like all of the others, the feather was never in a hurry to arrive; it was never in a hurry to be released; it was never concerned about how far it had to fall.

The Longest Distance Between Two Points Is A District Line

THE NEWSPAPER ARTICLES REPORTED THAT a white male in his late twenties, with sandy blond hair, estimated to be six feet tall and weighing about 160 pounds, walked into the Langley Park branch of Lenders Savings & Loan Company prior to closing and pulled a pistol on a young teller. He demanded she hand over all of the money in her cash drawer. The robber drove off in a late model white Mercury Comet with the license plate number obscured by mud.

The robber, smelling of liquor, got away with only $300. He also took a moment to confess he was doing this because there was no food in the house, and he had two small children who were going hungry. The first part of the statement was true, because he was once again out of work. The second part was extreme hyperbole. There's a good chance my father would have gotten away with this asinine act if he hadn't gone bowling afterwards, distracted from attending to one important detail: he forgot to remove the mud he used to cover the license plate…another poor bastard moment brought to you by Bowl-a-Rama All Thumbs Ten-Pin Alleys with Gutter Compensators.

Later that night, a Greenbelt patrol officer making his rounds randomly glanced into 53 Court and saw the car. There was a statewide all-points bulletin out on Dad and the car with the muddy plate. Dad's long-time lawyer was a prominent D.C. attorney named Stanley Dietz. (It was Stanley's wife, Aleta, who set up my parents for their first meeting, which, upon reflection, brings to me a whole new meaning to the term blind date.) Despite Dietz's pleas for leniency, Dad was found guilty and sentenced to a year in prison, followed by six years of probation. Why we left Greenbelt soon after his incarceration was never explained to me. All I knew was we had to leave. One thing was certain: Mom needed a full-time job to support her three children. The public humiliation of my father's felony conviction—as the capstone of years of publicly displayed dysfunction and violence in this small town—was likely too much for her to bear.

We took temporary shelter with Mom's parents. One day, to my good fortune, I found solace when I found a guitar belonging to Uncle Lee, on the bed in the back-porch room. I sat spellbound and distracted from all of the turmoil, as I endlessly strummed back and forth across the strings. I focused on the low E string, watching the same hypnotic harmonic wave form effect I experienced with my rescued and water damaged first guitar. The beautiful low E never stopped resonating throughout the room. I imagined what it was like to be inside the string from the beginning to the final moments of the wave. This time, no one asked me to stop as I sat peacefully in such a time and space.

———

WE EVENTUALLY LEFT NANNY'S AND landed in the District, but not where you could easily see the Washington Monument or the Capitol. There were no museums or wide open green spaces or memorials to our founders. We were in Southeast Washington, off of Wheeler Road, in High Point Apartments—the first of many ironically named apartment projects awaiting us for the next 10 years. High Point living was for those who have hit an all-time low point, with those dark red brick buildings, and cramped hallways smelling like oil soap, Lysol, and stovetop aromas arguing in stark disagreement while seeping through those crank casement windows. From Cheverly to Greenbelt to the District, in seven short years we went from the squalid to the charming, to the squalid with variations. The music—as the fugue of our life—was now in development; repetition of a primary theme evolving as a succession of contrasts.

Dad was in prison. Granddaddy found this apartment and promised us this residence was temporary. Mom got a full-time job working as an order clerk for a floor covering and tile outfit located in Maryland. In the meantime, Granddaddy gave her money to hold everyone over until she got her first pay-check, as well as covering the first month's rent.

During this difficult time of abrupt change and adjustment, in an act of unsolicited brotherly love and protection, Ronnie stepped up and escorted me to my first day at my strange new school. Ronnie introduced himself and me to my new first grade teacher, Mrs. Pheffer. She asked him if I had any special interests, and he replied, "He loves to read the newspaper." The teacher looked astonished. "Seriously," Ronnie insisted. "He reads the newspaper every day. He'll read it out loud if you ask him." She escorted me into the classroom and got the class ready for a reading lesson.

The lesson started with each of us reading from an easel with pages of phonics—consonant and vowel sounds next to a little drawing of the object the sound represented. I burned through the exercise while others struggled. Once Mrs. Pheffer saw this simple display of my skill, she decided to hold me in for a few minutes at recess and brought in several teachers to observe how well I could read. We went through vowels, consonant blends, sounding out strategies, reading compound words, whole sentences—you name it, they threw it at me, and I swatted it away as so many minor sonic annoyances.

One of the teachers was a reading specialist and from what she witnessed, determined I was reading at a sixth-grade level. When asked how I did it, I simply answered, "I hear it." What I didn't understand at the time was a deeper psycho/acoustical process I was experiencing. When I made an empirical connection with the letters or words and I heard them once, I could always remember the visual/aural relationship. My lack of sonic filters and the way I comprehended the interactions between the whole and its parts was at work in an important and useful way. It always came back to the music. I could hear the music transfer to letters becoming a word, and a word became combined with other words to make sentences, and so on. Nothing more was made of it.

———

ONE EVENING, AN ODD-LOOKING dark green device, standing vertically and held in place by spring tension, was lit and doing a random and indifferently directed incandescent illumination thing. The early 1960s American pole lamp was the finest in post-modern, lower working-class furniture. In the center section were three fixtures with a conical metal shade. Each lamp was unified but independently controlled—romantic mood lighting for under $20. This was the only light on in the apartment while Mom and a strange man sat closely on the couch. He had a high forehead with thinning, shiny black hair, and a large, oddly shaped nose framed by large basilisk eyes. He was well-dressed and smelled of Old Spice aftershave. She said with a dry and flat delivery, "Stevie, this is Willie." He was a local business man with money, a wife, and two children.

This was the man Dad caught in bed with Mom the night he came home from the railroad and reduced our home and lives to splinters and rubble. She wasted no time parading Willie for everyone to see. He was everything she wanted in a man. I was never sure if she was everything he wanted in a woman. Willie became a somewhat kindly, cipher-like presence in our lives for the next 11 years.

Ladybug, Ladybug, Fly Away Home...

I DON'T RECALL WHEN I first noticed Mom's shudders and shakes. Her tics may have begun during the five years she and Ronnie were on the run from Ronnie's notorious father. Maybe they began with the beatings and abuses Dad heaped on her. Or, it could have been a mild case of Tourette's, exacerbated by the stresses in her life. Whatever the reason, she displayed these distracting and disturbing mannerisms with no self-consciousness. I also recall several women on her side of the family displaying these out-of-control spasms. I found these twitches fascinating and it was difficult for me not to stare, mesmerized at such neuronal displays.

I noticed a change in me with the shift in energy from the placid Greenbelt days to the hyperactive world of the inner city. I liked the constant energy, and there were enough kids my age living in High Point to share the contagious effects of being surrounded by so much mechanized liveliness and spirit. Ronnie fell in with a group of school friends and did a lot of hanging out on the streets around Wheeler Road. I typically stayed close to home. Mom trusted that Ronnie was old enough to stay close and keep an eye on Karen and me when she was out gallivanting with Willie. She also trusted me to heed her words about not wandering too far from the project. An emotional vesication was also beginning to form in me, followed by the customary callous, especially when it came to Willie's presence in my home.

ON MANY WARM NIGHTS, I would go to the roof and stare out at the skyline of the National Mall and downtown area. In my solitude, I always felt a sensation of what I have come to know as melancholy or yearning; feelings inspired by my early memories of Greenbelt and trips into the District, especially during Christmas; travelling by streetcar among the asymmetrical choreography of cars, busses, taxis, and people; going to department stores like Woodward and Lothrop, or Hecht's. Stopping at a lunch counter for a sandwich and a milkshake gave me a sense of security because I was participating in an important social convention—a message of likeness to everyone. The fact that I was a kid didn't matter. I was learning by example a valuable life skill from the adults—this was how you comported yourself in a civilized society—with respect and consideration for the individual.

The soft, percussive notes of leather-soled shoes on the worn wooden floors of the old stores created a hypnotic, calming effect; if I stood still and listened long enough, I became drowsy and would slip into moments of deep reverie. Riding in crowded elevators, operated manually with a large handle and a scissor-like door, created a sensation that we were all sharing a purpose as we moved silently from floor to floor. Sometimes, the way the elevator gently lurched to a stop created the fluttering effect of butterflies in my stomach, like falling into the Greenbelt blanket.

The elevator operator was usually an elderly black man or woman who always offered a kind word for the passengers, especially a child. The adults were always well turned out: women in dresses and long flowing coats, men in suits wearing hats; women wearing cloying, penetrating perfumes, supplementing a polite yet lingering desire to attract the men of the world, while men smoked cigars, creating a self-distracting vapor affecting indifference to the passive attention demanded by women's fragrances.

The sidewalks always seemed crowded with adults of many colors going about the day, some nodding hello—men tipping their hats to whomever would gladly receive a moment of unqualified and unsolicited kindness, as a salute to their existence—conceivably motivated by the reality of neither person ever crossing paths again. "So here, brotha, take this moment with you, with my compliments, and no lingering commitment, but only the respect you deserve for simply being, with no expectation for a return. Go ahead, I insist, and please pass it on."

Here I was, a child in a world of adults presenting themselves as an eternal weighing of time and always with things to do. I, as a life looking up as others looked around—all in a mid-20th century world of discovery while still in recovery. I believe what I felt for the first time on that roof was love for the city, in as much as a six year old can foster such a feeling. What a shining hour, and within it was born a solitary moment of self-awareness. I became a city kid. I would never let it go, and I would never apologize for embracing such an identity.

THE TERM LATCHKEY KID DIDN'T EXIST in 1961. The circumstances were such that Mom had to work and Ronnie and I had to go to school. It wasn't complicated and there was nothing to negotiate. She got out of work at five, we got out of school by early afternoon. All of her free time and thoughts seemed to focus on Willie as we fended for ourselves.

The relationship she was developing with her boyfriend brought a twisted lesson in amorality. I never understood until many years later: it's apparently okay to live your life as an adulterer. Mom rationalized her choice on two facts—he was unhappy in his marriage and she was desperate to always have a man in her life. Willie promised he would leave his wife once his youngest child finished school. Mom had to accept this condition with a rare reserve of patience. We were nothing more than kids; something she had to get from point A to point B. To him, we were three step kids-in-waiting, and that wasn't going to happen.

True to Granddaddy's word, when summer vacation began, we moved to a place about two miles over the District line, back into Prince George's County; a small community called Kentland. Moving day was a surreptitious event, slipping out under the cover of early morning because Mom owed a month's rent, yet another abject lesson in amorality: it's acceptable to cheat on your obligations. It was time to say goodbye to 1064 Barnaby Terrace, S.E. Washington, D.C.

Once again, we packed the wagon. I was in charge of safeguarding the pole lamp while riding shotgun for the first time ever.

Your House Is On Fire...

Sprawling over 6.6399 acres, Kentwood Apartments were a low-rent version of our Greenbelt home. The adults living there seemed transient and desperate, especially our immediate neighbors. The transposed location from Ridge Road to 3007-A, 75th Place, was a lower class, blue-collar encampment. It was also a foregone conclusion we would fit right in with all of the other refugees from the backroad shows and dime tent revues.

Gone were the streets with pastoral names. The intricate network of pathways connecting the backyards laced with beautiful gardens with grape arbors and rose trellises, so reminiscent of 19th century English gardens, were gone. The Center and the beautiful "Mother and Child" statue were also gone. How I loved that immortal tribute to motherly protection and love.

Across the street were rows of small houses spreading in all directions, as far as the eye could see. This was the Kentland, Inc. development. The houses were like pieces on a Monopoly board, but at least the families in these tiny, board game dwellings had the advantage of being in a fenced-in yard from the houses on either side. Hard-working and seemingly stable families filled these homes.

Our quadplex row faced the barren, sign-less rear of stores in a continuous, one-story cinder block building, like being backstage in a theatre where all of the framing and bones of the staging betray the illusions of the scenery from the seats. With the uninterrupted line of service and delivery doors, we watched the early morning arrival of the waste removal trucks attending to the dumpsters receiving the daily refuse, beginning at one of the first 7-Eleven stores built on the East Coast and making their way to Howlin's Bar and Restaurant. A small dirt path adjacent to a dusty rock and pebble-strewn field, doubling as our ball field, separated the apartments from this string of low-rent suburban goods and services.

Across another street, slightly to the south, was the beginning of Kent Village and its shopping center. The huge, sprawling project of pre-World War II townhouses, small two-story apartment units, and those gulag-inspired three-story structures—all in red brick and located next to the railroad right-of-way—echoed the early days in Cheverly.

Kent Village boasted the impenitent Prince George's Country Club, a racially and religiously segregated 18-hole private membership golf course. The two-lane Route 202, known as Landover Road, defined the north boundary, starting from the Cheverly Theatre and stretching many miles to the east to Upper Marlboro, on the way to the land of pleasant living, the Chesapeake Bay—the land of blue crabs and rednecks. On the other side of Route 202 was nothing but a few trees and an old white mansion sitting high on a ridge overlooking Kentland and Landover Road—a compliment to the country club as part of the plantation tableau. The mansion was an indisputable reminder that we were in the South—and so much a part of the penumbra cast by the Southern Democrat culture. There were no good reasons to cross this highway in 1961, short of squirrel hunting or to watch the gandy dancers working the rails near the Landover switch house.

Kent Village shopping center was the main center of social gravity. Among the stores, Kay Cee Drugs was the anchor, with a soda fountain and lunch counter operated by white-haired older women, many of whom were the mothers and grandmothers of local kids. Kay Cee was a hangout and loiter trap, especially for those close to Ronnie's age. Once everyone was forced to vacate the fountain seats, they'd gather at the small bridge behind the store spanning the dirty, bank-breeching Beaver Dam creek to resume all of the posturing and showcasing required of teens auditioning to become adults.

A small, standout destination between the upper and lower shopping centers was the Hi-Hop trampoline center. A local man with a dubious reputation—depending upon the person with whom you were speaking—owned the trampolines, among other quick-buck spots in the area. He was a strong man circus performer in his heyday, so his post-circus vocation providing gravity-defying recreation, with the potential to result in several months in traction, made sense. Tall with huge earlobes and a slight stoop, he seemed to always have a tan. An unfiltered cigarette hung from his lips as he spoke with an oddly affable combination of Southern genteel, New England blue blood, and Mid-Atlantic drawl. He knew everyone and everyone knew him. Before too long, his trampoline center was where I would forever lose my young life.

***

OUR FIRST SUMMER IN KENTLAND was relatively quiet. I was nervous with anticipation about starting at another new school. With the arrival of fall, I began second grade at Kentland Elementary, a short, three-block walk from the apartment. The school was built like a low-slung state reformatory. Ronnie started 11th grade at Bladensburg High, which was built like a long, three-story state reformatory—industrial, utilitarian, and designed to intimidate the most snarling adolescent. Karen wouldn't start school for another two years. The usual trio of characters continued making their way in and out of the apartment—Willie, Granddaddy, and Dad.

Dad, freed from prison for a few months, often came around on weekends to take Karen and me for overnight stays with his bar-fly girlfriend and her two kids, who were a perfect parallel of Karen and me. He was good about spending time with us, but we often finished the day in some local shithole dive bar. I was bored to death as we endlessly ate pickled pigs' feet and drank untold amounts of Coca-Cola, often with his girlfriend going off on a drunken rant questioning whether or not Karen and I were good Catholics. The quality of these outings may have done more harm than good. Weekends with Dad gave Mom the relief she so desperately needed to demonstrate to Willie why she was such a good catch.

I spent the summer living entire days and nights at the trampoline center. The give-and-take tension of bouncing through gravity took me to distant mental climes, with gravity bringing me back to where it wanted me, then starting the cycle again by letting me win for another moment. This activity enabled me to continuously recreate the joy and sensations I first experienced in the blanket. The trampoline provided the perfect combination of self-control along with the unending repetition of practice. It was also my first formal introduction to Jake's second law of physics stating, "Never measure the outcome of an action before the action ends."

The trampoline was a way to learn confidence, balance, and control with my large motor skills—all essential attributes for anyone who desires to succeed beyond the average—but especially for the musician who endeavors to transfer from large to small motor control. The greatest value from this first-time experience was an immutable lesson which forever imparted this concept: you must love the repetition. If not, then step off, pack up, and move on.

In the fall of 1961, I started school with an entirely new wardrobe, courtesy of Granddaddy and his American Society of Composers, Authors, and Publishers (ASCAP) checks. He wanted me to start my studies with the same sartorial stateliness the Rochinski men enjoyed through two generations. I enrolled in the second grade class of the formidable Mrs. Helen Borden. She was the kind of primary school teacher a kid hopes to have at least once in their life. Mrs. Borden knew that my boredom was a serious distraction for me. I didn't find the boilerplate work for a second grader challenging. There was some discussion about putting me ahead, to skip a grade or two and see how that fit; such was the protocol in 1961 for handling a child in my position. The decision to stay put in Mrs. Borden's class eventually came down to me. I wanted to stay because of her and the friends I made in class.

———

Two indelible historical events during my second grade year began with the continuation of the NASA Mercury flights, starting the year before when Alan Shepard and Gus Grissom launched into sub-orbital flight. These flights were America's response to the Sputnik 1 event we all witnessed in Greenbelt. The Space Race was now in full flight.

On February 20th, 1962, Colonel John Glenn launched into the first American orbital flight. We took time out in class to wheel in a television and see for ourselves this exciting and unprecedented event. We sat in reverential silence as the countdown went from 10 to lift-off.

The name John Glenn became synonymous with American hero. Up until the moment he broke free from Earth's gravity, all of the real people who were heroes to me were either dead, or nearly dead historical figures. Their accomplishments were second-hand information, after-the-fact realities told in a history book or dramatized in pictures and movies. This was the first time we, the baby boom generation, got to see a hero actually born before our young eyes—in four hours, 55 minutes, and 23 seconds, with Glenn witnessing three sunrises and sunsets in one-sixth of a day, at close to 17,000 miles per hour—a space pioneer on top of a gigantic firecracker with a capsule called Friendship 7, resembling a really cool tree fort—a man who was transformed, and in turn, helped transform a nation and the world.

In little more than three months after Glenn's flight, another important space travel event unfolded. On May 24th, 1962, the television was again wheeled into the classroom. We watched a Navy test pilot named Malcolm Scott Carpenter sit on the same type of firecracker that took Glenn into space, ensconced in the same type of capsule, except his was named Aurora 7. This time, the flight would go around the Earth three times. Although Glenn's flight experienced a dramatic moment on his re-entry, Carpenter's would be evermore dramatic because of mechanical malfunctions resulting in overshooting his splashdown point by several hundred miles. It looked for a while like we might have lost the second made-before-our-eyes, real-life American hero to orbit the Earth.

Our *Life* magazine subscription was running story after story on the lives of these seven pioneers. I spent a lot of time looking at the issues covering the inside story on the Glenns' and Carpenters' personal lives. The story on the Carpenters was particularly interesting because the children in the pictures appeared to be my age—two boys and two girls. The younger of the girls was laying on her dad as he lounged in a poolside chair. She was staring at the camera smiling and clearly happy to be in her father's arms. Her name was Candace, and I was drawn to her eyes.

The arrival of the summer of 1962 brought many profound and destructive changes for me. Karen and I were constantly entangled in some kind of brother/sister shit. Sometimes the fighting was intense and very physical. Any sidewalk psychologist would attribute it to the blow-back from the constant day-to-day anxieties Mom wore as her lorica to Saint Agnes, and to the fact there was no father around to balance things out, giving us a different perspective on the world, and to shake things up if we got too out of control.

One of her favorite Ma-rant mantras was, "I have to chase that son of a bitch father of yours down for my lousy $25 a week child support." She also enjoyed railing against her job and the people who worked there—her invective was always a pot on slow boil. She often fought with Willie over their differences in expectations of one another: she expected him, a married man, to be at her beck and call and made her feelings known when he wasn't, and he expected her to maintain her availability and platinum hair color.

In the meantime, Ronnie was running the streets and hanging out at Kay Cee every chance he could. He was taking on the look and feel of the greasers who were a constant presence in our neighborhood. I, on the other hand, spent a lot of time meeting other older kids in the neighborhood while hanging out at the trampoline center. Granddaddy bought me an unlimited season pass for $25, good for the entire summer. I could go jump as long as I wanted at any time of day. My unlimited use drew unexpected and unwanted attention because it created the false impression that I somehow came from money. I was also the youngest kid to ever have such carte blanche access. The pass also came with lessons on how to jump and do basic moves and stunts. In a short time, I mastered many moves including the ever-elegant and advanced Barani flip. My accomplishment was real and it was mine. Sometimes a crowd of parents with kids gathered to watch this little kid do complex maneuvers in endless combinations, like a monkey doing tricks for pennies, minus the little red hat. Instead of an organ grinder, the record player in the plywood shack blasted throughout the facility all of the outstanding pop music of the late 1950s and early 1960s—Little Eva, Chubby Checker, the Shirelles, the Drifters, Nat King

Cole, Perry Como, and Elvis (these would be my back-up bands to develop my rhythm on the mats).

On the fringes of my newfound joy, life with Mom became even more difficult and Ronnie, Karen, and I became increasingly distant. As Mom grew more and more impatient with us, she increased her physical abuse using her hands, hairbrushes, wire coat hangers, anything she could find. As much as the physical hurt, the verbal and emotional abuse stung even more, with lasting pain. "Sometimes I hate you kids," and "One of these days, I am going to get in that fucking car and take off and become among the missing," were two of her favorites. The latter was the most serious threat because the implication was she was always at the ready to abandon us. In such moments of desperation, she would concede her control, or lack thereof, and call Dad to intervene.

Giving her some benefit of the doubt as a struggling single mother should have been easy. After all, she was presumably doing her best to raise three kids on a meager salary. One glaring contradiction was that she could never live up to the standards she held up against everyone else. In her mind, what she had to suffer was a far greater cross to bear than what people had to endure in dealing with her or in their own lives. Mom's circumstances were nothing more than the result of her informed choices and the consequences that naturally follow. Such a lack of self-examination was never more on display than with the shame and venom Mom spewed at Dad; certainly in some ways justified, because physical abuse is never a good choice for any reason. Yet, there was a sanctimony behind her double standard which was entirely lost on her. He admittedly allowed her venom to intimidate him from making regular visits to simply be a presence in Karen's and my day-to-day life. So, we had access to Dad only on his terms, usually when he took us to his regular bar haunt—a sleazy, no-way-out house for dipsomaniacs called Paul's Tavern. I learned some indelible and wondrous characteristics about adults under the influence of alcohol, and human nature in general, in this proverbial shithole. For a time, this jive-dive was like my second home.

One evening in 1961, as Ronnie was following in the footsteps of his notorious father on a fast track to nowhere, a car pulled up with the driver scoping out the Kay Cee teen scene. He called Ronnie over as he flashed a badge identifying himself as a detective with the county police. He insisted that my brother get in the car and Ronnie complied with no questions. The detective announced, "I'm going to introduce you to some real men." A short ride later, the detective, named Baeschlin, escorted Ronnie into the side door of a large, official looking building. Ronnie took immediate notice of the immaculate fire trucks parked in two orderly rows waiting to take off at a moment's notice. They walked over to where several older men stood around talking. This was the new location of Kentland Volunteer Fire Department, Engine Company 33. For the next several hours, Ronnie learned about the operations.

The moment Ronnie set foot in the building transformed him. My brother knew without question this was going to be his life's work—a warrior against the flames. This was the night Ronnie's life calling was awakened.

When the detective learned of Ronnie's tumultuous home life, he came up with an unprecedented solution: the first-ever junior fireman program created specifically for Ronnie became a reality. Baeschlin gave Ronnie permission to build a bedroom in the basement as a home away from home. When Ronnie broke the news to Mom that he was joining the fire department, she unleashed every form of emotional resistance and extortion she could excavate. This was an existential threat to her pathological need to keep my brother all to herself; a co-dependent life she spent 16 years cultivating was about to go up in flames. She posed legitimate concerns about the dangers of such a job, but all of life is a risk when one chooses to participate and live. It was time for Ronnie to move into the real. Her handwringing and gnashing of teeth fell on deaf ears because his mind was made-up, most likely years before this gift of opportunity came into his life.

Ronnie got a good jump off the blocks and not a moment too soon. For the next 29 years, he would spend his life running into the flames as the unfortunate fled the heat, destruction, and certain death. The love and admiration I felt for him would always burn quietly in my heart, regardless of any time and distance separating us.

Your Children All Roam

As a seven year old, I was enthralled with the oil paintings gracing the walls of Howlin's Bar and Restaurant. One of the two most memorable paintings portrayed a fisherman entangled with reeling in a large-mouth bass on a rock-strewn seashore. The picture projected a bright intensity ringed with hope. The other picture was dark and stormy. It was a three-mast ship about to run aground with a desperate captain struggling at the wheel to keep it from smashing against the rocks. My later memory of these pictures led me to believe that this artist possessed a high level of artistic scope and skill rivaling the Dutch masters. In the lower right-hand corner, I saw the scrawled signature of the artist—it read "Joe Danner." Joe Danner was a formless and meta-physical image to me. He always existed outside of my life experiences. Mom, or some other adult in the family who knew his story well, told me everything about the man.

Joe was born to a well-to-do family in Newport News, Virginia. As far back as anyone can recall, he was always involved in a life of crime. He was also an artistic savant, whose skills with many musical instruments, especially the piano, were as highly developed as his ability with a pen or paintbrush. Joe could play anything he heard after hearing it once. He was an outstanding dancer and an all-around natural entertainer. He proved on many occasions, as documented by Washington, D.C. newspaper articles, that he possessed a natural and gifted legal acumen rivaling F. Lee Bailey. He was successful in defending himself in several major trials, and on one such occasion, was able to convince the judge to dismiss the case, in spite of his guilt.

Elegantly dressed, articulate, funny, charming, flamboyant, and a neo-Romantic that Ronnie once described as physically resembling a young Jack Nicholson, he was also the leader of the notorious Pimple-Faced Gang, a group of young professional gangsters who were responsible for many armed robberies in the Mid-Atlantic region. For a brief time, he hired himself out as a contract killer for the New York mob. Joe took the job seriously and relocated a very young Ronnie and Mom to a basement apartment in Newark so he could take his careful time to plan how he would carry out the hits. In short time, Mom and Ronnie found themselves on the run from him, lasting for several years. He eventually gave up and moved on, but never too far from his only son.

One day in 1962, he contacted Ronnie out of the blue and invited him to spend an extended weekend in Newport News. After much resistance from Mom, she agreed and arranged for Ronnie to take a bus to Virginia. As a boy in his mid-teens, there was much that Ronnie experienced in the ways of life, but the lessons and examples he was about to live through during this short odyssey with his father would be forever seared in his consciousness, underscoring some life-defining moments as he came to a better understanding of this stranger and all that he lived for. There was one nagging question that kept running through his mind: *why does he want to connect with me now, after all of these years of being absent and completely out of my life?* The bus pulled into Newport News in the dead of night. My brother stepped off with a small suitcase, a few dollars in his pocket, and a major case of anxiety in meeting a man for whom he had no memory.

Joe arrived late and found Ronnie sitting alone on a bench. Fighting through all of his travel fatigue, he was running on high-octane adrenaline. As his father approached him to get his bag, his mind was racing about how to greet this stranger. A handshake? A hug? A left to the jaw? Joe relieved my brother from having to make the decision because he was the first to stretch out his hand and offer a firm handshake. He said, "Hello my boy, and welcome to my city."

After an awkward and silent car ride, they finally pulled into a long drive-way in front of a beautiful old Southern-style mansion. Ronnie immediately settled into one of several guest rooms. The adrenaline was still surging and sleep was the last thing on his mind. As he laid in bed, many things went through his mind, but the one thought he couldn't shake was, *Why now? Why now after all of these years?*

Daybreak came too soon. Ronnie was able to get past the lack of sleep and come around to some semblance of presentation, and he made his way downstairs. He couldn't help but take notice of his father's artwork—his paintings were hanging everywhere; sculptures stood in lit corners on pedestals. The formal living room that he passed through to get to the dining room had a beautiful grand piano. Joe and an older lady named Mrs. Williams were there to greet him at the breakfast table. After being introduced to her as his grandmother, the conversation centered on what Ronnie had been doing as a boy growing up in the D.C. area. The biggest news Ronnie shared was his appointment as the first-ever junior member of the local fire department. He also mentioned that Mom and Dad separated, without divulging too many details. Ronnie also mentioned Karen and me, and he boasted on how much of a voracious reader I had grown to be.

From the moment Ronnie arrived, the one thing that kept coming back to him was how cold and casual, to the point of indifference, all of the interactions and conversations with these unknown relatives were. Ronnie had some expectation of his grandmother being a person who was staid and emotionally reserved, for this was the story Mom always told. He was now experiencing this firsthand. Both acted as if they had known Ronnie all of his life, and this was just another day and another conversation, as a continuation of other days and other conversations.

That evening, Joe invited Ronnie to a nightclub. Everyone treated Joe like a don, and Ronnie being underage was not a problem. All eyes were on this gangster and this unknown handsome young man. They sat at the best table in the house with the most expensive bottle of champagne waiting on ice. The next night offered more of the same, only a different location. One can imagine how all of this adult attention was affecting a young teenager who, as a junior rank fireman, kept one foot in the world of adult responsibility, and as a kid barely the age of consent was now caught up in this heavy whirlwind of adult sensibilities, brought on entirely by this father-man.

Later that night, the duo stopped in at a local diner for breakfast. Stragglers sitting at the counter and tables were reminiscent of Hopper's "Nighthawks."

Suddenly, Ronnie was in pain; scalded by a full cup of hot coffee. Before anyone could react, the huge plate glass window shattered, and the man who went sailing through it landed on the sidewalk, in need of major medical attention. As the guy working the counter called for an ambulance, others rushed out to help this poor exsanguinating soul.

Once they got to the car and took off, Ronnie asked, "Why did you do that?"

Joe replied, "Because he spilled hot coffee on you."

Ronnie assured him it was only an accident. Joe pulled the car to a curb. He turned to Ronnie and said, "The power and respect I expect and enjoy in this town comes from fear. If your reputation rests on punishing someone for an unintended injury, imagine what people will think can happen if someone intentionally goes up against you. I expect airtight respect and if putting some asshole through a window is how you keep the leaks under control, then so be it."

As they continued driving around, Joe was less talkative, as if deep in thought. Joe took a long road and ended up on the edge of one of many bodies of water off Colonial Beach. Out in the middle, not too far off shore, was a large, partially sunken barge. The barge was a business venture. It was Joe's attempt to get into a legitimate line of work. He converted it into a floating entertainment venue—putting on shows with him singing and playing piano, dancing, telling jokes. The place was well-appointed with everything needed for success: high-end waitresses, a full bar and kitchen, and a huge dance floor. The barge became a featured, major entertainment destination for the well-heeled of Newport News. Joe enjoyed a brief honeymoon with the local politicians before the municipal romance ended when the barge broke loose in a storm and collided with a major bridge, bringing unpaid damages.

They drove on and arrived back on Interstate 64. Without warning, Joe again stopped the car. He said, "Let's have some fun." He got out and opened the trunk. Ronnie could see Joe was cradling something in his arms, but the trunk lid was obscuring his view from knowing exactly what he carried. Joe walked several hundred feet down the shoulder and after a several minutes, returned to the car. "Now we'll sit and wait."

In a few minutes, the road ahead from where they sat became empty of cars. Joe turned to Ronnie again and said, "Before you get out of the car, I want to tell you why what you are about to see happened: from the time I was a kid, I've believed that most of the people in this world just go mindlessly along and never question anything getting in their way. They'll go wherever the crowd takes them, like a bunch of fucking sheep being herded to the slaughterhouse."

Joe turned away, staring ahead into the night. His eyes narrowed down to a thoughtful squint, and after a couple of moments, he took one last drag of his cigarette. Without diverting his gaze from the windshield, he flicked the Lucky Strike out the window. As he continued staring ahead, he said, "Now go ahead and get out and take a look." At first, Ronnie hesitated to leave the car. He was afraid to see what his father did to wreak such havoc on this highway. He opened the door and stood looking over the car. His eyes widened in absolute astonishment as he was left speechless. Joe got out and closed the trunk and they continued the drive home. The lights bathing the highway faded into darkness with their headlights as the only illumination for miles around. Before long, Ronnie was asleep.

Ronnie awoke the next morning with an enormous hangover, not limited exclusively to booze, from all of the excitement and energy. He made his way down to breakfast and before long was ready to get to the bus station. He was not sure if he couldn't wait to get home or if he wanted to stay for good to bask in and eventually inherit his father's legacy.

After saying his thank you and goodbye to Mrs. Williams, he and Joe headed out to the car. Once they were outside, his father said, "Don't put your bag in the car. Follow me." In the garage, there sat a clean, beautiful, black 1947 two-door Chevy. On the top edge of the driver's door, painted in flawless Old English script, were the words "The Duke." Joe flipped Ronnie the keys and said, "Head north, my son." Without a driver's license and barely able to drive a vacuum stick shift, Ronnie found his way back to Kentland.

Once he returned with the memory of the trip still fresh in his mind, Ronnie was rarely at home, being either at the fire department or out with Linda. She turned 14 and he turned 17 and from the beginning, they were forever bound as quintessential childhood sweethearts. By bringing Linda into his life, Ronnie's first and only true love would become the force to pull back the remaining cover on Mom's borderline personality. The dark symbiosis Mom created in her relationship with Ronnie, beginning with the time they spent running from Joe, had been disturbed by this young girl who caught Ronnie's attention and heart—the female interloper, the uninvited, the gatecrasher—encroaching on Mom's sole claim to the only man in her life she trusted unconditionally to let her, and her alone, be his only caretaker and he as hers. The truth was the emotional extortion Mom forced upon Ronnie. Being the loving and dutiful son, he never knew what hit him until years later.

Mom's sense of entitlement made it easy for her to justify creating such a toxic existence that impacted everyone. When Ronnie and Linda were in a position to move on and up in their lives, she was there, hitching her Good Lawdy Miss Agnes wagon to his limited-slip differential. After more than 50 years of being torn between fealty born solely as an outcome of birth, and his unflagging commitment to make a good and independent life for himself, Ronnie's relief from Mom would one day come. As long as she had air to breathe, our birthmarks, as furrowed scars, would never run dry of her tears, and no one, no matter how close or distant, would escape her reach, especially Ronnie and Karen.

One morning, an expensive convertible pulled into our parking lot. In the passenger seat was a well-dressed man with a young woman driving and two other women in the backseat. The man asked me if I was Stevie. He introduced himself as Joe Danner. "Your brother tells me you love to read." I again answered yes, as I stood there awestruck by the primal essence exuded by this strange man. He asked if Ronnie was home. Ronnie soon came to the car and greeted Joe warmly, with a tinge of reservation, like he couldn't for the life of him figure out why his father would show up unannounced, especially in such an ostentatious style. Joe and Ronnie finished their short visit and said goodbye. Joe and the girls were on their way to the Jersey Shore for a week. They invited Ronnie to come along, to which he politely declined.

Not too long after Joe's pop-in, two huge cardboard boxes arrived, addressed to me. When I opened the first box, scores of books and magazines came spilling out. The other box contained a brand new 10 volume, multi-colored hardbound set called *The Junior Classics.* Joe wrote me a short note, with small, detailed drawings along the margins, expressing how much he enjoyed meeting me. He told me that reading is the surest way to open your mind to all of the wonder the world has to offer.

Ground Zero

"Evil requires the sanction of its victim…"
—A.V.R.

"…unless you happen to be an eight-year-old child…"
—S.J.R.

…AND IN MY CASE, THE only requirement was to unwittingly place myself in the position as the perfect target, in a time and space not of my making, for someone whom I trusted by default—he was a fringe part of a larger group of older boys, close to Ronnie's age, who, in my mind, possessed a collective identity. What made this executioner stand out was the unusual attention he paid to me, more so than others. He engaged me more directly than the others, sometimes with mean-spirited teasing, laced with the kind of sexual innuendo that was commonplace in adult male locker rooms. Other times, he stared at and through me, without ever saying a word. He drove a dark blue 1949 Ford coupe, and he often sat in his car in front of the trampoline center, talking for long periods of time with a very old man.

Myr worked behind the counter in the small plywood shack at the center, cramped and built for no more than two or three adults. The shack also served as a storage space for miscellaneous equipment and cases of soft drinks for the soda machine. As was customary, Myr often opened and closed the place, and he never jumped on the trampolines. Myr allegedly had a girlfriend, but she was never seen in his company.

Whenever the owner wasn't there, he would close the place for the night. Closing began with a five-minute warning for the jumpers to get in their last bounces and then clear out. One particular night, I kept jumping and before long, I realized Myr and I were the only ones there. I was never told to clear out after the five-minute warning was up. As I put on my shoes and headed for the gate, he asked me if I'd stay behind and help him restock the soda machine.

I never questioned why he locked the gate with the padlock while I was still inside—I never questioned why he turned out the huge lights ringing the chain link perimeter. It never entered my mind that he locked me in and made it appear the place was closed for the night. The long front door on the shack was also closed and locked. None of this seemed odd to me because there was nothing to compare it with, so it all seemed normal. The only open door was on the side. The only burning light was inside the shack—a bare, harsh, unshaded light bulb hanging from an unsecure fixture on the plywood plank pretending to be a ceiling. Once I stepped in, Myr closed and locked the door behind me.

As the increasing and irreversible darkness of my executioner descended upon me, I, a boy who wanted to be a man—whose life was about to be taken by a spirit-crushing, soul-killing physical and sexual assault—gave up my last fleeting thought and feeling to the last desperate struggle to remain in my mind a child, even as I could see my own light slowly growing dimmer. I never thought of my mother, or father, or sister, or brother, or grandfather, or anyone, or anything, except my own life—because in one-half of my next heartbeat, my life would be gone forever.

I reached in vain for the one tear that paused on its journey seeking its lowest level, a tear that caressed the small scar located slightly above and to the right of my upper lip, left behind long ago by the impalement on the bookcase spire as I reached for a favorite toy, lost my footing, and hung there in the balance—without a tear. Like a feather of solace I pulled from my Greenbelt pillow, making its way down to the floor ever so slowly to join the countless others, this considerate and loving tear was never concerned about when, or how far it had to fall.

Because no one could ever know what happened to me, under the threat of being killed by this twisted, evil annihilator…a true-to-heart eight year old, born with the gift to live and love the rhythms and music of life…a boy who loved to read and loved to laugh…a boy who loved the good company of all people, who loved to observe and understand all of life's intricacies…a boy no one would miss because so few people ever really knew this boy. The evacuated shell of my former self would have to continue on, as if nothing ever happened, and be forced to endure, absolutely alone, my immurement in an inextinguishable silence on fire as I entered a living after-life forever trapped in a halfway world.

The Two-Thousand Yard Stare

I FLEW HOME AS FAST as my legs would carry me. My mind was reeling as millions of abstract synapses fired off at once. I walked in with a sense of dread, believing that somehow everyone in the room knew what happened and I was to blame. Mom and Willie were sitting on the couch listening to a new adult comedy album called *Pardon My Blooper*. She asked where I had I been, and I answered that I was at the trampolines. She asked no further questions, and I went to bed. Once I got to my room, my biggest concern was where to hide the two-dollar bill Myr gave me, like I was some cheap streetwalker who was out looking to snag any trick who happened by. The last of the uncounted feelings I remember, before I drifted off to sleep, was the heaviness of inconsolable shame and fear of death.

Many changes came over me in the weeks, months, and years that followed. The first was to never again set foot in the trampoline center. My escape from the strife, as a constant presence at home, was gone. I no longer had a place where I could continue to sharpen my skills of self-control, balance, and hitting the mark with those short, gravity-defying ballets. My ability to fall asleep and stay asleep became erratic. I was having problems of incontinence, especially bed-wetting. The feathers of solace that accumulated under my Greenbelt bed were now replaced with soiled underwear.

Facial tics, a characteristic of my mother, soon began appearing in me. A chronic, anxiety fueled short-windedness fell over me, lasting for decades. Through Mom's eyes, all of these manifestations of my trauma translated as a boy becoming more and more difficult, maybe even mocking her infirmities, as if my grand plan was to make her life increasingly miserable.

As my symptoms became evermore frequent, she became more punitive. It was not uncommon for her to rub my face in my underwear before making me clean them in the toilet. Upon seeing my tics, she'd call me out in her most humiliating manner, often while others were present. I didn't have the adult insight to make a cause and effect connection in the aftermath of what I experienced. Even so, the threat of being killed by Myr guaranteed my silence, along with my sense of shame and fear growing stronger with each passing day. All I could do was focus on staying alive and staying safe.

I was in desperate need of professional attention and intervention, despite a non-existent medical establishment in 1962 for treating such childhood traumas and abuse. If there had been such treatment, and Mom was aware of what took place in the shack…no matter. Mom came from a generation and a background of cynicism fueled by ignorance that would never allow such a concession because it would be a sure sign of weakness in me and neglect by her, so the only outcome would be the scorn of family and others.

I existed in a total state of fear, panic, and shame. I didn't want to go out, I didn't want to go to school. The start of my episodes of serial truancy lasted for many consecutive days. I didn't want to venture into the world with anyone, even with adults, because I believed they would be powerless to stop my killer. The more isolated I made myself, the more attention I brought on from Mom and Ronnie. Occasionally, Mom would ask me to run an errand to either the 7-Eleven, or to take the short walk over to Kent Village shopping center, further risking exposure. I planned and developed escape routes, in case my killer drove by and saw me.

It was inevitable that I would see him drive past as I walked to Kent Village. Myr would direct his laser-like eye contact through the windshield. He would swerve to pull off the road, attempting a U-turn, but, like the meerkat, I had access to my bolt paths before he could catch me. My initial reaction was to freeze in abject terror, but I was able to quickly shake free from the grip of fear and trembling and take off. I was too small to fight, but always quick to flight—Dr. Amy G. Dala always had my back.

As confidence in my ability to avoid my killer grew, I took greater chances going out and doing the normal things I wanted to do—the concept "false sense of security" was not in my vocabulary. The next change I noticed was my constant need to scan my surroundings, especially at distances way beyond my immediate field of vision. Years later, someone explained what I had developed to a high-level, especially for a child, was something called hyper-vigilance—a similar defensive mindset developed by soldiers in combat. Another disorder, developed by soldiers in extreme combat conditions, is something called the 2,000 yard stare—a disassociation from the reality of the violent conditions on the battlefield. A less severe form of this condition started to manifest itself in me when I was in elementary school. By the time I reached junior high, these episodes were more defined and intense. For a split second, I believed I was dying before my eyes.

The stare started like a shade slowly pulled down over my brain, followed by not knowing where I was or who I was; the not knowing who I was created my greatest fear and anxiety—it was as if I ceased to exist, and yet, at the same time, I was a human blank, totally aware during this out-of-body experience that I, this Other, knew nothing about me. I had entered a psycho-fugal state of being.

My awareness of duality triggered a panic attack. Somewhere from deep down, a corner reserved for me, the one person I knew and trusted, was rapidly collapsing in on itself. I had to find something benign and safe before the final implosion, or I would no longer exist; something familiar like singing the jingle from a commercial, or the theme song to a favorite movie or television show. A musical trigger often brought me out of this waking dream state. My pulse and heart rate pounded to the top of my head for a few minutes and then a tepid, clammy calmness and relief would return. Ironically, the one image I never called on was the Mother and Child statue.

———

ONE DAY, I LET DOWN my guard and paid dearly for it. As I walked along Kent Village, suddenly, with no warning, there he was—confident he had snagged a deer in headlights. I knew there was no getting away, so I acted like nothing ever

happened. He reassured me he wasn't going to hurt me or do any
Myr convinced me that an older kid we both knew had hidden a rⁱ
of the golf course, near the railroad tracks parallel to Route 50. I
let me fire off some rounds, an irresistible lure for any kid. He kept pac̲
yards ahead of me as we walked through the neighborhood—maybe a strategy
to create the impression we were not together, or maybe an unconscious action
that betrayed his belief that I was not, and never would be his equal.

He kept me against my will and assaulted me for a far longer period—what
seemed like hours. I was too numb and young to feel a sense of relief at not
having been beaten or killed.

It was the perfect setup for this evil incarnate. Because I had kept silent
about the first attack, out of fear for my life, he was free to pursue me at every
impulse, but ever so careful so as to not draw any attention to himself. I was a
prisoner without physical restraint. If I kept quiet, he wouldn't kill me. Guilt
was now setting in from all sides. I felt guilty for having let this happen, and
guilty for not trusting Granddaddy, or Dad, or Ronnie—the men in my life who
would and could protect me and bring me some justice. I felt guilty for hiding
my torture from anyone with official power to stop this living hell—guilty for
the lying and deception I created by making false excuses for not doing ordinary
day-to-day things, like any other kid my age would be happy to do.

From now on, trust was something that would never come easy, if ever. It
didn't take me long to learn to read the signs of anyone who bared intentions of
inflicting this kind of abuse on me—the body language and the verbal signals,
all the way down to the sound of their voice. I had developed the same instincts
that dogs and other animals possessed to survive.

Child sexual predators were as rampant and malignant in 1962 as they
are today. The only difference was the shame and the guilt, the feeling of helplessness, and the coerced silence of the victims who kept quiet for far too long.

———

"EVIL REQUIRES THE SANCTION OF its victim…" Catholic doctrine teaches evil
as "the lesser good." This specious semantic sleight-of-hand accomplishes only

one thing: the denigration of the word good. I wonder which letter "o" in good would sacrifice itself to become a silent placeholder?

The word sanction fascinates me. It's one of those semantic rarities with two meanings in opposition to each other—to approve or allow an action, or to bring punitive measures against an unapproved action. As an eight-year-old child, I was smart enough to know I didn't approve of the assault and the subsequent long-term stalking, nor was I in a position of power to not allow it, having been forced to submit by a much stronger physical force. As for the punitive side of the word sanction, it would take me 45 years to summon the courage to take such a step in reclaiming my soul.

I survived the attacks, but the real work lay ahead. I would spend the rest of my life working to survive the recovery, surrounded by life in a 20th century post-war, halfway world in its own state of recovery, controlled by adults always weighing time, and always with things needing to be done.

Point Of Departure

As 1962 started to wind down, the 22 days between October 16th and the 28th left everyone with the growing fear that what started as a Cold War between the United States and The Union of Soviet Socialist Republics, going back to 1947, was about to get very, very hot. The real possibility of a nuclear war loomed for nearly three weeks, and everyone from school kids to adults was made equal in the helpless belief that carbonization on a massive scale was looming over us.

It seemed all of the nuclear attack drills we practiced in school would now be put to the test. "Remember kids, stay under your desk, with your knees tucked under your chest, and your arms over your head, with your eyes covered. Don't look at the sudden bright flash. Everything will be okey dokey." Uh huh. If "okey dokey" was a euphemism for "…evenly distributed, in its most vaporized molecular state of existence, over an untold number of incinerated acres," then everything would be so. The Cuban Missile Crisis was arguably the start of the national anxiety and handwringing over nuclear annihilation that would last for at least the next 27 years. It was all about the A-bomb. My annihilation was not only in my immediate sphere of existence, but also a possibility on the world stage.

ONE DAY, WHILE SITTING IN third grade music class singing from a song book, I noticed for the first time how the notes on the page would go in an upward direction as the melody went from low to high, and when the melody went from high to low, so did the notes on the page. I also noticed the insignias used in the notation. Of particular interest was the treble clef and time signature. The treble clef was especially attractive—elegant and graceful curves curled around and back onto itself. It looked like a familiar combination of a letter and a number,

/ unique. The idea that you could write the music by moving the aper in the direction of the melody was a revelation.

ιn I got home from school, I immediately opened the dictionary. I red seeing different tables of signs and insignias in the back of the book with an entire page of music notation symbols. With this information, I believed I could write a song. I took a blank sheet of paper, a ruler, and a pencil, and drew five horizontal lines close together. I copied the treble clef on the left side of the lines, and put in 4/4 next to it, exactly as it looked in the music books. I hummed a melody and wrote the note heads in the direction I was singing. I put some words below the staff and gave it a title. My next challenge was how to send it off to a record company. The only address for a record company was on the label of one of our albums. I chose one from Capitol Records. I addressed the envelope, mailed it off, and then forgot about it.

One Saturday in the following spring, Mom and Ronnie were sitting at the table having a laugh. Mom said a letter addressed to me came in the mail, which she had opened. There was a type-written letter addressed to Mr. Stephen Rochinski, and it was on Capitol Records letterhead. This is how it read:

Dear Mr. Rochinski,

We received your song and we thank you for your submission. While it does have merit, we are not at this time seeking any new song submissions. Thank you.

Sincerely yours,
Capitol Records
A&R Department

The A&R people had no idea this incoherent scribble came from a nine-year-old kid. The derision I received from Mom and Ronnie burned. I don't believe they were kidding to be mean, but it hurt nonetheless, because I took this seriously.

I got through the rest of 1962 and most of 1963 safely and unscathed, because it appeared as though my stalker had disappeared; or maybe my survival strategies had been successful. I felt modest relief from my hyper-vigilant state of mind, but my guard was still up, and the radar was still on—it was always on and it would always be on.

ONE DAY, I GOT UP the nerve and asked Granddaddy to buy me a guitar. He bought me a cheap, second-hand cowboy box. Over many months, the guitar fell by the wayside due to a variety of abuses and transformations, in large part stemming from my frustration with not knowing how to play it. I asked him for another guitar, so he broke down and bought me a new instrument. Other than the way I played my rescued guitar, there wasn't much I could do without guidance. Once again, I asked for guitar lessons and was again refused. I banged around on it to my inevitable frustration.

During one Granddaddy visit, Ronnie happened to be home, and he pulled a fast one—he set me up by asking me to play something for Granddaddy. I faced two choices: either refuse and risk embarrassment by disappointing Granddaddy, or attempt to make some kind of music come out of it. So, I chose to take my chances and sit there with the instrument resting on my knee and do my best to play something—anything.

For the first couple of moments, all I did was strum the open strings with down strokes. Then, something happened that caught their attention and went through me like a jolt—I used an alternating strum of down and up, and instead of hitting all of the strings, I focused on only the first string, the high E, the string closest to where the guitar was resting on my leg. Before I knew it, I had placed the first finger of my left hand on the first fret and played the note—to my surprise, I started to alternate the open string with the fretted note. This flash of my future unfolding lasted for only a second or two, but was enough for them and me to know, however rudimentary it may have been, that I was in the act of playing the instrument. Granddaddy and Ronnie heard something that sounded like I was starting to play a song—their reaction was so shocking,

I stopped playing. They encouraged me to keep on going, but I didn't want to continue. I was too consumed by the rush of a complex of feelings of surprise, excitement, awe, and the desire to keep this experience to myself, to protect these first-time feelings, and to be in control of what I had done.

This ephemeral moment became the sound of me stepping ever so briefly across a threshold into a world I have heard since the age of three. What I knew to be true flashed in an instant of sonic vividness and clarity. I was aware that what I could hear in my head went way beyond what my hands could create, and unless I had formal lessons, getting my hands caught up to my inner hearing was going to take a long time. No matter how long it took, I knew there would be no turning back, even if I had to go it alone in the face of indifference by those around me.

RONNIE AND OUR COUSIN MIKE graduated high school in June of 1963 and both were free to further pursue their life's ambition to become professional firefighters. Mike was the only son of Aunt Helen, who died of tuberculosis when Mike was an infant, followed by his father's passing shortly after his mother, leaving him an orphan. My grandparents truly loved their only grand-child from their first-born daughter, so they formally adopted Mike and gave him their last name. Like Ronnie and so many of their friends, he worked as a volunteer fireman. With Mike's graduation and subsequent position at the fire department, his character continued to grow and increase in everyone's heart. Everyone believed Mike, like Ronnie, would go on and become the flame warrior that destiny demanded. He and Ronnie became even more inseparable by the summer of 1963.

It was a Friday afternoon, the weather was clear and around 70 degrees, an unusually balmy for a day in November. This meant that our recess after lunch would be more active than usual. Suddenly, one of the custodians came running out to the playground screaming, "Get the children inside. The president has been shot."

The concept of a political assassination was so new and abstract to us at this young age, we didn't possess a historical frame of reference for such an event. In fact, there were few alive in 1963 that would have remembered the only other time in the 20th century when this happened, in 1901. All we knew was something was terribly wrong. We sat huddled in the multi-purpose room and watched the aftermath of this fixed and permanent calendar moment unfold on television. The man we believed was the most powerful and important man in America and the world was dead—shot and killed by a young, deranged gunman.

On this dark and infamous November day, all rational adults knew the conflicting gravity of this event, as witnessed by the tears scoring through their own 2,000-yard stares. With the warm-up act of the Cuban Missile Crisis still looming in our collective national consciousness, Act 1, Scene 1 of The Masters of The Tectonic Slip and Slide Political and Popular Culture Ride began. Everyone who was alive on Friday, November 22nd, 1963, at 12:30 p.m., Central Standard Time, was forever tattooed by the three-dimensional stain of a nation's blood—shown to the entire world, from start to finish, through a two-dimensional electron transmission translated in black and white—spilled in the shortened life of one man.

IN THE DAYS OF LIMITED hard-wired communication, our home telephone and the time of day it rang was a reasonable predictor of why someone was calling. If it was a weekday evening, then it was either Willie or some family member or friend calling for Mom, Ronnie, or me. A bad time for the phone to ring was either late at night, while someone was still up, or even worse, after we were all asleep, and the earlier in the darkness of morning, the more ominous the call was expected to be.

In the early morning hours of Saturday, the 23rd, one day after the killing of the president, the telephone rang. Mom went into a complete and dysregulated meltdown, and this was before she answered it. Her state of mind after she hung up the phone was beyond description, and this time, for good reason: a drunk driver going 55 miles per hour lost control of his car and crushed Mike between the front end of the car and the back step of the fire truck. Mike was rolling and stowing hose on what turned out to be a false alarm at two in the morning.

Surgery lasted for nearly four hours, and there was still no word on his condition. Within the next hour, the head surgeon appeared and announced his having to amputate Mike's leg up to the waist. There was so much residual damage and massive blood loss, it was too early to know of his surviving such a devastating accident. They were contemplating the option to remove his other leg if it would help save his life.

Ronnie went into the recovery room and waited for Mike to come out of the anesthesia. Now a senior member of Kentland No. 33, 18 and helpless to do anything, my brother was bound and determined to see it all the way through with Mike. As Ronnie stood there, he saw Mike's open eyes, but he was unconscious. Mike slowly turned to look directly at Ronnie, as if to say in his penetrating gaze and silence, "Thank you for all of your love and companionship. Thank you for being such an important presence in my short life. Thank you for sharing the example of your dedication to this righteous calling of the flame warrior. Please do not let my life end in vain. Carry on for this fallen brother, and through you, I will see another day, and another day, and a thousand days of running in to save a life, or 10, or a thousand, without concern for the value of who or what they are, other than the common threads of humanity we have all shared from the moment we could think and feel and understand."

In another moment, Mike's quintessence turned and left behind his young and broken body. In the irrevocable last instant of this child-man's life, he kept his eyes open, as a lasting symbol of his courage to face the slowly fading light of life, as his existence transformed with the rippling wash of ultimate release to welcome him to the unknown—all without fear or tear. With a final, infinite gaze at Ronnie, as if to say that it was all going to be okay, Mike left a world where he would be forever 18; a world that knew him all too briefly.

FOR THE NEXT FIVE YEARS, between 1964 and 1969, we would be traipsing, in our best white gypsy fashion, from one encampment to another. I never knew

Mom's reasons for putting us through such a needlessly transient experience—maybe it was a matter of economics, rents going up and the like, or maybe it was the "we're-off-to-see-the-wizard" or the "grass-is-always-greener" syndrome. The greener rationale is certainly reasonable, because the Kentwood flop was small and without air conditioning. Our brief time in the District was gone in my rearview mirror. However, Greenbelt was a place I continued to think about and often yearned to visit, to relive memories, see old friends, and to visit the Center and the statue.

Shortly before our move from Kentland, a life-threatening incident happened involving Mom and me that was never spoken of afterward. One evening, Mom lied and said she was going over to Howlin's to meet a girlfriend. She had established a history of threatening to leave us to become, in her words, "among the missing." I lived in constant fear of this threat becoming a reality. I believed this was the night she was finally going to leave us. Willie hadn't been around for several days, and she was oddly quiet, like she was hiding something.

After she left, I waited to secretly follow her to the bar. Crowded with drunks and thick cigarette smoke, it was impossible to differentiate the limits of the barroom. As I worked my way in deeper, I saw her sitting at a table having a drink with two men I never before laid eyes on. The three of them seemed to be having quite a cozy time, sitting close and having some laughs.

Something in me snapped. I don't know how many adults in this place ever experienced what they saw and heard coming from an eight year old kid, but I'm confident this is a story they told for years thereafter. In my breakdown, all I could see was the blinding heat of white-hot raging anger. As I approached their table, I may have been speaking in tongue or something close to it. I let loose with an unbroken volley of profanity and more motherfuckers than you'd ever hear in 10 cell blocks of solitary confinement. What I experienced, considering all I had been through since leaving Greenbelt, and especially since living in Kentland, was a palpable sensation of sustained rage, fear, and release. It's amazing I didn't lose consciousness as all of my physical actions concentrated down into the essence of a kid in a paroxysm of flailing, swinging arms with tiny, clenched fists, and assorted spasms of bilious outrage.

bar was now in a state of total pandemonium. I imagine all of the
were thinking they were unexpectedly set upon by a pissed-off, unem-
alcoholic munchkin from the Lollipop Guild, with the fear there may
ore of the same clamoring to break down the door. Mom was in an utter
state of shock—eyes wide, and mouth struggling to stay off of the floor. She
was found and exposed by her little middle kid. In the process, I set off a small,
but dirty verbal nuclear device and the radiation was everywhere. Lookout
motherfuckers, I'm 40 pounds of trouble, and I'm headed your way.

The two guys she was with took matters into their own hands. It was
obvious that whatever they had planned for my mother was not to be. As they
escorted me out, harshly I might add, she was following closely on their heels.
Mom soon lost her way in the crowd as several others followed us out. In the
meantime, the two thugs were taking me to their car, arguably to either beat me
unconscious or worse. I knew with my newfound danger radar something was
not right, and I struggled to break free. As they were forcing me into the backseat,
Mom heard my screams and came running over to beat, scratch, and claw these
two kidnappers into a stupor. Once I was free, she grabbed me by the hair with
one hand, pulling me on the entire three-minute walk home, while beating me
nearly unconscious about the head, face, and body with the other hand.

The physical punishment I received when we got home was an Old Tes-
tament kind of event. The verbal excoriation she also laid on me was as intense
as what I had unleashed, that which had landed me in this unpleasantness in
the first place.

I caught her red-handed doing something unseemly and suspicious, and
if mentioned by me, denigration was waiting to set upon her from all quarters.
After the next day, nothing else was ever said; it was like nothing never happened,
in spite of my aches and pains. This was now our little secret.

Dodge Park

In January of 1964, the wagon was once again loaded. One thing I packed well ahead of time was the pain associated with the Kentland location. For me, it will always represent where I lived and died.

We were on our way to the next encampment of the "Good Lawdy Miss Agnes' Rope Show and Shit-Jyeah Defiance Revue." I was again in charge of safeguarding the pole lamp as I rode shotgun with my guitar at my side. Ronnie had Linda. Karen was still too young to have any responsibilities, so she stayed in the back counting the chickens and their eggs. There was always room for one more of anyone or anything. However, there was one item that was noticeably absent. It was a gift from Willie—a small, white decorative plate that hung on the wall. In the center of the plate was a rudimentary drawing of a black dining room chair. Around the edge of the plate read the mildly sarcastic plea, "God Bless This Lousy Apartment." Maybe there was hope for us yet.

The travel time took all of five minutes to arrive at 3303 Dodge Park Road, No. 103, because the project, located across Landover Road, was only an eighth of a mile to the east. Dodge Park contained no park—another example of a deceptively spurious name, most likely invented by a real estate developer. The closest thing to a park was an acre of trenches dug for the foundations of Dodge Park shopping center 200 feet from the front door of my building. Like the view from our Kentwood spot looking at the back doors of the stores, we had the same view, only more intimate and up close, with delivery vehicles and the Humpty Dumpster trucks making their biweekly rounds.

By the early 1960s, the apartment model shifted from the red brick gulag-lite World War-era construction to include a more contained and off-street quality. It was a softer and lighter look and feel—a garden feel—from the sandstone color of the brick, to patios for ground floor residents, to wider and brighter hallways, without the smell of Lysol and oil soap. The kitchen smells escaped to the outside with exhaust fans located near the kitchen window. Entrances sealed out the world beyond the hallway, with space heaters/air conditioners located near the horizontal bank of vertical mailboxes displaying a variety of makeshift name labels—a controlled and efficient existence to help make the world in recovery a bit more comfortable.

This project centered on the goal of squeezing the most people into the least amount of stacked space, with the objective to eliminate as much of the tenement feel as possible. After all, who wants to smell what delightful flavors someone may be concocting after a hard day at work? I can imagine how the planning meeting might have gone down: minimize the presence of others in close proximity to create the illusion of exclusivity in an otherwise high-density, moderate-impact, and non-exclusive suburban environment.

One innovation inspired by inner city public pools and bath houses was the apartment swimming pool. This was as close to luxury living as any of us would experience at this time of our lives—a multi-purpose gathering place in the hot summer months that kept temperatures and tempers cool, while teenage and young adult libidos heated along the makeshift runways of the pool's edge and diving board.

The project was the perfect pre-adolescent playground to run completely amok—a luxury we didn't enjoy in Kentland. Dodge Park was at least two cuts above Kentwood. We were now living in gulag-chic, and happy to be there. For me, an important added benefit with this setup was feeling relatively safe from the stalking of Myr. I never let down my guard, but I had some breathing room. I don't believe he knew where we moved, if at all. I rarely saw his car up at this end of Landover Road. Avoiding another attack was a constant. Surviving the recovery was still submerged deep into my subconscious.

I was living in the classic grey area between being a little kid and moving into the bullpen to warm up for my debut on the adolescent mound. I met a boy named Mike who lived in the next building on the patio level. His mom was as a waitress at Howlin's and his dad was a Prince George's County cop. I loved spending time with Mike. His parents called him Mickey and he had about two years on me. In the world of coming of age, two years difference felt like five. They were always doing something fun in the summer, to which I was sometimes invited. Having these experiences with him and his family gave me a welcomed feeling of relief from what I would otherwise have to face at home. Unlike many of the friends and acquaintances I developed during this unusual time, Mike came from a solid and stable family. Whatever baggage they lugged, if any, the family possessed the grace and class to keep it between them. Mike never came off like he had something to prove as it related to our slight difference in years. He simply accepted me for who and what I was. Many years later, I developed a deep and abiding appreciation for his friendship during those turbulent times.

A girl around Mike's age named Carol was another standout who lived in the project. Unlike Mike, who was an only child, she had several younger siblings to help keep in line. Mike was typically quiet and understated in his personality, whereas Carol had a more animated and outgoing quality in her personality—it wasn't typical silly adolescent shit that was so universal for that age and time. She had a self-confidence beyond her years that came through in her quirky sense of humor.

Carol was my first adolescent crush, fueled not solely by the fact that she was a slightly older and attractive girl, but that she was so interesting, funny, and outgoing. Attraction to someone of the opposite sex because of the quality of her personality was conceptually lost on me—I accepted it as a matter of fact and never gave it a second thought. In a perfect world, maybe a Thornton Wilder moment, someone would have sidled up to me and whispered, "Pay close attention to this feeling kid, because this is the way it should always be. Physical attraction will speak for itself." I chose to keep those feelings locked away in my secret chamber. Even then, I knew Carol and Mike had each other's hearts.

It was inevitable that they would marry. Like Ronnie and Linda, they remained together for more than 50 years—two good and decent kids who escaped the monsters hiding under the bed and choosing to build a wonderful and lasting life together. For every kid who succeeded in dodging and weaving through the minefields of dysfunction and evil, there were two coming from a family life similar to mine. Those are the kids to whom Karen and I typically gravitated—misery breeds misery. We were always parading some kind of inherited impairment, which enabled us to create our own emotional contagions—fighting among ourselves, starting fights with others, petty theft, vandalism. These were the blueprints of what my surroundings established as a normal existence.

Ronnie was pretty much out of the picture by now, but when he was around, he was put in the middle as Mom's enforcer, and he grew tired of it. Although he and I still shared a bedroom, my late-teens brother worked a full-time job, drove a beautiful 1964 Bahama green Chevy Impala, with a saddle tan interior, and always spent his free time at the firehouse or with Linda. By now, Linda, her mom, and her two sisters had packed their wagon and moved from Kentland to Dodge Park, close to our location. It was beginning to look like one big happy family.

The presence of older kids running the streets, many in their late teens and early twenties, was rampant in Dodge Park. I was living a schism that was tearing me between what mattered in my heart as the kid who wanted to make his music, read his comics, and go off into his little fantasy worlds of make-believe, and this tough street-kid in the training cage who was always expected to display his bravado, especially as a preemptive strike.

A dual identity began to emerge in me. However, I was no stranger to the concept, starting with Clark Kent and Superman. The dichotomy was that Superman existed to eliminate evil, whereas in my little world of duality, I emerged from the priming of the street to blur the lines between what was right and wrong. My parents reinforced my conflicted values and behaviors because they lived their lives so much in the cracks and crevices of established moral codes. Both had a strong work ethic, but I believe, like so many who shared a similar station in life, if ever an opportunity came along to get something for nothing, they would jump at the chance. That was especially true with Dad and his gambling habits—why bust your ass scrapping out a living every day if you can't cut out and spend a few hours and risk a few dollars at the track?

There was no escaping the continued widespread sexual predation. This time Karen was the victim. She already transformed from girl to womanhood by the age of eight. She looked at least five years older than she was. The long-term brain damage doctors feared would develop from the jaundice treatment at birth was beginning to show in her emotional development. She was acting more impulsive and erratic, and she loved the attention of boys. This was the beginning of Karen's long and difficult slide, taking her through the next 45 years.

Before long, adolescent sexual predators next-door, along with their friends, and a maintenance man, set upon Karen and others. I was helpless to save my sister. Anger and frustration were all I could bring to bear, because I knew all too well what she and other girls had to endure.

The fighting between Karen and me intensified; we were completely adrift and desperate for stable parental supervision. We competed for whatever attention was available, positive or otherwise, wherever we could find it. If she and I had been shown cooperation and compassion from the ones closest to us, we would have likely developed closer bonds and seen these horrors through together. Such sibling support was not to be. I at least had the positive example set by Mike and Carol's families to offset the dysfunction inside of our walls. I don't recall Karen having such an example in her circle of peers. She was no less deserving of such relief. My time in Dodge Park was the stage setting for many turning points in my life, some with long-lasting consequences, especially in my world of sound and music.

THE NEW MUSIC ON THE top 40 stations was so unusual, stirring many new emotions in me, especially the chord changes. At the time, I didn't specifically know what chord changes were. All I knew was something besides the melody was stirring new feelings. I wanted to hear more. The vocal harmonies were beyond ethereal beauty. All of this was ironically supported by a marvelous rock and roll groove. This was my first perception of transformation of style. One day, the DJ announced that this was the latest hit from a British group called The Beatles. The first picture I saw of them was in the newspaper, as a preview to the start of their U.S. tour, beginning in Washington, D.C. at the Washington Coliseum. They wore long hair, at least by the standards of 1964. They dressed in unusual suits with high-heeled boots. One thing was certain: you either loved them or not. The adults typically fell into the latter camp. Most of us were completely swept up in their uniqueness and irreverent attitudes. At the heart of it all was this unforgettable music, sounding both new and familiar.

On Sunday, February 9th, at 8 p.m., The Beatles would appear on *The Ed Sullivan Show.* That was all I needed to hear. The worldwide transforming impact of this moment was on the same level of firsts as seeing Sputnik, or John Glenn and Scott Carpenter blasting off to orbit the Earth, followed closely by the Cuban Missile Crisis and the assassination of John F. Kennedy. Like a tsunami that starts small then engulfs everything in its wake, these events possessed a self-generating energy no one ever expected.

After the initial shock of hearing the live performance not sounding like the record, I soaked in every detail. This was the shot I needed to push me to the next level. I bought all of their records and listened constantly. Without lessons or guidance, my efforts would remain an uphill trek.

May 6th, 1964, at D.C. Stadium: a baseball game between the New York Yankees and the Washington Senators was in progress. Dad was in the stands with two friends. Sitting next to him were two women, one of whom was a lovely 20-something redhead who bore a small resemblance to Patty Duke. Her name was Carol Taylor. She would become the only life force capable of adding a much-needed dimension of clarity and discipline to Dad's increasingly downward trajectory toward self-destruction. Carol was born and raised in the small eastern North Carolina factory town of Tarboro and was a fast-rising secretary at the Central Intelligence Agency. She learned that he drove a beverage delivery truck, had a 10 year old son, a seven year old daughter, a 19 year old stepson, and a growing criminal record. She gave my father choices that would only improve his life. He was an occasional millstone around her neck. Whatever the attraction was for her to hitch her wagon to his star is one of the great unspoken and unsolved mysteries. Maybe there really is such a thing as a guardian angel.

Even as a young boy, I immediately fell in love with Carol's stellar example of independence, her unflagging work ethic, and no-bullshit attitude. Her love of family and children was foremost in her heart. She was the quintessential Southern girl—if given a choice, sitting around talking or playing a game was preferable to watching television. After four long years, Dad's divorce from Mom was official. Carol and he married on November 7th, 1964. She was born exactly 13 years to the day of my birth. Oh, how the Spiral loves the convergent repetition.

Dodge View

I LOVED 007. AN ADULT neighbor introduced me to Ian Fleming's British spy character James Bond. Yet another character possessing a dual identity found me lying in wait. The attraction for me went beyond the romance of always living life on the edge with a beautiful femme fatale, who eventually comes around to his way of doing things. I loved all of the self-confidence it took for 007 to pull it off. It all came down to being about the secret.

I could relate on some primal level to the concept of the secret identity that must, at all costs, be kept secret. I abandoned my infatuation with Superman. I was embracing a more realistic vision of what it would be like to live as someone whose professional concealment was not to deceive with a costume worn under a costume, but to infiltrate as I am—to hide in plain sight. It was time for me to leave the world of the comic book superhero. By sixth grade, I owned all of the Fleming books and read them with great fascination. Having a stepmother working at high levels in the CIA made this clandestine world even more attractive because for her, it was all too real.

The big move was once again upon us. In the summer of 1965, we packed up and set off for the next encampment, directly next to Dodge Park. It was an effortless downhill coast by a distance of half a football field. Dodge View was the name of the project, and like High Point, Kentwood, and Dodge Park, with their misleading names, Dodge View had no view, except for the back of another 7-Eleven store. However, we now had a balcony. This feature marked a serious rise in class. Full-scale gulag-chic arrived in full glory and sixth grade was about to start.

I soon absorbed into the periphery of the street tribes. The hierarchies were made up of older alphas. They owned hot cars with girlfriends who went all the

88   STEVE ROCHINSKI

way. They also wore tattoos and owned rap sheets, including any number of misdemeanors salted on the rim with a felony or two. These were the baddest of the badasses, short of having membership in the local chapter of an outlaw motorcycle club—a whole other level of tribalism requiring more from their members than any of these guys could afford.

The alpha echelon tribal tattoo read, "God's Little Acre—Kentland, MD." The required tribal dress was called block. Depending on the time of day, day of the week, and the occasion, the typical block uniform consisted of Chuck Taylor tennis shoes and Ban-Lon shirts. Pants were any color of works held up with a tweed belt. Headwear was a cotton knit cool cap. A Peter's brand jacket, with your name in cursive stitch on the upper left, or a black leather coat finished the ensemble. Hair was short and greasy. Badass-approved fragrances came down to English Leather, Canoe, or Brut.

Our music was soul, soul, and more soul—sweet soul music. The two venerable AM soul stations located in the District were WOL and WOOK. WOOK featured a DJ named the Moon Man. His opening patter was classic 1960s inner-urban pre-izzle: "What's happin'n at WOOK, everything in the book… the nitty gritty in the Capitol City, I'm the Moon Man with the Bald-Headed Baby." No translation was required. One of my great joys was dialing into one of the two soul stations on a Saturday night with the radio under my pillow, and waking up to the Sunday morning gospel programming.

The block style was stolen directly from the black inner city street culture going back to the 1930s. And therein lies the Great Lie and Contradiction. One group, who isn't confident enough to create something to represent their own unique experiences with their stations in the world, absconded a style and culture from a group for whom they held nothing but learned, third-hand contempt and hatred. The hypocrisy bothered me, and any questioning of it would not go unpunished.

I made choices to survive the streets, adding one more layer to compound the desire for the secret identity. As one of many betas and omegas waiting in the shadows, I fought and challenged among the others for the next spot in the order of succession into the ranks of the alphas. Everything was subjective and zero-sum—period. It was all a fucking charade and I hated it. Someone said that civilization is the process of setting man free from men. What reasonable argument can possibly stand against such an axiom? I wish I knew that then.

Ronnie and Linda married in 1965 as he moved into the ranks of the professional firefighter. He trained his sights on the D.C. fire department because that was the big show in the world of flame warriors. He and Linda found an apartment on the edge of Kent Village, directly behind Jimmy's Crab House. It was here they would start their family. In June of 1966, my nephew, Michael, was born. My niece, Michelle, was not far behind. Life for them was holding its own. I was excited to be an uncle; another rite of passage into the world of adults.

Dad and Carol married and moved into the third and final apartment project bordering Landover Road, next to Dodge View. The time Karen and I spent with Carol and Dad were the happiest and calmest in our sibling lives. There was a sense of uncomplicated fun and joy; it all seemed so normal. However, I could always feel the dark pull and pall of Mom's anger and negativity. She always took time to subject both of us to the third degree. If we expressed anything in the positive, she destroyed it with her negative judgments.

My NEWFOUND INSULARITY SERVED ME well: to carve out a single focus on following the music, and what I had to realize in the security of sonic wonderment. Ironically, I enjoyed some comfort running the streets in my beta/ omega block-wearing and shit-jyeah sneer. Secret dual identities came with a price because the deeper current was a lack of confidence and trust in the world around me. In the long run, the most damaging impact is that being without such convictions becomes a normal state of mind. I was the only one to whom I could turn. The ideal image of the Mother and Child statue was, by now, starting to dissipate, like a windswept sand sculpture fighting to maintain some semblance of its original integrity. Five years on, my fear of Myr remained.

I loved summer Sundays with Carol watching Dad play on a softball team sponsored by none other than Paul's Tavern. To describe this place as a toilet or a sewer, or any other foul image, would be an insult to all hard-working waste containment systems. The education I received in this place and others like it was priceless.

Dad spent time in this shithole partly for the comic relief. He was always laughing at something or someone—maybe as a sign of malicious joy he got from the suffering of others. The company of the regular broken-down men and the occasional woman, who lived such pointless and perfunctory lives, consuming more than they created, was enough to challenge anyone's sense of life—even that of a kid. By comparison, Dad's life choices looked pretty good. The most emblematic statement on this entire spectacle of letdowns and disappointments was an abandoned 1958 Edsel, rusting away on the side of the tavern in a ragweed-covered industrial waste sculpture garden, strewn with old freezers, transmissions, and drive shafts.

Besides the holes kicked into the bottom of the bar, there were holes punched into most of the walls and all of the souls. The trenchant smell of garlic breath from one regular, who was breaking new medical ground in treating heart disease, among the redolence unique to a beer joint, made this a seminary for the urban drunk—where a man could stop in on the way home from work to unwind with a beer or two, and when he got home, may be too out of sorts and less inclined to break his wife's arm for burning the rice (although liquor has been known to have the opposite effect when filtering the emotional response of a drunk to an unsuccessful dinner plan).

One of Dad's blunders was using the cover of Paul's to hatch plans for establishing a major bookmaking ring—a big-time operation covering the entire D.C., Maryland, and Virginia area. All of the actors were eventually busted in a major raid, resulting in Dad doing more jail time thanks to the uncontrolled chirping of a washed-out courtesan known only as J-Bird. She was one of the rare female regulars who kept her glass full by taking guys out to the abandoned Edsel to test the shocks and change the oil. Dad rebuked her advances. As payback, she dropped a dime on him and the entire gambling ring to the FBI.

On the evening the big bust went down, Carol happened to be driving home in D.C. rush hour traffic. This was just another day of doing her part to keep our nation's secrets safe from our foreign enemies. Making her way to the South Capitol Street Bridge, she noticed a major traffic jam caused by dozens of police vehicles. Carol had no reason to think her betrothed was at the center of this civic upheaval. As Dad later described it, "…everyone's fucked up on Bennies for three straight days, and we're counting nearly a quarter million dollars in cash—all of a sudden, these sons of bitches started crashing through the ceilings, doors, floors, and windows with guns drawn, screaming and hollering, telling everyone to stay put with our hands on our heads."

A fitting epitaph for my father's continued ungraceful fall was found written on the back wall of Paul's: "When J-Bird comes a-knockin', make sure the Edsel's rockin'."

———

THERE WAS A KNOCK AT Ronnie and Linda's door. It was the prodigal father, Joe Danner, standing at the threshold. Four years passed since he appeared in the Kentwood parking lot. Since then, no phone call, no card—nothing. Ronnie invited him to join them for dinner. For the next several hours, they all enjoying what turned out to be a pleasant evening. No drama, just sitting around talking and sharing a few laughs. Joe got to see and play with his newborn grandson. Ronnie noticed how much his dad liked babies and thought what Joe lacked as a father, maybe he could make up for it as a grandfather. The evening drew to a close and all said their goodbyes. Joe gave a prolonged and tender goodbye to his grandson. He said there was some unfinished business in Baltimore, and then he would be disappearing for a while. After saying their goodbyes, Joe Danner drove off into the night.

Later that same night, Mom and I were watching television in our usual locations. At a little past 11 o'clock, Mom bolted from a dead sleep on the couch with a scream. This time, there was no imaginary prowler at the balcony door or an unexpected phone call. What startled her was the 11 o'clock news. The announcer reported that the FBI, after a brief gun battle at a downtown

Baltimore hotel, shot and killed Joseph Crawford Danner, the one-time leader of the notorious Pimple-Face Gang from Newport News. After several attempts to let him surrender, he escaped down a string of bedsheets into an alley. Agents were waiting and after Joe opened fire, they killed him on the spot. The reason for Joe's appearance in Baltimore and why the FBI was in pursuit were not yet known. During what turned out to be the last time father and son would ever see each other, Ronnie recalled that night four years before in Newport News, "Before you get out of the car, I want to tell you why what you are about to see happened. From the time I was a kid, I've believed that most of the people in this world just go mindlessly along and never question anything getting in their way. They'll go wherever the crowd takes them, like a bunch of fucking sheep being herded to the slaughterhouse. Now, go ahead and get out and take a good look." It was traffic cones! Joe Danner pulled traffic cones out of the trunk and spread them across the highway. He brought Interstate 64 to a mindless, grinding, and detoured halt with traffic cones in the middle of the night, with no indication of official state highway activity or police presence. It was simply traffic cones; sheep to the slaughterhouse.

The next day at work, Ronnie picked up the morning edition of the newspaper and saw the headline announcing his father's demise. In the moment of receiving this shocking news, my brother found a second to laugh at that memory.

The FBI had been on Joe's trail for weeks with a charge of attempted murder. The agents also happened to be hiding in the parking lot when he stopped in to see Ronnie. The reason they didn't apprehend him then was the risk of Joe either taking a hostage or a gun battle.

A couple of days later, Ronnie got a call to pick up Joe's black 1958 Chevy. When he arrived at the Baltimore police impound lot, he saw a beautiful '58 Chevy in showroom condition fitting the color description. Having not seen the actual condition of Joe's car on that last night, Ronnie assumed Joe would not have been driving any vehicle that was less than pristine. Joe's car turned out to be a complete piece of shit on the backside of the lot; a total wreck. Ronnie was barely able to drive it the 40 miles back home. Next morning, he opened the trunk and found a suitcase filled with all types of disguises, hair dyes, and wigs.

When Joe left their apartment, Ronnie had a foreboding sense that would be the last time they would ever see one another. Yet, with this man whose only claim to fatherhood was biological, there was a moment of poignancy in their final embrace. With an apologetic tone in his final statements to Ronnie, Joe's last words to his only son were, "Live clean." As Ronnie went to sleep, the last thing he remembered thinking about was traffic cones. Ronnie always believed his father chose suicide by cop over life without parole.

———————

WHEN I FIRST HEARD THE opening guitar riff in the main title music of *Goldfinger*, I knew it must join the other riffs I was picking up along the way. The orchestrations I heard during countless viewings of the Bond movies at the Cheverly were captivating. They awakened in me an appreciation and a vivid awareness of something more than pitch and rhythm. What I heard was the importance that instrumental color had on the notes. I needed to hear this music again and again, so I bought all of the soundtracks. This acquisition was another thing I believed was best kept a secret—this was music by adults for adults, and not the music my peers would listen to.

Night after night, I sat in my bedroom playing the records. Once I figured out the riff, I spent more time listening, subconsciously absorbing every detail of the music, especially the brass and the majestic beauty of the French horns. In a short time, I had worn down the frets and developed bleeding callouses on the tips of my fingers—a small, but necessary price to pay.

One night, angry pounding came from the apartment directly above. What an unexpected surprise. As the weeks went on, the pounding from above stopped, replaced by what sounded like a tribal mating ritual with drums, maracas, bells, whistles, claves, and possibly a sacrificial virgin. If the playing surface was made of metal, wood, or with skin stretched across it, they played it loud and long, usually starting at 11 at night.

Mom thought they were doing this as a deliberate attempt to drive her out of what little mind she had remaining. Each night she would reply in kind by pounding on the ceiling with a broomstick, accompanied with a string of expletives sounding like she was purging demons. This pissed them off even more, and so the battle wore on and on. It wasn't until a week or two into the skirmish when I made the connection that what started this battle of the bands was in all likelihood my guitar. The tribal standoff gradually subsided, for the time being.

Not long after, an official-looking envelope arrived in the mail. It was from the Dodge View management company. The letter was requesting possession of our apartment. Eviction was swiftly upon us and all because of my guitar. Instead of the traditional picking up and moving every year or so falling entirely on Mom's shoulders, I was now doing my part to keep the show and wagons moving on.

The path of least resistance was to relocate several hundred yards to the west, to the last apartment project on Landover Road. This was the same project where Carol and Dad lived, but had long since vacated. The final twist was almost too ironic: this rather milquetoast-looking young couple, pretending to be members of the Igbo tribe, were the music teachers at Bladensburg High School.

So, we beat on, wagon and guitar against the current, borne back ceaselessly into the past with the help of the Good Lawdy Miss Agnes' Rope Show, featuring Little Spleetus and his E Chordestra—with all due apologies to F. Scott Fitzgerald.

Landover Gardens

THERE WASN'T A GODDAMNED GARDEN in sight, earthly delights or otherwise, unless you want to count the poison ivy patches living on the edge of the grass lines, mixed in with some greens from the Paleo pre-construction period. Landover Gardens was the last in line of the three major encampments along this static stretch of Landover Road. If we moved any further west, we'd be living at the railroad tracks with the gandy dancers.

In 1967, I entered seventh grade at Kent Junior High in Palmer Park—a major milestone in the world of adolescent rites of passage. (Palmer Park actually possessed all of the missing attributes found in the fallacious names of the projects I lived in since 1961. The town had woods, a park, a view, and gardens.) Kent had a reputation for churning out the baddest of the greaser street culture, which impacted anyone enrolled in this out-of-control environment. Ronnie was fully ensconced in the D.C. fire department and Karen was in fourth grade. Karen's emotional state of mind continued on a slow and steady burn and downturn. Life at home was never more difficult and my emotional state was no better, but I was able keep it reasonably contained with a less impulsive nature. Karen and I were beyond salvaging any kind of a normal sibling relationship—a not-so-peaceful coexistence was taking hold. Many of my Dodge Park friends had come and gone, but I still had infrequent contact with Carol and Mike at Kent. We drifted further apart and went our separate ways for the next 50 years.

Junior high was an adjustment on many levels. Instead of spending the entire day in one classroom with the same 20 kids, we started in homeroom, creating the day's scripts for pubescent posturing and maneuvering for alpha dominance to carry one through the day. Once released, we went through the day to different subject classrooms until lunchtime, and then we would resume the shuffle until dismissal. Subjective academic sections established hierarchies ranking intelligence and peer identities. Sections 1 through 14 were a sliding scale that would mark you for the duration.

It's reasonable to think that once I got into junior high, I'd take advantage of the music class, however, that wasn't the case. The class consisted of a lot of singing of songs of little interest to me. There was some focus on music theory, such as the names of the notes in treble clef, time signatures, and basic rhythmic values. The problem was the abstract presentation of this information. If I had been told, "Here kid, this is what you can do with this information," then I would have shown more interest.

THE GUITAR AND AMP THAT helped evict us from Dodge View was unplayable. For most of the year or so that we lived in The Gardens, I owned no guitar, and no one was offering to buy me one. To my surprise, on Christmas, I found a new guitar under the tree.

I continued a major push upward to the next level of musicianship. It was also my good fortune there were a lot of older guys living in The Gardens who were quite good for being self-taught players. One of them owned the gold standard of equipment—a Fender Jazzmaster guitar and a Fender Twin amp. He knew all of The Ventures tunes, as well as a lot of pop standards. He often raved about his favorite guitar players who played jazz—names like Tony Mottola, Johnny Smith, Howard Roberts, Barney Kessel, Herb Ellis, and someone named Tal Farlow. That name really stood out because it had such an interesting sound—like that of a Western storybook hero. My exposure to jazz guitar players was very limited, but I knew if they played jazz, they must be the best.

The instrumental guitar music of The Ventures was an absolute requirement for anyone of my generation claiming to be a guitarist. It was accessible, simple, melodic, and memorable. I learned their music along with as much of the music on the AM radio airwaves as I could assimilate. I played wherever and whenever I could—usually in someone's backyard for the surrounding neighborhood, much to the approval of the kids and much to the dismay of the parents. My first public performance for money, for a birthday party, came at the age of 12. Another kid I knew could sing only two tunes, which I also happened to know. Our pay was cake and five dollars each. I didn't ask for any girl's phone number, but the gig was otherwise a rousing success. The buzz from the day lingered long. Not a bad night's take for a 12 year old.

Before receiving the new guitar for Christmas, I had to find ways to gain access to a guitar, any guitar. One day at Capital Plaza, I discovered that Montgomery Wards stocked various musical instruments. There was a wall filled with their Airline brand guitars. I figured I didn't need permission, so I sat there and played. A salesman suggested I plug in to really hear it. Actually, his strategy was to have the sound amplified so customers would gather to hear the products in action; the true mark of a good salesman. Because I could play a little, I became a de facto demonstrator and an unspoken partnership began. Anytime I was in the store, I was welcome to come by and plug in.

In my quest to learn more Ventures songs, I discovered a "Play Along with The Ventures" album. This was a brilliant variation on what was called Music Minus One. The album contained the original tracks of several hits, like "Walk, Don't Run" and "Tequila," with the lead guitar track removed. You learned a basic fingering for the melody from a booklet notated with tablature and neck diagrams. The cost of the record was out of my range, so I did the next best thing, starting with 35 cents that bought me a five-mile bus ride to Montgomery Ward.

On the other side of the store was a record section which happened to stock the play-along. I opened it with great care, memorized small portions of the diagram, then I hurried back to the instrument side of the store to practice the melody. When I was ready for more information, I went back and memorized each section until the entire tune was captured.

These auto-didactic moments verified important insights into my learning style—from a constant observation to details and their memorization and retention, to the sonic connection of the complex and tessellating visual nature of the fretboard. This was my solitary path to a deeper understanding. There was nothing in a traditional classroom environment that would give me the sense of excitement or accomplishment than these crystalized moments. I was also planting the early seeds of learning how to teach myself—for me to be responsible for what I needed to know. I came to conclusions I knew to be true, and there was no one around me who could tell me otherwise. In nine years, the virtuoso studio and jazz guitar legend Howard Roberts would validate my conclusions.

———

I NEVER WORRIED ABOUT OR lamented how my family life wasn't the same as that of my friends. I was too distracted with my hyper-focus on the guitar, as well as my adolescent diversion with girls. Fitting in with the ever-evolving stream of alphas in my street life was another distraction. The fact that there were so few single mothers raising kids wasn't something I considered odd or out of place.

After all was said and done, there were only two or three in my life I entirely trusted, with me at the top of the list, followed by Granddaddy, and then Carol. Eventually, I would be the only one from that short list left standing. I still lived in fear of Myr, despite my day-to-day functions and demands. Creating the conditions for one's own recovery doesn't guarantee success. I was simply driven by my need to survive, with desire at my back as a silent and unseen force.

Kent Village, Act 1

AFTER SEVENTH GRADE, WE MOVED the show several hundred yards across Landover Road to a cracker box, second-floor red brick apartment in Kent Village. We nearly squared the circle in six years—we were a scant 200 yards from the Kentwood unit. Our family troupe had taken a four-year, one square mile journey. The rest of 1967 was reasonably uneventful.

By contrast, 1968 was a banner year for assassinations and every other social, cultural, and political upheaval any country could endure. In the throes of such rapid change, the adults still seemed clueless about how to live life through the lens of objectivity, like putting reason before emotions, or regarding people first as individuals and not as some faceless and feckless representatives of a collective or group.

We, the kids, were oblivious to our error in thinking that secondhand awareness of adult realities was commensurate with firsthand experience. We believed that such awareness was the only requirement to prove ourselves as equals to the grown-ups. Age of consent never crossed our mind, until we crossed the line before our time.

The adults had a good head start with figuring out the shit of life, but they demonstrated greater skill in creating lasting negative consequences than we, the kids, usually at the cost of sacrificing individual accountability.

I BEGAN NOTICING HOW THE outward appearance of many friends I knew from earlier years took on new and unexpected costumes, particularly in the wholesale embrace of the hippie and flower power movements. I was still in full-blown block and greaser mode. The choices I made at the start of eighth grade took me to the darkest side of the sneering and defiant. The bottom of my academic life collapsed and sent me in a free fall. The whirlwind changes in the world paralleled the changes in my ever-increasing social life.

Word soon spread about how well I could play my instrument, which bought me some unexpected cache among the older alphas. They were intolerant of the fringe dwellers, and any opportunity to single out someone from the edges and keep them in line was never passed up. However, they didn't fuck around with me—they showed a small shred of respect because I was younger and could do something they admired. I usually kept a safe distance and only moved into their orbit if I was invited and the coast was clear. Many of these guys were on their way to an early death by cop, car, drugs, or some serious prison time; few got out alive or intact. Rampant heroin use was also on the rise among this crew. There was nothing they wouldn't do to get their fix.

My first steady girlfriend—if a few months qualify as steady—appeared during this time. She was the first girl I ever declared to anyone in my family as being my girlfriend—a major step in trusting others to not judge my burgeoning romances. She was a bit of a wild child who possessed many of the same traits as my mother. She defined her self-worth through the approval and desires of boys and men—an all-too-familiar song. All we were doing was going through the motions as the currency of the example from those adults closest to us.

School became nothing more than a stage for social interaction and playing games of dominance. Learning was the last thing on my mind. The teachers concluded I was a lost cause. I went from section 7-2 in seventh grade, down by two to 8-4 for eighth grade. Like the Richter scale, this simple two-digit drop betrayed the true exponential increase in the severity of this fall from academic and social grace.

Kent Village, Act 2 and Epilogue

Tattoos, one on each upper arm, made their inevitable appearance to balance the first one Ricky C. jabbed on my right hand the year before. I also began putting them on friends. Being a jabber with a good, controlled hand wasn't a top requirement for jailhouse-inspired body staining. Another year or so would pass before I ventured out under the radar to get my first and only professional tattoo as the last of my tribal markings.

Between finishing eighth grade and moving into the ninth, everything moved at a supersonic blur. I established a home base when I started working at the pizza shop in Kent Village. I also landed a highly coveted job for anyone in my peer group: shining shoes and sweeping up at the Kentland Barber Shop. The attrition rate for the latter position was low, and you had to do a lot of hanging out and show some initiative by helping without pay—a kind of barber college/janitorial internship—all for the honor of bragging rights and on-the-life training.

———————

T&G Pizza was, from all outward appearances, your average non-descript lunch counter, just like any other on the planet. It was small and narrow, with seating for only four. Other than the stools, the only furniture was a jukebox. On the inside, what went on with the owner and the central cast of characters that made up this odd tragicomedy troupe bordered on the pataphysical. Bernie, the owner, was in his early forties and married to a wispy blonde who resembled someone's second grade teacher. They appeared to be your average American couple. Bernie developed a reputation for being a benevolent friend to all, going out of his way to assist anyone with money, shelter, or whatever the need happened to be. He was also one of the biggest fences for stolen property in the county. The shop was a working front for clearing and cleaning hundreds of thousands of dollars a year in stolen bonds, jewelry, storm doors—you name it, he moved it.

Among the regulars was Charlie, the Lonely Wolf. He was short, thin, and in his thirties, who enjoyed his reserved perch at the end of the counter; not sitting hip to hip with everyone else facing the ovens, but at the turn of the counter with room only for Charlie, like the period at the bottom of an exclamation point. He stared hard at the profiles of those at the counter, acquaintances and strangers alike. He enjoyed the dominant position of seeing only what he needed to see in each individual, believing half a face told the whole story. He was well positioned to control all eye contact and interactions. If they wanted to communicate with him, they must turn their heads and meet his already full-on countenance; everything was on his terms.

Most of the time, Charlie just sat there in wistful silence, staring into his Coke on ice, which he served himself. As a customer, having behind-the-counter access gave one an air of status and cache; almost an air of privilege and invincibility. The Lonely Wolf always kept his pack of Pall Mall cigarettes neatly to his right with his perfectly maintained silver Zippo lighter positioned squarely on the center of the pack. He pumped endless quarters into the jukebox and the only button he ever selected was B-9, "Lady Willpower." Every time the chorus line, "…Lady Willpower, it's now or never give your love to me. I'll shower your heart with tenderness, endlessly…" was sung, Charlie, with his slight under bite, madras print shirt buttoned up to the top, and green work pants with an old brown belt cinched two notches too tight, would look up from staring into his Coke on ice and the lit cigarette in his nicotine-stained fingers, portraying a look of deep-seated poignancy, tinged with a gaze of defiant self-assurance, and an occasional tear. The piteousness in his eyes turned his soul inside out. It was often too much for me to witness.

There was a steady stream of adolescent girls who frequented the shop. When they took their rightful spots at the counter, they reminded me of fragile figurines perched in a grandmother's shadow box. They all had an unhealthy attraction to the avuncular personality of Bernie. I learned years later that he was one of the busiest sexual predators in the neighborhood; one more in a seemingly endless deep vein of local sexually depraved men with sad and desperate lives. He was filling a vacuum in the lives of these girls, most likely created by the absence of, or maybe abuse of, a father or some other male influence. It seemed that few, if any, in positions of power or authority were trustworthy.

One fateful night, a fever of hippies in full freak regalia came in and thoroughly upset the place. The alpha freak was a tall bearded guy wearing a brown fedora. He looked like Shakespeare doing an impersonation of Walt Whitman, replete with hat and an animal skin tunic. Charlie happened to be listening to B-9 when the interloper dropped in a quarter and selected Steppenwolf's "Magic Carpet Ride." Charlie was unhappy that his little romantic fantasy world was upset with this far-out tune, and he made it known to all with a squinting side-eye glance and scowl. Little did I know that I was witnessing a prophecy that would forever impact and seal my life as significantly as had my abuser, Myr.

———

THE CHILDREN'S CHOIR PART OF this carry-out troupe consisted of many players, some of whom were the alphas from the Dodge Park/Kentland tribes. Bernie always had some job or scheme to put us to work to do his bidding, like running errands for the shop, or pulling some kind of larceny, which gave him distance and plausible deniability. I learned that Bernie was in way over his head with the cost of running the shop, along with his losses from bad jewelry he fenced to some local mobsters.

One night, Bernie enlisted the help of Ricky C., his two brothers, and me to join in a heist he planned. A new housing development was going up east of Kentland. For weeks, he surveyed what building materials he could steal to sell. Fencing new storm doors was the new flavor of the week. One problem was that only the occupied houses had such doors. So, the plan was for the brothers and me to take a midnight ride.

We parked in an easy access spot near the targeted houses. I went along with Ricky as the flashlight holder/lookout. The escapade was going off without a hitch for the first three doors. While the other two were getting a fourth door, we were about halfway around the frame of our final door when suddenly, the front porch light came on and the door opened with a man holding a shotgun. Instead of being thrown into a panic and attempting to outrun 12-gauge bird shot, Ricky, by some temporary stroke of genius, was able to think quickly on his feet.

He convinced this guy that we worked for the developer. Our work order required us to replace all of the iron screws with aluminum to prevent rusting. When the homeowner asked why we were working at such a strange hour of the morning, Ricky explained there were 200 doors to fix and his was the last on the list. Payment was by the screw, and the one who showed up the next morning with the most iron screws would get a bonus. I stood there swaying in disbelief. Ricky must have thought this out ahead of time. The man said to keep quiet and left the porch light on. Once we finished, the door was off, as were we.

The pizza shop became a gathering point for the varlets of the world with an apprentice program for the kids. As long as Bernie approved, so did everyone else.

ONE AFTERNOON, I WAS WORKING a busy lunch rush. The place was three deep, packed to the windows with hungry people of many occupations. Bernie asked me to make the pizzas. Charlie sat there playing B-9, staring into his Coke. I looked up and my legs buckled. My head and ears began to pound with a surge of fear-driven adrenaline. There he stood—Myr. It was my first encounter in nearly seven years. I thought I had escaped his shadowing tentacles, but there he stood…dressed and disguised in a Wackenhut security guard uniform, staring a hole right through me without once diverting his gaze. My peripheral vision quit working; it was as if we were the only ones in the room. Everything I feared came rushing toward me like a runaway train, where one stood frozen in fear and resignation and waited for it to kill you, because running would do you no good.

My last encounter with him went back five years, while walking through the field behind Kay Cee. He seemed to have appeared out of thin air. He called me over, asking for help in getting something from the basement storage room of the apartments. By then, I was smarter and wiser. I ignored him and went about my business. I believed with utmost conviction, that had I been stupid enough to again fall for his mendacity, he most assuredly would have murdered me as his final act of control and assurance of my silence.

I couldn't bear the stress of standing there any longer. I dropped what I was doing and retreated into the back to lock myself in a small bathroom. I was now a trapped and frightened animal—every sense I had was on high alert, and escape at any cost was all I could think of. Bernie was calling in a panic for me to come back and help him. I was too terrified to respond. The only way out was for me to climb up a long airshaft to a skylight—an impossible task, because there was no way to get high enough to grab onto something and start the climb. Assuming the worst and being in a state of emotional reduction, with my lower brain engulfed in flames, I would have killed anyone who came through that door.

I don't know how much time passed—minutes or days, it didn't matter. Eventually, Bernie came banging on the door asking if I was okay. I told him I was sick, which I was. I cracked the door to listen for crowd noise; it sounded like the lunch rush was over. I emerged from my shithouse cell and—except for Charlie at his spot on the corner of the counter, listening to "Lady Willpower," the place was empty. I left trembling in silence.

The place that I believed was safe, the place I thought of as a home away from home, where adults and kids were essentially on the same level, was now breeched by this monster. I was once again running for my life.

CHILD SEXUAL ABUSE RAGED ON rampantly and quietly in this day and age. I recall Dad telling me a story about his encounter with a priest when he was a boy in Catholic grade school in the late 1930s. It happened in broad daylight on the playground during school hours—such a brazen act of betrayal, and without compunction on the part of this vestment-costumed swine. There was no one to whom he could turn, because of the fear of God coming at him from all directions. There was no one for me to turn to because of the threat of death.

And then, there was poor Dottie, a dark-haired girl with black horn-rimmed glasses, in her late teens, who was physically well developed, but under-developed in cognitive and emotional skills. She lived with her father and wheelchair-bound mother in Kent Village. We heard rumors that she was being sexually abused by her father—it was all speculation and hearsay until one day, someone cruelly raised the question to her face. She confirmed the truth with the same flat, stoic delivery you'd hear from someone reciting a grocery list. She spared no details about how her father would make sure her mother was asleep in her wheelchair before summoning her into his bedroom; the various acts she was required to perform; how he made sure she contained the semen to dispose of it in the bathroom sink, taking care to never leave a trace of their activity; convincing Dottie that if she ever told her mother, the revelation would surely kill this infirmed woman where she sat.

Dottie's abuse was a daily event of emotional and physical torture and extortion which went on silently for years. The derision she faced from those who knew her story was heartbreaking, but appeared to have no effect—it was as if any feelings of dignity and self-esteem she may have possessed had long since died with her innocence, and in their place lived her 2,000 yard stare. It was the same blank stare into eternity found in the eyes of a female figurehead carved and placed on the prow of a ghost ship forever wandering the seas.

In the 1960s, those who were getting away with these unforgivable violations of trust against kids were often people in positions of authority—deputy sheriffs, scout masters, security guards, merchants, and parents. On and on it went, with each young soul searching for answers to questions they could never ask, and no one to hold accountable.

The most notorious of these sadists wasn't in any public position of authority or trust. He was the father of three boys—an obscure nobody whose existence most people would never give a second thought. He was Mr. R and a legend among the male street blossoms. I never knew what a stag film was until the day he showed me one in his basement. I eventually figured out the intention of the entire operation. Mr. R, who was in all likelihood sexually abusing not only his sons, but also their friends, sent the son I knew out to recruit boys and bring them back to the Palmer Park house—such a young, corrupted master of deception, replete with bad skin and bad teeth. When I arrived, his father was there to greet me as if I was a long-lost family member. We went to the basement to a small partitioned area with a large bed—another lurid detail of this outfit that escaped me, and understandably so.

Mr. R came down the stairs and immediately went into his shtick starting with bringing out humorous sexual novelties and pages of dirty jokes. We then went over to a partitioned area with a projector set up and ready. I let down my well-honed defenses because I trusted that because his son was present, this sick creature would not try and pull any shit with me. Nevertheless, I was still bothered with a gnawing thought about how strange it was for a father and son to be giving sanction to share in such an extreme and taboo form of adult entertainment.

Although overwhelmed by the nonstop bombardment of unending sexual imagery, I never lost control. I sat there calm and cool until it was over. I stood up at his behest and he could see there was no outward impact. Bewilderment contorted their facial muscles, with the old man's eyes showing an eerie, mystified glaze. He saw this was going nowhere and returned upstairs to the kitchen to finish cooking a pot of braised meat. I left on my bike, never to return.

I fell into the lair of Lucky Pierre and emerged intact, unscathed, and victorious. For the first time, I controlled the threat. Kentland alphas often made regular weekend visits to let Mr. R have his way with them. Each departed with three dollars in their pocket. I learned later that Mr. R began recruiting his boy toys when, from time to time, he caught one of his window display assistants attempting to have sex with the mannequins kept in a store room.

I BEGAN EXPANDING MY SOCIAL life to outlying encampments such as Riverdale and Hyattsville. These locations were well outside of walking distance, so hitch-hiking was my principle mode of transportation—a high-risk event that continued my history of chasing DDT foggers and playing in polio-infected puddles. Most of the time, the ride with a stranger was uneventful, but on occasion, I was forced to choose drastic measures to survive harm and possibly death. Broadening my social circles into the border towns was another step toward asserting more and more independence from Mom. I often went to Hyattsville on a Friday night and wouldn't return until Sunday evening, without even a phone call to let her know where I was. I was playing defense with a good offense—after all, she was the one who was always threatening to take off and leave us so that she could live among the missing.

The girls in the Hyattsville tribe were nicer and more accessible than the Kentland girls. During my time with this crew, I dated several girls with a lot of necking and handholding. There was, however, a small, but nagging problem with my self-esteem: I was still technically a virgin, which was unacceptable in the unforgiving world of teenage kids breaking and entering into the adult world. My lack of experience wasn't something I would admit to, nor would anyone ever question it. I'd wager most of the boys and nearly all of the girls fit this category, but we all wanted to think the best of those with whom we bonded.

One night, scores of us gathered at a carnival across from the P.G. Plaza. We arrived like a cloud of locusts on a wheat field ready to search and destroy. With a significant police presence and a lot of motorcycle gang members, we showed self-control and displayed our pinfeathers and baby fangs when it was reasonably safe to do so.

I met a girl named C.K. and of all the girls I met in Hyattsville, she seemed the most approachable. After some time, we split off from the rest of the pack and headed toward a park. We had no destination in mind. We were simply following our eyes.

As we made our way deeper into the park, holding hands and talking about anything and nothing, we came upon a softball diamond. Arriving at the pitcher's mound, she stopped and turned to me with gentle affection and an understanding look of a girl living well beyond her years. We instinctively knew there was only one way to do this—to let her control my fate. No words were spoken as she led me to join the continuum of boys becoming men from the beginning of time—to experience a lifelong ritual that always comes with a price.

In a few moments, what started as a conquest over the eternal drives of human beings ended as quickly as it began. Once we got off the mound, my first impulse was to run the bases and scream and holler and then slide into home. If I had followed through with my urge, it would have counted as one of the foremost pleonastic literary statements-in-action of the 20th century. All other metaphors aside, we continued on aimlessly, holding hands and saying little.

I now officially crossed the line to becoming my father—the tattoos, the booze, the company I kept, chasing girls. I was living the whole package, except for one thing—the music. The music was going to make the difference in how my life would turn out, but only if I made some changes and choices, but time was fast running out.

The time had come for me to choose: either honor myself, or continue down this path so well-trodden by my father. At this age, I only knew how to live moment-to-moment, day-to-day, and before long, I'd probably end up in jail or dead. But there was something else going on; it seemed I was being guided by an interior force or will. The less I questioned it and simply did my part in keeping my focus on my instrument, the better off I was. Was it possible that Granddaddy and his claim to have been born with a caul was somehow working an unforeseen influence? Such mysticism is too incredible to ponder. I still had many gauntlets waiting to unfold before me.

———

My SHOESHINE BOY/SHOP ASSISTANT/GOFER GIG at the barbershop promised a fascinating cast of characters. A double amputee named Buck was the owner. As a kid, he traded his original legs for two wooden ones the day he chose to play around some train tracks and turned his back at the wrong moment. His claim to fame was an undefeated record in the 10-yard dash, using only a pair of crutches against other crutch runners. Buck loved playing nine-ball at $500 a rack on the pool table in the back room. At a quarter a game, anyone could come in during business hours and play. Buck also hosted after-hours games with a $5,000 minimum in the pocket of each player who wanted access to the festivities. We'd sneak into the service alley and hang out while window watching some serious high-roller nine-ball players arrive strapped on the hip, wearing $500 custom tailored suits, and sporting thousand-dollar custom pool cues at the ready. It was like watching outtakes from a Paul Newman movie.

The shoeshine job was the best of all the duties and I became good at it. It was soothing to sit there and concentrate on making leather look like glass, but I couldn't shake the uneasy feeling that this barber shop was possibly staffed by child predators. There was also the risk of Myr showing up. The shop also happened to be next to the infamous Howlin's, where I nearly shut the place down all those years before with my meltdown and the subsequent kidnapping attempt on me. I'd wander in from time to time and stare at those amazing paintings of the late and infamous Joe Danner, and get a free Coke from Mom's cousin Billy, who was a permanent fixture as the long-standing bartender. Even after the place was sold and the name was changed, those paintings remained, like some kind of weird museum for the artwork of the criminally insane.

One morning, Buck opened the shop and discovered it had been burglar-ized. Oddly, there was no sign of forced entry, as if someone with a key showed up in the middle of the night to ransack the place. The police arrived, looked the situation over, and listed the missing items, which were small and of no serious monetary value. Subsequently, the shop was hit several more times with no pattern of activity. The break-ins were always random, and the items taken were randomly chosen.

The police initiated a midnight-to-six stakeout with a rotation of detec-tives armed with binoculars across the street in the parking lot of Dodge View apartments; a rare moment of convergence between name and purpose for one of my former dwellings. They were expecting to see someone enter through the front door, which never happened. Whoever this thief was, his secret to getting in and out of the shop seemed unsolvable.

One night, a detective was concentrating his magnified gaze at the back room door. Suddenly, he knew he had the thief right where he wanted him. He called for uniformed backup and met them at the rear door. There they found a kid named Perk ransacking a supply closet. When the detective came by the shop later, everyone was eager to hear how he caught this thief. The detective explained his habit of always checking the clock mounted above the back room door, as a way to keep track of the time. He noticed the second hand stopped, but the power in the shop remained on. He figured someone behind the wall must have unplugged the clock.

Perk later explained how the skylight above a short airshaft was always unlocked. The entire scam worked perfectly until his foot snagged the cord to the clock. When asked why he did it, he explained he was seeking revenge because Buck fired him as the shop gofer. The damage and items were minimal, so the matter was dropped. He was forever banned from the premises.

Perk eventually ended up doing a lengthy stretch in prison for assaulting women. The assaults were not a power-is-sex-is-power motivation. He was under the spell of an intense women's shoe fetish. After being fired from the Thom McAn shoe store for using it as a proving ground for his odd tastes, he went on a short tear with a string of minor assaults. He approached women sitting alone in some public place and after a few minutes of engaging in harmless small talk, he'd lunge for the foot closest to him, snatch the shoe, and take off running.

While in prison, women who read the story sent him pen pal letters, offering to send him their shoes. He welcomed the offer but requested they send him only one shoe of their choosing. Perk amassed the largest collection of non-matching female shoes in the history of the Maryland penal system. He also developed into something of a cellblock philosopher and became quite well read, at least evidenced from the message he carved into the wall of his cell, a quote from Seneca the Younger, which read:

"If I accede to Parmenides there is nothing left but the One; if I accede to Zeno, not even the One is left."

It was never clear if he was referring to his shoe collection, or the stopped second hand beginning his life's downfall; only his ontologist knows for sure.

ONE FATEFUL DAY, I CROSSED paths with a slightly older kid named Kenny. Although we exchanged a friendly glance of acknowledgement to one another, a rarity among the Kentland street blossoms, we were never formally introduced. It was as if we didn't need an introduction—just crossing paths was the minimum for some sense of familiarity and acceptance. My friend from Kent Junior High named Billy also knew Kenny. Billy was unique among us because he was the only guitar player I knew who took formal lessons. He also owned a Mosrite Ventures model, the epitome of badass guitars, and he could read music. I made regular weekend trips to his house to jam along with a drummer he knew named Jimmy, who also knew Kenny. As it turned out, Kenny also played guitar, and they all knew this guy Norman, a much older guitar player in Kentland with a reputation for being pretty good. Suddenly, my circle exploded with guitar players. It seemed that everyone in Kentland owned a guitar and played a little.

Billy invited me to a jam session Jimmy often hosted in his basement. I could hold my own with these guys, so I started to regularly attend the sessions. Norman soon drifted off, leaving Jimmy, Kenny, Billy, and me to form one of many short-lived basement teen club bands. Having no bass player, Kenny took on that responsibility, initially on the last four strings of his guitar before he committed to buying a real bass guitar. My first group was complete with a band business card, a strobe light, and one wannabe groupie. For a brief time, we covered several local Friday night teen club appearances, as well as a few private parties.

My fledgling performing life began as 1969 came in more quietly than 1968, although political turmoil was still taking hold and festering, especially as the Vietnam War peaked and the protests became more organized and strident. After doing a successful stint in summer school for a failed math grade, ninth grade started the fall of 1968. I still wore the "shit-jyeah, fuckin' A, B, and C, tippintude," but I soon embraced a more easy-going, less hostile nature.

With the neck of my guitar so warped as to be unplayable, I again turned to Granddaddy for help. He located a guy who sold Gretsch guitars as a sideline out of his basement. For one $125, I could own a Gretsch Clipper. With the help of Granddaddy's ASCAP check, I bought my first professional grade instrument. As circumstances would determine, 26 years would pass before I ever again had to pay cash for a guitar.

My impending introduction to drugs came by way of two guys Kenny knew who returned from a tour of duty in Vietnam. Returning soldiers never came home empty-handed. One of their favorite commodities was pounds and pounds of Vietnamese reefer smuggled in the bottom of a duffel bag. High-end stereo components also accompanied the soldiers on their long trip back to the states; an important accessory for the stoner to plug in a headset and lay on the floor for hours, blasting Jimi Hendrix from the reel-to-reel tape deck.

In 1969, you couldn't get much better quality weed than from overseas. Compared to everyone else, I was a late arrival to this tribal ritual. In the company of such constant users, I would have to partake of the toke…some joke. In the backseat of Norman's car, I crossed over from the last vestiges of the shit-jyeah sneer to the more contemplative and self-examining world of the "we are stardust, we are golden, let's go open a headshop and name it 'the Joint Possession'" generation. Woodstock happened to be coming to life during the weekend of my impending arrival in the Land of Enlightenment; the Crossover Handover in Landoverandout." There was talk of going, but no one wanted to fight the traffic and crowds in Bethel to participate in the making of pop culture history at the great counter-culture implosion and sell-out. Besides, everyone was broke.

The one-half square mile marking and defining my world from 1961 to 1969 would soon be coming to a close: starting in Kentwood, the camp with no woods; followed by a parkless Dodge Park; a viewless Dodge View; a gardenless Landover Gardens; and finally Kent Village, the camp that pretended to be a village, complete with the gulag-inspired structures. All of these places amounted to nothing more than a metaphor for the three-dimensional development of the original thematic call and response of the blues for my family dynamic.

Like those string games, such as Jacob's ladder or cat's cradle, played for millennia by kids the world over, our lives started out with an interlocking order, then became entangled, and then disintegrated with the slightest wrong move from either side of the strings.

I had my own special strings, metal and shiny, that cut into my fingers and drew blood, leaving endless friction blisters that transformed into beautiful, splendid callouses—the price, the reward, and the badge of honor proving you love the repetition, because you love the repetition, because you must love the repetition, keeping the unending vigil to remain in a constant state of observation.

The further I moved along the infinite grid of the neck, the more revealing and still mysterious everything became. Anyone could play along, if they knew the minimum requirements for doing so. Otherwise, they would have to settle for passive participation—to sit and watch and listen, preparing to anticipate the next sonic event, the outcome of which was never guaranteed.

The art of listening to music has never been well understood by most people. It's been said that expectation is a function of music. What makes that reality so incredible is that music creates its own expectations, based on tonal gravity driven by a hierarchal order—entirely non-egalitarian and undemocratic. The human mind is brilliantly hard-wired to receive the sonic information translated by the musician, into a lasting emotional response, instantly and without thought. Therein exists a double-edged sword: attach a lyric to the music, and there's your Trojan horse, your malware. The message and meaning of the words burrow deeply into the human psyche, to influence and form one's sense of self-worth and world view. How did we go from the optimism and outward expression of requited love from a Johnny Mercer lyric, to the dark, dour, interior grindings of much of the songwriting in the 1960s and '70s? Our world in 1969 was poised to consign multiple never-ending entanglements to a mid-20th century world still in recovery and seeming never to recover.

The Village In The Woods

THE FIRST THING I NOTICED was the tiny applique—such an unusual embellishment on the door of the apartment directly below ours, and kind of weird, actually. Below the tiny door knocker, in a small space reserved for placing a label with your name, was a small type-written piece of paper with a Sir Walter Scott quote: "Oh! What a tangled web we weave, when first we practice to deceive."

The first image that comes to mind when I think of a Village in the Woods is Danny Kaye playing some excessively ebullient character in a Hans Christian Andersen fable. This final encampment for our old and dying family show was located several miles east next to the Capital Beltway. An unusual village it was, with its own fables and myths—Mr. Andersen by way of R.D. Laing, in collusion with R. Crumb and Zap Comix. We finally breached the roughly one-half of a squared circle mile which encompassed my entire world since 1961, although it was more a Caesarian delivery than a yonic arrival.

Starting in high school in 1969, with the excitement of an impending new decade, my present and future converged. I felt the unrelenting lure of the counter-culture movement pulling me in further and further. The music was always the center of attention. The superficial trappings of the costumed and coded dress and mannerisms, and the drugs, were all distractions, especially for a 16 year old who was still in the throes of coming to terms with history.

On a purely gut-level, I still kept my well-guarded secret under the evermore distant threat of death. Such long-standing pain was a constant presence, like the 60-cycle hum from a florescent light interrupting and demanding your attention—a reminder of no matter how much you direct your mind and thoughts elsewhere, the pitch, somewhere in the cracks between B and B-flat, is always there seeping in, finding its level to eventually settle in and burrow like a tick. I was living an interstitial life, yet always active and seeking resolution as I made my way through the spaces between so many grains of sound.

On most days after school, I sat alone in my living room and ran my Gretsch full out through the Ampeg 200 amplifier and open windows. I soon got a reply from the people in the unit below us, far different than the Dodge View fiasco. They opened their slider, pointed huge imported speakers into the yard, and blasted The Band and The Who.

There were four men, with anywhere from 10 to 15 years on me. Dan was a grad student at the University of Maryland studying biology. He was in the military for a short time and turned his attention to science. The other two were indefinite houseguests. One was a sociologist, and the other was Aaron, or Steve, depending on the time of day and drug of influence. He was the alpha freak poet and guru. Clark, a college buddy of Aaron's, soon appeared to round out this clowder. Clark was a wannabe poet and singer/songwriter with one foot still in a non-descript middle-class life, try as he might to unshackle himself from that legacy. Once they knew me, Clark was particularly taken with the fact that I, this punkish kid of 16, could play circles around him on the guitar.

As these men settled in with memorized parts for hitting their marks, their identities soon changed into self-anointed, freaky personas. Dan was now and forever Uncle Hunny, the Terrible and Beneficent; Clark took on Wee-Wee Head. Aaron was still Aaron, or Steve, again, depending on what head was under whatever hat he was wearing. He became the nonsexual incarnation of Myr. The stage was now complete, as the prophecy of that night in 1968 in T&G Pizza came to pass. This was the very same freak show who infiltrated on that fateful night in Kent Village.

Phase one of the Stanley Milgram Invitational Tie-Dyed Amygdalae Tournament, featuring the Albert Hofmann Unicycles and Granfalloon Balloons was complete. These guys were on a mission, and I was their first catch. "Oh! What a tangled web…"

How Do You Tune A Granfalloon?

GRANFALLOON—WHAT A WONDERFULLY INVENTIVE AND musical word. It's a technique of coercion, brought to you by Kurt Vonnegut in his novel *Cat's Cradle*. Vonnegut, along with Kerouac, Burroughs, Ginsberg, Hesse, Mailer, Vidal, R.D. Laing, Carlos Castaneda, and J.R.R. Tolkien, was part of the required reading list to belong to this little club of leftist radicals. Their head cook and bottle washer was Saul Alinsky, by way of Gramsci.

This outfit wasn't some collective of love-beaded, peace-sign flashing, Three Dog Night 8-track, Frederick S. Perls poster-posing, tinsel and glitter glamor weekend hippies taking small tokes while pontificating about how reality was infinitely malleable when subjected to the slightest tilt of the head. These good and dutiful soldiers were frontline fighters for The Cause.. They were the natural continuation of the leftist movement going back to the 1920s and '30s during the Red Scare—Stalin's useful idiots. They were the intellectual grandchildren of the Norman Podhoretz/Lionel Trilling/Lillian Hellman generation of American left-wing radicalism, on which Podhoretz eventually turned his back in the late 1960s because of the emergence of the New Left. Podhoretz breaking ranks, in turn, ignited the Neo-Cons—liberals who had been mugged.

These New Age centurions worshipped their drugs. They knew all of the techniques and strategies to wear down anyone they perceived as vulnerable and primed for an extrusion of change to their worldview. Their solipsism magnified a sense of self-righteous indignation, which knew no limits. They were out to burn it down, baby; up against every fucking wall, brick by brick.

One fatal flaw in their tribal zeal was the absence of a realistic plan to restore anything they destroyed—to replace the dominant paradigm presumably for a better, evermore dominant, acid-washed paradigm. In their rush to clean the lint traps of their conscience and those around them, they also rejected certain irreducible fundamentals. One axiom against which they stood in absolute denial was that reality is real. Eastern mysticism and Western existentialism, combined with subjectivism, created this confusion. To deny any aspect of reality, they first had to accept the premise that reality exists in order to deny it—otherwise, what is it they are denying?

That's a tough one.

Another bind was the rather prickly problem of who was going to rewrite the ancient rules of trade—trade being the one constant motivating mankind to interact with one another, in ways that mutually benefit everyone, without force or coercion. Trade is arguably the reason economics exists in the first place.

It's easy to avoid the challenge of truth—truth being the recognition of the existence of facts in reality—when you are too invested in substituting reason with emotion, or an even more tortured Mobius view by believing there's no reason for reason; a classic bind.

None of this mattered to me at the time because I was too ignorant with the truths of history. I was seeking the validation of my keepers and was too wrapped up in my own agenda of living in the moment. Added to that was my increasing appetite for smoking dope and doing a variety of drugs, especially speed, of which there was an endless supply. And, of course, the warm embrace of a female.

———

FROM DAY ONE, UNCLE HUNNY insisted I walk right in, sit right down…no need to knock—we'll just kill 'em with kindness. Although their communal apartment was directly under mine, it might as well have been a parallax second away. I became the official mascot/houseboy/minor domo/drug procurement officer with free run of the place. I was naïve to believe these men accepted me into their tribe without conditions and prejudice.

The further into their tangled web I went, the more I experienced their true agenda. I took their humiliation as harsh currency for the privilege of having a seat at a corner of their roundtable. I attached my every gesture to their examples. I grew my hair, I changed the way I dressed, acted, spoke, thought—you name it. I became a parasite-turned-poacher in their world, with their approval always just out of reach. All I cared about was having their imprimatur. I was their formless clay—their novice urban monk.

I recall my first big league, gold standard protest event was the upcoming march on Fort Meade. Abbie Hoffman, the flamboyant star and court jester of the Chicago Seven, was the guest speaker and instigator. After a crowd of about 30 had heard his call to arms, we marched dutifully behind the slow-moving pickup truck in which he stood, tossing marshmallows to the adoring, following masses of the correctly pissed-off. He was much shorter in person than the cameras showed, or was this also all in my mind? I expected we were going to ram the front gate and flood the fort with daffodils. All we did was eat marshmallows and listen to Mr. Hoffman excoriate in a vacuum, for a modest fee and a per diem.

———

BETWEEN THE DAYTIME PROTESTS AND nights at Uncle Hunny's getting stoned and listening to Aaron reading his poetry, I was also putting in street time with the Kentland junior hippie league. A major explosion of drug use had occurred among those I knew from my younger years. Whenever I ventured out to wander among them, I felt like I was coming from a lofty retreat high in the mountains where cruel, but well-meaning giants and wise men would grant me a reprieve to head to the low land. Circulating among the sleeping and the waking dead was the backdrop for measuring my progress. Testing new sensibilities and spreading the message was my charge.

The make-up of the Kentland crew was unusual: psycho wannabe bikers, Earth mother types, and unformed weekend hoppies. The outstanding, award-winning soul burner was Crazy Eileen. She was 23 and always high, with a pack of shuffled tarot cards and a strong desire to sing like Grace Slick, and—completely out of her fucking mind—a card-carrying psychotic and proud of it. She enjoyed reminding her parents that she was on a mission to kill prior generations and that she may kill them in their sleep.

One auspicious day, while passing by the dumpster behind old Doc Hutchins' office, a kid named Durt hit pay dirt. The old doc had discarded dozens of unopened, seven-day sample packs of diet pills—speed. Durt figured there must be more inside the dumpster, so he and two others went back and did some major dumpster diving. They came up with untold packets of high-quality and high-potency speed, sealed and sterile, waiting to tear-ass through our neurotransmitters to free all of our dopamine from solitary confinement—nootropic heaven for all. After we divided up the loot, they used the rest to sell to many eager suburban customers.

I returned to the Village and presented a sacrificial offering to my guardian lords and masters—a relief for Aaron, because he was in the middle of a poetry writing binge and exhausted all of the speed on hand. During his week without sleep, he resorted to smashing open Vick's inhalers, which contained a cotton swab saturated with Benzedrine, and then swallowing the entire swab. The inhalers were tearing up his stomach and my fresh supply of packets of electric Good & Plenty was just what the shaman ordered.

———

IN ANY COLLECTIVE, GROUP-THINK ENVIRONMENT, the expectation of someone seeking the imprimatur to join the Cult of Personality is proving one's willingness to sacrifice individuality. You proved your worthiness by repudiating every conclusion you ever came to that led you to their definition of a flawed worldview.

Up to that moment, everything you knew was wrong, and the sooner you accepted their reality, the sooner you'd have a place at the table—no room for negotiation. The freakier you presented yourself to the straights in public, the more convincing your commitment. This natural progression from the interior scrubbing and replacement of values and virtues, to the public transformation and expressions of guerilla theatre, attracted a lot of fucked-up, psychotic personalities. I'm sure a few new burnouts and causalities were also created in the process.

I presented as the near-perfect vacuum for Aaron and the others to fill with their perfect storm of influences, which were not unlike the Manson clan and the

Weather Underground. Drugs were the perfect detergent for them to scour my squirmy young mind down to nothing. This permitted the catalysts of cerebral modification through the time-honored technique of ego stripping to have the intended effect. The Village in the Woods became just another Siberian gulag only with balconies, a swimming pool, free-flowing drugs, and required reading.

Neither Confirm, Nor Deny

(But…But…Everything Is *Sooo* Significant)

AARON EXPLOITED MANY WEAKNESSES IN character among those in his orbit, especially the rocky marriage of a young couple across the way. He snared a young mother of 18 and with little resistance, turned her against all she believed was right and true. She was as easy a mark as I, but with the added attraction of her willingness to do his sexual bidding at any time. Soon after her scouring, she divorced her husband and received custody of their toddler son. Aaron was now free to move in and become further entrenched in this girl's psyche. All he had to do was stay home, get high, and write poetry while she worked to support the three of them. Her ex-husband never knew what hit him.

One remaining challenge I had to confront was living my life as a serial truant during my next to last year in high school. Instead of continuing my studies in building pads with 6013 low-hydrogen welding rods and running groove seams in sheet metal shop, the time arrived to be set free of my obligations to finish school, by way of permanent expulsion with extreme prejudice. This was done by none other than the inimitable Mr. William Laurich, vice principal of the Bladensburg Senior High vocational tech program. This is exactly how it went down one memorable morning:

BILL (officiously clenched jaw): …and because you won't go to school, you can't go to school!

ME (in stoned, blanked-out silence): *What the fuck!? Did he really just say that!?*

MOM (snarling): I'll tell you one goddam thing—you will start working for a living.

Instead of taking this moment of institutional rejection to question if this was another example of how the forces of life in an adult world will often work both for and against you, I saw it as pure liberation. I was set free to spend my time as I saw fit, to pursue what mattered to me. The Dahl-like irony in the principal's obverse, self-cancelling statement of bureaucratic blather has lasted unabated for all of these years, like gum you chew your entire life and it never loses its flavor.

On the heels of my expulsion, Aaron suggested it was time for me to experience my maiden LSD trip; the final phase of my ego stripping. He was a devout acidhead who began his forays into the mysterious world of the sub-conscious in 1963, under the guidance of a New York City loft dwelling swami, complete with ceremonial swords and turbans, straight out of central casting. His staunch commitment to turning on to the higher and loftier goals of blur-ring the lines of his inherited reality was the oxygen for his flame—to change the world, one fucked-up mind at a time, with a complete and total invasion of the human conscience.

After much reassurance that the trip would be safe under their Yaqui Indian guide-like watchful eyes, I caved and said I'd take a hit of Purple Dou-ble Dome. The plan was for several of us to go to the Biograph Theatre on M Street in Georgetown to see *The Yellow Submarine*—the perfect first foray into chemically-induced psychosis to claim the finished product; cleaned, ego stripped, dipped, and ready for post-submerge imprinting, courtesy of the Firesign Theatre, complete with fuzzy follow-ups and Tessa Late's Double-Overs with climb-ease switchbacks.

The moment the movie house went dark and the projector started to spin, I knew this was the conclusion of the death of my childhood by a sexual predator, and the start of the death of my conscious. I had to remember the mantra I was told would help me maintain my composure, just in case: neither confirm, nor deny, and remember: you are a creation of the universe.

Oh, yeah, and…just in case that doesn't work Clyde, here's some chlorpromazine to bring you back to…reality. Oh…so it does exist?

———

By the age of 16, I was living away from home with greater frequency. Older guys with their own apartments and crash pads made their space available to anyone who contributed drugs and maybe something toward rent, food, or utilities. By 17, I had left home permanently. Home was a euphemism for Mom and Karen living in complete emotional meltdown. In the meantime, Mom's boyfriend Willie died in 1971 from brain cancer. He promised her the world, especially after his never-intended divorce. All he left Mom was empty promises, a broken color television, and a broken heart. He went to his grave knowing my mother's bestowment of time and energy in their decade-long charade was tender she could neither afford nor borrow. He strung her along as his concubine with an endless supply of platinum hair. And now, devastated and 43, Mom was alone without a man for the first time since the age of 17—a hell of her own making.

Karen was in an uncontrollable state of existence. The long-term negative neurological effects of her total blood transfusion in 1957 resulted in deep emotional problems. Mom did more harm than good to Karen's already fragile state of mind through a lethal combination of negative emotion and ignorance of my sister's history. Mom not being aware of Karen's jaundice transfusion at birth gave Mom some reasonable cover, because she lacked important and missing pathological information. However, she was told, in no ambiguous terms by state-appointed psychologists, that Karen's problems were a combination of probable organic and environmental factors. Environmental was a genteelism for, "Lady, you are a major contributor to your daughter's problems."

Committing my sister for six months to a state institution for uncontrollable girls was another of Mom's colossal blunders. Any semblance of what I knew of Karen before her release changed forever. The distance between us was long in the making because of the destructive forces and influences we absorbed all of our young lives, emanating primarily from Mom and her untreated pathologies, along with Dad's parental ambivalence and common vices. The gulf between us would remain insurmountable for the remainder of her tragic and all-too-short life.

———

THE RIVERDALE STOCKYARD AND VILLAGE bump-out was a filthy, quasi-commune crash pad. Uncle Hunny moved in with Ken, the Grand Mal Leprechaun; Dave, the Straight; Little Bobby Piss-Off; Big Chris, head of the Spider's Web Head Shop and Transcendental Tanning Salon; their old ladies; and a troupe of transients. The Stockyard was my next port of call.

Most of these freaks worked for a landscaping company, which gave them some control over the quality of their outdoor environment. One of the most glaring hypocrisies in this commune was all of the standards they demanded for a clean and livable exterior environment didn't apply to their squalid interior living conditions. I could never quite wrap my head around that one.

———

IN THE MIDST OF ALL my distractions with chasing my head and tail, a pixie named Larry Miller just sort of appeared one day—poof! There he stood, a modern incarnation of Frodo Baggins meets the beautiful people of the Georgetown salons. Larry, like Crazy Eileen, was an early but ephemeral influence in my life; an indelible representative of my increasing circle of alter-egos. I've no recollection of his connection to the immediate crew of Kenny and the others. He may have come by way of the periphery, but I really think he just simply, inexplicably appeared.

Larry had five years on me. He continued living at home with his parents and sister well into his twenties. He enjoyed the perfect sugar mountain set-up; he could come and go as he pleased, with dinner on the table, clean clothes, and an unending supply of rose wine in the back room pantry. He slept in a bohemian-chic bedroom with a pedestaled round bed, his own artwork, a nice component stereo, and a Hofner Beatle bass. Larry had no fucking clue how to play the bass other than yanking on the open strings while posing ever so elegantly on a stool with one leg crossed over another. He also possessed an attraction to the dark arts and mysticism. Shooting junk whenever the opportunity crossed his path was Larry's delight. I sat with him in bathrooms on many occasions, watching him boot the shot until he flashed. Even when he was puking into the bowl, he did it with turquoise-emblazoned style and panache.

At five feet, five inches, with a blond shag haircut, green snakeskin boots, and an all-out Carnaby Street-influenced sense of style and fashion, Larry was in a class by himself—a perfect Rod Stewart and David Cassidy look-alike. He straddled two different worlds—making a living selling clothes and cutting hair in the ootsy Georgetown fashion boutiques and balanced with slumming and running with the grubs; his term of endearment for all of the inelegant, grubby musicians and wannabes he knew. The girls, their mothers, and all the boys found him alluring, and he always returned the compliment. He could go either way and was proud of it. Early on, he learned from my signals that I held no interest in examining his sexual wares.

Nevertheless, Larry and I established a mutually validating friendship. We could talk for hours about anynothing, with a highly stylized form of pseudo-intellectual gibberish, replete with its own airtight syntax made up of strings of at least three prepositions, preceded by one or two conjunctions, then finish with the subject. This was a favorite: "…since, as to for the concept in and of reality negates reality itself, as a concept, for that to be such, irregardless of the thing as a, you know, a concept…you know, reality…"

Deep down, Larry knew he would never become a legitimate bass player. Nevertheless, he was desperate to be a rock star and would go to any lengths to advance his goal. While Larry hung out with Kenny and me, he began reinventing himself as a singer, because Kenny had the bass chair covered. It was a natural progression for Larry because his true heroes were the British rock and roll front men.

After Larry settled on his new persona and we all bought into it, the time came to upgrade the instruments. The first problem was the Gretsch I bought in 1969. It was in such an unplayable state, I had to replace it. My need was something Larry became invested in because I could play, and if this band idea was going to get off the ground, I needed his connections to find a better instrument for little to no cost.

Larry made a call and arranged to go into a notoriously dangerous part of the District. Larry's friend offered to drive us to the middle of a war-torn ghetto to see what magic Larry would conjure. We sat there for a few minutes and when Larry got a signal, he insisted Kenny and I wait while he and his pal went in with my guitar. As I saw it fade into the night, I felt a small pang of loss. After all, it was my first professional-grade instrument.

Kenny and I sat trapped in the car for an hour with no sign of Larry. We had no car keys to make a quick getaway if such an emergency arose. The situation was now going from a short-lived risk of life and limb to all-out panic. Then, like a scene out of film noir, emerging from the steamy shadows came two figures moving very slowly toward us. Larry and his friend calmly got in and put a long, unfamiliar guitar case into the backseat. We never looked back.

I was now the owner of a stunning new 1968 Fender Telecaster. I couldn't believe it. It was mine and I paid not a dime for it—no strings attached. Removing it from the case, I could just as well have been pulling a sword from a stone. This magnificent piece of wood and metal felt like perfection; a new professional-quality instrument representing a new level of expertise into which I had to grow. No more faulty instrument excuses. The Telecaster coaxed me to work harder than ever before as justification for receiving such a magnificent gift.

I asked Larry how he was able to swap a total piece of shit for this instrument. He said, with a sullen and tired voice, "Don't ask." Something about this wasn't right; it didn't make any sense. I thought he may have stolen it, larceny being one of Larry's favorite past times. I never again asked, and he never offered an explanation. I had to wait 45 years, long after Larry was dead and planted, before I learned the mystery of the buckarooty switcheroo.

Time Compressed and Formatted to Fit Your Screen

One June afternoon, Crazy Eileen and I were hanging out in the small park in Kent Village. It was a beautiful summer day: perfect weather, perfect drugs. I was playing a song as she sang along. She seemed to be deep in thought and wasn't her usual ebullient psychotic self. When I asked what was wrong, she confessed she missed her old man, a 30-something professional guitar player named Sweeney. He was waiting for her in a rented brownstone off of Flatbush Avenue in Brooklyn, just on the edge of Brooklyn College. Their big plan was to start a band.

"So, what's keeping you from heading back?"

"Yeah, dig it. I don't have the money for a bus, and Sweeney is starting to get really bugged with me being away."

"How much is the bus?"

"Three dollars."

"I know where I can get my hands on some money."

"Yeah, dig it. Hey—why don't you come with me and you can join the band?"

She didn't have to ask me twice. The bus was leaving from the New York Avenue station at seven and getting in around midnight at the Port Authority terminal. I told her to hang tight. I would return with travel money and possibly a ride to the bus terminal. I arrived back at the Village and sought out Marilyn, who lived in the building next to mine. Marilyn was 30 and hailed from a small town in Iowa—a classic Eugene McCarthy liberal who stuck with him to the end, especially after Robert Kennedy was killed. With a penchant for breathless talking with conviction and earnestness, she also harbored a soft spot for the downtrodden. She believed there was hope for me because of my music. Marilyn's role in the Aaron and Uncle Hunny show was relegated to fifth business.

I explained my opportunity to join a band in New York City. She was only too happy to lay several rolls of dimes on me for our bus tickets. She drove us to New York Avenue in time to catch the bus to the Big Apple. All I had was my Telecaster, a rare copy of the entire *Lord of The Rings* trilogy in one volume, a toothbrush, and the clothes on my back. I considered that my first-ever trip to New York could become permanent. For now, all that mattered was this: I was in the company of an extremely free-spirited, crazy, 23 year old acid casualty tarot card reader, who desperately wanted to sing like Grace Slick, and for some reason known only to her, she thought I was some young diamond-in-the-rough who would benefit from being in the company of her older and experienced guitar player old man.

It was getting close to midnight. The ride up the New Jersey Turnpike seemed to have gone on for days. Isn't that the way it always is with a never-before-traveled path? The more you travel it, the quicker it seems to go—just another aspect of living with memory in time and space. Once you are no longer enamored with any first-time experience, the law of diminished returns settles in and you head off to uncover another first. I began to jot down what a drug-fueled, run-on, hyper-active monologue on the topic of Firsts would sound like:

"...D-i-g-g-g-i-t!! One of the most overlooked aspects of our lives is the fact that life is an accumulation of firsts: a first kiss, a first dog bite, the first day of school, the first time eating dirt, the first time eating ice cream, a first injury, the first time driving, the first time having sex, the first time defying gravity, the first time getting high...you know what I'm saying right? [Huge gulp of air.] It's the firsts that motivate us to keep on going and we always bring along the potential to become distracted and derailed by insisting on dwelling on selected first firsts while we look for second firsts, third firsts, and on and on. The quality of these firsts does have an impact on how we make choices, especially when measured in how their impact on us impacts the lives of others. Good firsts, bad firsts what the fuck, (grind, grind). If bad firsts are a matter of fact, then what is the optimum ratio between bad and good firsts to create a balance? How out of balance does the ratio have to be in order for the good to be reduced and ultimately realize the bad? Is there a minimum amount of bad that must be present to give definition and meaning to the good? How does the Church handle this or would Jesus even give a shit? Whew. Does anyone have a cigarette? Man I need some fucking water I'm firsty…Wow did you hear that I said 'firsty' for thirsty. There must be a name for that like something-convergence. Shit, if there isn't, I am making one up right now, which is no longer now but was a moment ago. My mouth feels like glue. Am I talking too fast because if I am I can slow it down because you are now in the presence of some deep shit and I don't want you to miss any of this; goddamn I hope someone is writing this down. Do you hear what I'm sayin'? Why didn't someone tell me that everything is *sooooo significant* I need some paper and a pencil? You know I now know that I love all of humanity and I'm not just saying that I don't think I will have another bad feeling ever again. Whew! Am I grinding too much? I can't feel my fucking knees or teeth…"

BEFORE LONG, THE SOUTHERN TIP of Manhattan came into view. As I glanced to the right, the Statue of Liberty was lit from the backside, which was a view I never before experienced. In pictures and movies, it was always shown front and center, sometimes a little to the side. New York City always fascinated me. The countless movies set in the city portrayed an intense, distant romantic quality. Even those old Dead-End Kids movies, with all of the goofy and gritty street bravado, portrayed some of the New York magic and wonderment.

As we got closer to the Holland Tunnel exit, I noticed two massive twin towers that were near completion, called the World Trade Center. This towering monument was the newest representation of the greatness and unlimited potential of man's mind on Earth, and would be the tallest buildings in the world, surpassing the greatest of all the New York landmarks, the Empire State Building.

The imagery I always visualized for the most majestic city on Earth was one of men and women dressed in their best—men with hats and overcoats and women in skirts and dresses, strolling 5th Avenue window shopping. I imagined taxis busily pulling up to and away from curbs in the Theater District, with elegant people hurrying into a theatre to see a play by O'Neill, or rushing to their waiting table at the Russian Tea Room after a Carnegie Hall concert. Other than a Bernard Herrmann score, the only music that stirs those feelings and imagery for me is the 1957 Miles Davis classic *Miles Ahead,* and his immortal 1959 sextet recording *Kind of Blue.*

Man, oh man, to have been born several decades before the release of those records. I could have enjoyed their immediate cultural impact, not only on me as someone who would be nearing 30, but on the entire world of music as it was happening in real time. Maybe the women were right—maybe I was an old soul. I knew I was a city kid all those years ago when I stood on the roof of the apartment in Southeast D.C., looking out over the monument-filled skyline. My love of the city has increased many-fold since.

When we stepped off the bus at the Port Authority, I could have been stepping onto a movie set. The electricity and energy in the air had a three-dimensional quality. It was about one in the morning as we made our way to the subway for Flatbush. It could have been one in the afternoon, because there were as many people at such a late hour as one would expect on a busy work day, running to catch a quick lunch before heading back to their own special grinds. Of course, most of the people I saw on the graffiti stained and tattooed trains looked like strap-hanging stand-ins for a Clyde Beatty extravaganza: a woman dressed in a heavy fur and evening gown, with tons of makeup smeared on while talking to herself about needing more rehearsal, and junkies on the nod, splayed out on the bench lying in their own puke and slobber. I was getting nervous because my only possession was my guitar, and it wouldn't have taken much for a couple of shitheads to do a snatch-and-run. Eileen moved quickly between cars and across the couplings as the train rattled on for close to 45 minutes, moving deeper and deeper into Brooklyn. A high decibel rumbling accompanied the constant flickering of the ceiling lights. It was like being caught in the middle of a thunderstorm without the downpour. My excitement distracted me from fear and I was too exhausted and adrenaline drunk to sleep.

I AWOKE THE NEXT MORNING greeted by a hot and humid New York day. The floor I slept on was going to need embellishment. I gathered loose material and made up a reasonably uncomfortable nest to crash. I hadn't set a specific time limit on my stay—I was keeping all of my options, both real and imagined, open. Eileen's sister Helen was there with her boyfriend putting together a breakfast made from pokeweed growing wild next to the back stoop, and brown rice. That was pretty much the limit of our day-to-day rations. I had an idea of how refugees in the Congo probably felt when the CARE packages arrived from some UN delivery service. I was happy to have it.

Sweeney was 30 and from the suburbs of Westchester County. He was from a well-to-do family whose legacy he rejected long before I ever met him. He claimed to have a lot of background and experience in studio work in New York City. At that time, he was the best guitarist I ever spent my good fortune to meet. He saw something in me that motivated his attention—to push me to reach higher than ever.

Our daily routine started alone in the room, with guitars plugged in, standing back to back. Sweeney played a note, and I would have to find it on my instrument. After we got into a rhythm and groove with this call and response, he increased it to two notes, and then three, and on and on. This was a tremendous confidence builder. It verified that I was evolving to a new level of unity, whereby I could hear the instrument internally, as if the notes I heard awoke from inside the neck and reached up to guide my hand to the correct location. We also spent a lot of time listening to recordings. He was especially taken with a solo Dave Mason played on a song titled, "Look At You Look At Me." The moment where the tempo changes into a slow, half time feel was where the magic started. Mason's solo was a perfect study in slow-burn intensity, with sublime, unhurried pacing—telling a story using an improvised melody, sonic prosody. What a major revelation it was for me.

I spent an equal amount of time just sitting and listening to him play, observing how he covered the entire range of the neck; the way he used the blues articulations of bends, shakes, and smears; the way he handled the voice-leading of chord forms. This motherfucker could play, and I stole everything as rapidly as he was casting it off.

We eventually talked about his life, the details of which were scant. He pointed to an old footlocker loaded with reel-to-reel tapes, reams of paper filled with lyrics to his tunes, and sheet music. With a laconic catch in his voice, Sweeney said, "My entire career is in that box."

He was the most fully formed musician I knew because he was also a lover of jazz, especially such esteemed guitarists as Barney Kessel, Wes Montgomery, and Tal Farlow—and there was that name again, the one I heard the older guys around the projects mention from time to time. During these sessions, Eileen sat there observing, rolling joints, and chiming in from time to time with some gibberish, starting with her signature anacrusis, "Dig it."

The relationship between Sweeney and Eileen was volatile, especially when drugs and alcohol were in the mix, which for all of us was all of the time. When these two went off to play a few rounds of Psycho-Land, all the while fighting over the spinner and dice, it was time for me to disappear for a while. It seemed like that was all they did, fighting then fucking, but it wasn't beyond them to fuck and then fight—what a waste.

I began to silently question if this band was ever going to materialize. About a week into the stay, Sweeney and Eileen introduced me to a guy who lived on the next block claiming to be a bass player. Across the street was a much older guy who resembled Clyde Crashcup's sidekick. He was a chemist who experimented with infusing LSD with micro amounts of Potassium-40—he was manufacturing radioactive LSD, and we were in line to be his beta testers.

After we dropped the hit, we set up in his living room with the two guitars and bass and Eileen. We didn't get five minutes into this maiden session when, without warning, Sweeney slammed down his guitar and bolted from the apartment. I tried to process his sudden change of mood, and the acid with the nuclear-tipped warhead was not helping matters. Back at the house, he sat there seething, with no explanation. He wanted no further discussion, but nevertheless, his outburst colored my understanding of this mercurial soul.

After the acid began to really take hold, we all headed up Flatbush Avenue to Prospect Park and spent the next six hours flying and bumming for spare change. We didn't have a successful day with the panhandling, but the trails in the park were mesmerizing.

OUR MONEY SITUATION WAS BECOMING desperate. Not only was the food running out, which amounted to only the big bag of brown rice because the pokeweed seemed to have been grown from magic beans creating an endless supply, but the bills were also coming due. We also took on two strays. They came in the form of two Midwestern gentlemen in their mid-twenties. They lurked beneath our streetlight like lost souls, so we invited them to the house to get high, and as a consequence, they never left. They were harmless, in the spirit and style of George and Lenny meets the Tweedle twins.

Their story amounted to them taking a bus from the middle of the Midwest to the big city to find fame and fortune. The cinematic legacy of Joe Buck and Ratso Rizzo was probably lost on them. For a couple of guys who spent many Octobers loading the pumpkin truck, they had a big city appetite for drugs and possessed more street smarts than one would have thought otherwise. They got a job hustling Poppadoodle's Popcorn from a corner vendor cart in Midtown, which was a lot more than we, the precious, gifted, and talented few were willing to do. This shit with the band was going nowhere fast.

Early one morning, Eileen blurted out, "Yeah, so dig it. We need some fuckin' money and fast. I shared a place on Second Avenue with this broad who had a kid. I got a monthly welfare check, but the office fucked up my address change when I moved. I told her to forward the check, but I think she's tryin' to rip me off. Let's take a ride over to Second Avenue. I may need some back-up because this bitch is nuts, and if there's a check in there, she'll try and cash it." We headed to the train and soon arrived on Second Avenue.

"I'm going in. You stay here and if I need help, I'll call for you." Eileen's name was still hanging at an angle from a yellowed shard of paper, with a dry covering of Scotch tape about to give up the ghost of adhesion. I never imagined there was a living condition that would make those structures I grew up in and around seem like luxury garden apartments. I was missing the antiseptic reassurance and piquant bouquet of Lysol and oil soap.

A few minutes later she returned and said there was no answer, although she could hear the kid behind the door. Before we headed down Second Avenue, she impulsively turned to go back and declared, "That bitch isn't going to rip me off."

Eileen disguised her voice by posing as a maintenance worker. The woman fell for the ruse and opened the door. Like a racehorse in a starting gate, Eileen broke through and went into her tirade. I entered the vestibule and stood outside the door. I could hear a lot of crying and screaming from the kid, along with a lot of smashing and breaking and shit being thrown to the floor. Once the destruction stopped, the screaming continued and then the door flew open. Out came Eileen, walking fast, bug-eyed, red-faced, with spit on her chin. She sounded like she was speaking in tongue as she paced in circles like a caged animal waiting for feeding time. Ninety-seven degrees with about 80 percent humidity did nothing to cool the situation. Eileen gathered her anger, stored it somewhere between her head and her colon, and we resumed our walk down the avenue empty-handed.

We approached the Fillmore East Auditorium when I suddenly noticed that I was alone. I turned and there she stood, facing up the avenue in response to someone running toward her and screeching her name. I returned to her side as a man in the deep end of non compos mentis approached. He was the live-in boyfriend of the woman whose apartment she just reduced to category five wreckage.

"Eileen, you muthafuckin' insane bitch, what the fuck is your problem? I'm sitting on the got-dam toilet and all of a sudden I hear all of this screamin' and shit. And then you trash my muthafuckin' shit. And scarin' my kid? Bitch, I oughta' cut your fuckin' th'oat right here and now…"

I understood this cat's anger, especially being in the unenviable position of making the hard choice between pulling up his pants or just sitting there, trapped, a captive audience, helpless by choice in an effort to save whatever dignity and self-esteem remained in him, as a Tasmanian cartoon character came to life on the other side of the bathroom door. Then, without warning, he spins around to me and with a long switchblade, clicks it open and gets in my face.

"...and as far as you're concerned, I'll cut you where you stand muthafucka."

With my hands in the air, I confessed I was only along for the ride. Eileen stepped in to deflect his attention and in all likelihood, saved my life. He got quiet and put away the knife.

Eileen explained that his old lady forged her name and cashed her checks. He admitted forgery was exactly what she did, because she was cut off from her monthly assistance; it came to light she was using it to support their junk habits. The only way to get her payments back was to go into a methadone rehab program, which she wasn't willing to do because she had Eileen's check to fall back on. "Nothin' to it, and nothin' personal." Eileen offered no apology as we parted ways with the man of the house.

The most outstanding reality from this brief theatre of the absurd one-act play in the middle of the Lower East Side was no cops showed up and no crowd gathered. It was as if we slipped into some other dimension where we could see everything, but were invisible to everyone else. We ducked into a subway station, jumped another turnstile, and headed back to the house—another tough day at the office. It was time to harvest and boil the pokeweed next to the back stairs for the evening meal.

THE ROMANCE AND EXCITEMENT OF the journey was played out for everyone. There was no possibility we were going to have a band together in time to open for Jefferson Airplane in August in Gaelic Park. I finally understood Sweeny's sole motivation for hosting this summer band camp. It was his once-in-a-lifetime opportunity to shed some professional anonymity as a struggling part-time studio player, and stake his claim to a slice of the rock and roll pie. Maybe that was the reason for the tantrum he threw in the chemist's apartment. Let's see, a quick inventory of Sweeney's assets: an insane girlfriend with less than minimal music skills; a young, budding guitarist who was still too green for this kind of major league pressure; a bass player he hardly knew; not to mention having to scare up a drummer and a keyboard player; and get in enough rehearsals with some small venue gigs to work out the shit out of the corners of the show. It was all bullshit and he knew it. On the other hand, I was having the time of my life.

NEAR THE END OF MY stay, the bass player invited me to his apartment to get high. If the chemist was any indication of how these New York freaks like to fuck around with their drugs, I couldn't imagine what kind of genetic modification this shit must have been put through before this cat bought an ounce. I made my way up three long flights to his door.

My first impression was how dark he kept the place—no lights, no air conditioning. The drawn shades filtered the only illumination in the room. The translucent glow of another brutal summer day on the bottom of the Big Apple burned through window paper yellowed with the stains of change and life. I asked if this was his place. He explained he took it over from his grandmother just before she died. The place smelled like a combination of reefer and My Sin perfume. The furniture was vintage and well worn, with doilies and antimacassars draping the backs of chairs and the arms of an opulent and threadbare couch. These old world coverings never moved from the moment his grandmother put them in place, sometime around 1920. If you peeled them back, a persistent, ghost-like negative image would have taken its place.

The lamps looked like something in a palm reader's parlor with brittle, yellowed shades. Every stick of furniture rested on Queen Anne's feet. A vintage Philco radio stood in the corner with old *Life* and *Look* magazines piled on top. I flipped through the copy of *Life* on the top of the stack. It was the issue I remember seeing in 1962 featuring Mercury astronaut Scott Carpenter and his family. I opened it to again look at the young girl with the fascinating eyes. The entire space was like a museum diorama capturing the faded lavishness of upper middle class, old Knickerbocker New York.

A strange-looking machine on the table near the door caught my attention. It was a miniature version of an old raffle drum, surrounded by rocks and stones and cans of wet sand and cloths. He explained it was something he used to polish rocks and stones as a part of his lapidary hobby. Lapidary—it sounded like some kind of a tropical disease requiring quarantine deep in the tropics.

Remove a stone or crystal object from its natural surroundings, put it in a tumble drum for weeks and months, sometimes years on end, then viola—a cabochon possessing the subtlest grade of chatoyancy, accompanied by a note of sublime asterism, followed closely by a whispered aftertaste of almandine garnet. Or, run a knuckle of Stevland through the tumble and grind of the cult of Sweeney for two weeks and see what comes out. The setting may break, but the stone remains intact.

We smoked part of a joint while sitting across from one another. Not a single word was uttered, simply because we couldn't. It was impossible to make any kind of sound. This shit must have been hand delivered by some Yaqui spirit courier straight from the grave of Don Juan Matus. I felt like I was breathing through the bottom of my feet—and with not much success. This was a whole new stage of spifflication.

My host sat there staring at me with a strange, intense look on his face. Then, out came a long knife. He stared a hole through me, all the while flicking it open and snapping it shut with one hand, silent and unblinking. The only conclusion I found was that this crazy motherfucker was going to cut me to pieces and feed me into his little lapidary tumble drum. I'd be the wet-sand agent to create optimum shine and smoothing results for his next miniature, non-faceted fantasy world.

This was some seriously deep shit I stepped into, and I knew there was only one chance to get out of this alive. Somewhere, in an imaginary civil defense emergency kit packed away in my groin, was a pamphlet explaining what to do in such a situation. First, don't let your killer see you panic. Next, calmly stand, as if you're going to the bathroom, and then divert yourself to a point of mutual interest: the little tumble drum. "Hey man, so how does this thing work? You throw in a stone and flip a switch…?"

Fortunately, the table on which it sat was next to the door. That made going toward the door less conspicuous. Calmly open it and pretend you are Superman, flying down each landing without ever touching any one of seven consecutive steps on the way. I could hear him calling my name in a sardonic, taunting voice. I made it back to the band house in record time and sat there for hours as the rushing sound in my ears quieted. I never saw him again. I've always wondered if he was just fucking with me.

The following day I bid my keepers and mentor farewell. I headed back to D.C. and announced that if anything changed, to please let me know. Too much uncertainty without a coherent plan of action was enough to send me packing. Once the Poppadoodle Popcorn twins got wind of my leaving, they wanted to tag along. There was nothing but indentured servitude for their foreseeable future if they stayed around in this cartoon strip. I made it clear we'd be parting ways when I got to the 177th Street station. My goal was to make my way over to the George Washington Bridge and begin the hitchhiking ritual. I got to my stop and bid them a heartfelt farewell, thanking them for what they contributed to keep all of us from starving. They continued northward into the Bronx, hopefully finding what they were looking for before it found them. As the train door closed, I thought I heard one of them mutter something about an opening for a gazebo sweeper at Fort Tryon Park.

I was dirty, hungry, and thirsty, but I matured five years in two weeks. For all of Sweeney's burgeoning megalomania, I was grateful he gave me the chance to accept his challenges and send me on my way to continue working it out on my own. I proved that I was a quick study, needing minimum exposure to get a concept and apply it. My disappointment that I wouldn't be doing their opening set in August with the Jefferson Airplane lingered for a long time.

Standing stranded on the eastern edge of Othmar Hermann Ammann's masterpiece for four hours in the hot afternoon was a special kind of torture. Eventually, a guy pulled over and offered a ride, but he was going only as far as Fort Lee, which literally amounted to going from one end of the bridge to the other. I enjoyed a brief moment of success in catching a ride taking me four hours south—hey, it's all about the journey, and not the destination, right? Yeah—bullshit. The start of the journey is fine, but if that's all it's about, then your life is destined to be neither here nor there.

I briefly stood at the Fort Lee exit before a Plymouth Valiant pulled over and let me in. I looked toward the Manhattan skyline with a wistful moment of regret, but I knew one day I would be back for even better reasons than this maiden adventure. New York City is a place that demands you take your time to get to know it; a slow and seductive courtship, with all of the bumps and bruises that come along with any love affair.

The four guys who picked me up were fresh off of the Vietnam battlefield. They were all freaks and looked to be about the same age as the Village crew. Attached to the trunk of the car was a huge banner that read, "Vietnam Vets Against the War." They were several hours into a trip to a major protest in D.C., so it was clear sailing all the way in. We didn't have much to say, but they sensed I was broke, so they made sure I was fed. I slept unsoundly most of the way and didn't come around to consciousness until south of Baltimore, on the Parkway.

Driving past the exit for Greenbelt, I glanced toward the wooded area separating the Parkway from my first home at 53K. A pensive wave washed over me as I reflected on that lifetime. Fewer than 15 years had passed since that galvanic moment on top of the mound of destruction, stained with another's loss that led me to finding my first instrument—hearing the burnished two note melodies filling the air between the rusty gears of the sit-and-spin carousel, and the metal-on-metal clasps of its swinging singing partner.

I reflected on the damage created by the seduction of a confused 12 year old girl, casting my sexual innocence into an emotional free fall, and subsequently caught in mid-air by a vicious serial sexual predator, who stalked and instilled the fear of death in me for years. Another reality was the hyper-vigilant mindset I developed in my tortured survival. I always followed sound through the darkness with pitch, rhythm, melody, and harmony demanding to come to life through the ancient resonant glory of one grand single string, coursed and wrapped and then laced to become six, where one-plus-two-plus-three becomes one-by-two-by-three. Six strings, tightened and stretched, and constantly held to their near-breaking point over a head, a neck, and a body shaped with lines and curves that would make the daughter of Dione tearful and bitter with envy.

I thought about how the guitar sometimes patiently waits in silent empathy. Other times, it challenges with utter petulance, cajoling me to discover the secret point of entry to travel deep down into the center of each string; circular chambers with no beginning or end—circumferences expanding forever, regardless of the differences in their size and appearance. The individual notes have the power to not only duplicate their identity at different locations on the neck, but the ability to create entirely new identities, only on one condition: To transfer my energies into the strings to initiate and complete an unending process of duplication and generation—an endless penetrating circle becoming a cycle, becoming a scroll, becoming a spiral…

The next thing I knew, I awakened from my daydream because someone was telling me we had arrived in Cheverly. I thanked the vets for the ride and their kindness. I slowly headed down the ramp to Landover Road. For the time being, having no place to go, I hitched a ride east to the Village. I climbed onto the railing of the apartment where it all started with Sir Walter Scott's admonition—"Oh! What a tangled web they wove, when roped around the dying novae." Uncle Hunny's apartment stood empty. I shimmied up the railing to the top balcony, hoping to find Mom's slider unlocked. She was at work, so I made my way to a shower, some food, and then to bed, sleeping for 36 hours. Quite some time passed since I last stayed here, but the mattress was still on the floor, in the grandest freak fashion, and the old broken dresser stood unmoved from its original position.

During a brief encounter, I told Mom I wouldn't be staying long. Karen was home from the state correctional institution for girls. She took to spending her time floating in and out of D.C. drug dens. Karen was still checking in at home from time to time to keep the supervisor assigned to her off their backs.

Mom had long since given up on any further efforts to control her. All of Karen's pathologies became so co-mingled and complicated that no one could get a handle on how to treat her. One thing was clear: nothing was working. Her fate was now in her own hands. Like everyone, she possessed free will and was smart enough to read her moral and ethical compass reacting to the dynamics of cause and effect, right from wrong. Informed choices always impact others with consequences. Only time would tell what fresh torture she would bring on herself and others, forgone conclusions and all.

By 1971, Carol was more than 10 years into an ever-increasing upward trajectory of responsibilities demanded of high-level security duties at the CIA. The last thing she needed was for Dad's out-of-control gambling lifestyle to create a constant cloud of suspicion over her professional life. He already did jail time for the big raid on his interstate bookmaking operation. She decided it was time for them to separate. The CIA looks askance with burning eyes at spouses who pose a risk to any employee's security profile, especially as a path to being extorted into compromising sensitive intelligence to foreign enemies.

Carol was wise to initiate a preemptive strike by telling her superiors about her spousal problems. She submitted herself to a polygraph examination, which she passed with flying colors. There was one creed she always lived by, handed down from her factory worker grandmother to her factory worker mother and then to her: never put yourself in a position to depend solely on a man for anything.

She put Dad on notice, and he took this opportunity to put a plan of action in place that would evaporate like a mirage in the Nevada desert. He was leaving town to become a Las Vegas blackjack dealer. He lasted two weeks before making a tail-between-the-legs return.

In the meantime, Granddaddy moved from his old Northeast Brookland apartment, where he lived since the late 1940s, to an independent living facility in Takoma Park. He was 72 and in rapid decline.

Changes in my life and worldview estranged me from the one man who understood me better than anyone. To Granddaddy, I embodied the same motivations and creative energy he struggled to fulfill throughout his life. He had only one real tangible hit to show for his efforts, "Powder Your Face With Sunshine." His son had been a disappointment by squandering his prodigious athletic skills and a promising family and home life. Granddaddy believed I would turn out differently, even in the face of so many challenges. I held tight to his belief in me. I never wanted to disappoint him.

———————

FROM SOME OF MY EARLIEST memories, I always felt like two people. I could hear this lashing out, mouthy kid who went after the slightest challenge like a bodily function, but controllable if I chose to do so. I didn't like this other kid inside of me anymore than those who were downrange of my volleys. The imprinting from the adults closest to me had taken its toll. I used it as a preemptive strike against a world I came to distrust with great purpose and intensity. This was the worst kind of defense mechanism, putting up a fight before any reasonable justification required such an action. Was it possible that because of what I experienced in my early years, and subsequently suppressed deep inside, I was growing into a pathological personality?

I always needed the company of a female and often succeeded with that priority. They were usually older girls and women who were single mothers looking for a daddy. I wasn't always the hunter and I had no problem with being the hunted. With a confused sense of what were normal hormonal urges, all I could do was take the path of least resistance and default all of this attention to an ever-increasingly distorted and inflated ego. I was cornered before the turn because long ago someone called on my only surrender before I knew how love should begin. The best and the worst of a halfway world still in recovery lay before me, as I searched for new ground.

Anywhere From 52,560 Hours to Six Years...

THERE ARE NO ADEQUATE ADJECTIVES to describe the events and experiences I lived from 1971 to 1977, often with Kenny at my side—warp speed? A neophyte chewing neolite? Styro the tyro in overdrive pyro? None of that matters, because the Spiral snared me in its gyres and gimbals and all I could do was hold on, acquiesce, and pay constant attention to the details.

The first of the next 52,560 hours started in a hillwilliam dive bar on Route 5 South, deep into Southern Maryland. A country and western entertainer acquaintance had booked himself a gig at this joint. Anytime we knew someone with a gig, we'd pack our equipment and head to the spot with the intention of crashing our way in, turning it into a free-for-all jam session. One night, in late fall of 1971, someone beat us to the punch. It was a drummer unknown to any of us, and a more congenial fellow one would never meet. His name was Barry. There was something very familiar about this cat. It was later revealed that he was the photographer who was contracted to take my yearbook picture for my 10th grade class—such a small and Spiralized world.

Once the festivities in this backwater ran its course, the owner-bouncer ran us out of there because we ran out his customers with long hair, hippie-freak rock and roll. Barry offered, "Let's all go to Olney to my house and start a band and anyone who wants to live there is welcome." Oh yeah? No shit?

Olney is in upper Montgomery County, at the intersection of Route 97 and somewhere. Going south takes you to Silver Spring, where Georgia Avenue splits off to 16th Street. Continuing over the District line will deliver you to the front door of the White House. The East/West road intersecting with Route 97 is Route 108—hardly a nexus of the universe. Other than an overly ambitious traffic signal, the rest of downtown Olney consisted of an IGA grocery store on the southeast corner. On the northwest corner was Olney Drugs. Beyond that, it was all small farmland houses. This area was unambiguously bucolic.

Barry had six years on me. Recently divorced, his wife moved out with the baby and left his unfaithful ass for good. He lived on the top floor of a farmhouse in front of an old animal hospital. The downstairs neighbor was a wonderfully kind, patient, and possibly stone-deaf elderly woman. There was no telling how long she lived there, but from evidence in the attic, it was since before World War II. A live-in attendant occupied the animal hospital after hours; a sweet old guy with no teeth who walked with an unusual gait—an extreme high-step, similar to the ambling gait of a Lipizzaner stallion.

Kenny and I, without hesitation, accepted Barry's offer to move in and start a band. I was homeless and Kenny wanted to relocate from a temporary living situation. He was working a full-time government job as an apprentice pressman at the U.S. Bureau of Engraving and Printing, and spent long days commuting 40 miles to print money, food stamps, and postage stamps. Unfortunately, the Bureau frowned upon handing out free samples from the back door.

I attempted working construction. Weighing 125 pounds and tossing 12-inch cinder blocks up to elderly Italian masons was a non-starter. Kenny was willing to do whatever necessary to get a band off the ground, so he became the de facto breadwinner. I wasn't eating much of anything, and someone was always around with drugs.

Larry Miller—who was still sporting his shag cut, but further refined into a Rod Stewart look—signed on to sing and front the band. He brought along a kid from his neighborhood named Jackie to fill out the second guitar chair.

The local intelligentsia wasted no time making our place a nightly destination. Our rehearsals were the backdrop for every kind of drug-spun character. Old, young, male, female, black, white, rich, poor—you name it, the U.S. Census demographic list was in full representation. How Kenny got high, rehearsed, partied, and then on only two hours of sleep, drove to D.C. to print millions of U.S. dollars, drove home, and did it again, night after night, was one of the veritable unsolved mysteries of social and medical science. Kenny's unique occupation was part of a legacy going back to his uncle. He came to hate the work and soon resigned the cushy government job with a lifetime of benefits and a guaranteed early retirement.

My 18th birthday came and went in this band house. It's one of those imagined and over-sold "today I am a man" milestones, which meant nothing more than I was eligible for the draft. I got my draft card as a form of identification, an acceptable proof of age to drink beer in the District. Getting called up to the draft, even as the Vietnam War raged on, was not a concern of mine—with no fixed address, I was vapor in the wind.

Shortly after my birthday, we received the one-month notice requesting possession of the apartment, without fear or fanfare. Except for the kind and patient old lady who lived below us, we would all soon be out on the street. I was again homeless and resorting to crashing on a couch in Glenmont, or with Kenny in his van, or even back to the Riverdale Stockyard for a night or two. I was quite underweight along with the onset of gum disease.

Kenny eventually landed in College Park with Norman's tribe. Barry slept wherever he could park his van. Any place Barry could set up his makeshift, patchwork drum kit and wail away for hours was all he needed. I was crashing in either Norman's or Kenny's van, or sometimes on the couch in the basement. Living moment-to-moment was always my choice. In a strange, twisted way, my ephemeral existence helped me to further repress so many dark memories.

Someone that Barry knew owned mountain property at the northern end of the Shenandoah Valley, in a town called Star Tannery—seven miles north of Strasburg, and seven miles off of a dirt road at North Fork. This place didn't even qualify as nowhere.

At the turn in the road, in the Virginia/West Virginia notch across the creek on the side of the mountain, stood Birch's house. About 500 feet into the woods, a bit further up the mountain, stood the schoolhouse. The College Park contingent headed west and backward for a time to the mid-19th century. I went elsewhere, for the time being.

Larry Miller was still around the area, and when he wasn't shooting junk, getting laid, or flirting with black magic, he was always up to hitting the D.C. bars where live music was to be found. He introduced me to his other world with an invitation to a night of walking on the wild side, which ended with two very disappointed transvestites looking for a pick-up. Later on, he admitted the pick-up was set-up of his making, without their knowledge, to see if I would take the bait. At the last minute, he changed his mind and backed out of the prank—no small mercy. Just when you think you have someone pegged, they turn around and reveal yet another facet refracting an already complex collection of the bent and twisted light of the soul.

As Kenny and the Star Tannery marauders continued their time travel to the unspoiled corner of postbellum Virginia, I connected through Larry with a gaggle of grubs from the Bladensburg streets. Larry had a thing for grubby guys. I suppose that kept the competition down for the most elegant freak on the street, while keeping all of his options open for drug connections. There was one central grease trap for this collection of misfits and it just so happened to be an apartment literally a 10th of a mile down the hill from where it all started for me, behind the Cheverly Theatre. Yes, the Spiral always repays.

The space was occupied by a young married couple. I knew the wife from my elementary school days. I hadn't seen her in years, but it came as no surprise to know she was living the hippie married life. All of the required décor was in place to show they were far hipper in their world than all of the straights surrounding them—black light posters, multi-color beaded room dividers, bean bag chairs, incense burners, jade plants in the windows, and a collection of albums with the Bee Gees being their favorite. *Zap Comix* were strewn about for a real gen-u-ine, psycho-dellic experience. Her husband wielded a Svengali complex and she was fine with it. They both possessed an eye darting nervousness and frequently retreated to their bedroom, behind a locked door, for hours on end.

Among all of the floaters who came in and out of the place, there was one guy named B-rent who was particularly unusual—a manic personality and ever more so when dropping acid. The only thing I knew about him was that he was local. One evening, after we all dropped acid, the loving couple did their disappearing act. For the next 36 hours, B-rent and I remained planted and rooted in the living room, in all of our psychotropic glory.

By the time the drugs wore off, we were exhausted. I retrieved some level of coherency after a few hours of sleep and took off for a short while. When I returned, B-rent was gone. I knocked on the couple's bedroom door and got no answer, but I could hear them whispering. I grew tired of this hang and took off.

Several days later, I saw a few of Larry's boys and they were quite dark and agitated. I learned someone discovered B-rent's body off of an out-of-the-way road called Lottsford Vista. He was shot several times and carved up with all kinds of strange insignias.

One of the grubs knew the details because he knew who killed him. B-rent sold high-volume amounts of reefer. He started a partnership with some bad motherfuckers—bikers who settled in the area. They fronted B-rent the money to make a huge score and when it fell through, they wanted their money returned. The hunt was on and B-rent decided to hide out at the apartment. The husband knew the bikers and when they found out he knew their target, they arranged for the happy couple to set him up. Their plan was to give this dead man some incentive to stay around and get comfortable, then await further instructions.

The call came in—they were ready to show up and make the grab. The couple was told to stay put in the bedroom. They were also told, without exception, that anyone with him would suffer the same fate. All it would have taken was for them to come out and make some excuse for me to leave—accuse me of stealing a joint, leaving the toilet seat up, anything would have sufficed. Being the cowards they were, this couple let my life hang in the balance and only because of timing and circumstance, I left on my own accord.

There was no way for me to know how long after I left when the killers showed up, but any reasonable conclusion was they were in the immediate area, only minutes from making their move. They drove B-rent out to the remote area east of the Beltway and pulled him from the car, giving him one chance to run. After begging for his life, he turned and within steps of fleeing, they emptied a gun into his back, then finished him off with knives, carving his torso. As for me, timing was my salvation. I never went back to the apartment and all involved were eventually caught, tried, and convicted. The fearless couple got off the easiest with a substantial stretch for accessory to murder. I got away with my life.

———

KENNY AND THE BOYS RETURNED from Virginia. All they could talk about was how amazing this place was and that at some point, they were heading back for an even longer stay. From the pictures I saw, to say it was rustic would have been a severe misuse of the word. This place was possibly uncharted.

One night, a much older guy who owned a nice guitar and sported the mandatory Paul Williams shag cut came by Norman's with his date—a local girl named Helen. She seemed to take a liking to me. She was seven years older and a former heroin addict who was forced to leave Hawaii in lieu of doing some serious jail time. She was also a single mother struggling to make ends meet. It didn't take long for us to establish some intense mutual interest. I took care to make sure that the thing between she and her date was nothing serious. Helen assured me it was casual, but he had other ideas.

We were together for only a short time and I briefly took up residence at her place. We both took very well to playing house, but she had far more experience with this set-up than I did. Helen made it clear this was her space. I was a desired guest, and not much more. The un-air conditioned, sweat-box, one-bedroom apartment, that required her five year old daughter to sleep on the living room couch, was located in one of those ubiquitous gulag-like projects from which I never seemed to escape.

I was falling in love, or so I believed, because love was allegedly the sum of our choices, from which came actions. Realistically, there was no way I could gauge what I was thinking or feeling; another desperate outcry for some kind of loving attention from an older woman. I was playing the role of a real-life, love generation guitar playing knock-off of Goethe's Werther, albeit with a cleaner ending. I knew she had some use for me and I met her needs, which were as superficial as one could imagine. In fact, Helen could have any man she wanted. So, why this 18 year old guitar player? I was needy, and she was needy—everyone's needy. Beyond the routine and boredom of licentious sex, there was nothing of substance between us.

Any kid of my age and vulnerability would fall hard for a woman under these conditions. I believed I found an echo of my mother—unmarried with a young child, having a thing for younger guys, sexually promiscuous as a way to combat her lonely and aimless life, seeking constant approval for her physical attributes. All of this was perfect-bound with some measure of arrested emotional development.

Promiscuity is a trait that's not the exclusive domain of women, and yet, the eternal question for me always remains: why do women seem to hold all of the power when it comes to appealing to the call of the wild? The essential difference between us of the baby boom generation and my mother's generation was the influence of drugs and the new cultural paradigm of free love. Fuck, fuck, fuck, and then fuck some more. Consume yourself while you consume the one you're with. There was no accountability for the outcome of one's choices and actions—pants off to Mr. Stills. What else could it have been? What was the alternative?

I knew real emotional abandonment salted with threats of physical abandonment. For the first time, a woman who was as emotionally stunted as my mother allowed me intimate access. But immaturity ultimately explains nothing of reason, and looking back on it, it's clear that I was missing the bigger picture of pure sexual motivation as a means of controlling my surroundings and protecting myself as the person in need of protection.

This affair amounted to nothing more than self-imposed sexual and emotional abuse, sanctioned through a consensual relationship—the Spiral is unmerciful. Helen held all of the power and none of the responsibility.

Soon enough, she made it known in the most hurtful way, that we were through by inviting an older guy who lived across the parking lot to come and get high as I sat in the living room; one more conquest to assuage her famine for validation.

After Hurricane Agnes and Hurricane Helen came and went, I landed at the Rockville Rock and Chord Quarry, another outlier crash pad similar to Riverdale, under the auspices of a mysterious woman named Fredda. She ran a tight drifter ship with a couple of renters, one of whom was a combat vet from Vietnam—a gentle cat who played good blues guitar. We got along well. The Quarry had limited availability for me to flop, but tow-headed vagabonds can usually find a perch.

Fredda was unusual. She was the doxy of a wealthy hipster who didn't care what or who she did, as long as she was available when he beckoned. She was an uncanny body double for Debby Harry. Her ride was a new Cadillac, courtesy of Sugar Daddy, and she flaunted everything. Fredda owned high-end rock guitar equipment and couldn't play for shit, in spite of the fact she was taking lessons from one of the best multi-instrumental musicians in the D.C. area. It was all a front for whatever this set-up was intended to accomplish. Two Russian wolfhounds and an Italian greyhound rounded out the cast of this one-act play. I found less than no interest in pursuing her as a sexual conquest.

One late summer night, Fredda threw a party. Among the guests was a girl around my age named Joanne. We hit it off immediately and for the next five years, our fates and stars were cast under a tumultuous relationship. She came from a well-educated, upper middle class Jewish family in Silver Spring, consisting of her parents and an older brother. Her background inspired in me a lack of self-confidence. Joanne held the traditional Jewish cultural values portrayed in Philip Roth's *Goodbye, Columbus*. The only equanimity I felt was being the same age as she—no older women bullshit to put up with at great risk to heart and mind.

It wasn't long after she and I met that Barry was leaving to live in the schoolhouse at Star Tannery. Living in his van had reached diminished returns. Barry was born to thrive in a hostile environment—an expert at growing food and requiring very little in the way of creature comforts. He was a Spartan to the core. I was completely homeless, so he invited me along. We had to arrive no later than early September to make the place livable for the impending harsh mountain winter. Joanne and I were still in our best behavior phase, and I was torn to leave, so I invited her to join me in the mountains.

When we presented her mother with this idea, she calmly, like a good progressive liberal, suggested I stay with the family for two weeks to get to know one another. If I passed the audition, she would put us on a bus for Strasburg. I agreed, and once I proved worthy of whisking away her daughter to unknown hills and valleys, I received the Montgomery County Progressive Jewish Mothers and Daughters Association for The Approval of Late Adolescent Consensual Wanton Depravity and Ruin imprimatur. Barry picked us up at a predetermined day, time, and place…

Star Tannery…

…The schoolhouse served the entire valley in the 19th century. By the time I arrived in my new home, it was 115 years old—no electricity, no plumbing, and no insulation. The windows were small window-box types covered in heavy plastic to keep out the cold and bugs, but good for storing perishables between the months of November and February. The floor was rough-hewn timber laid on an uneven stone foundation, providing crawl space for skunks and other mountain wildlife to nest and listen to a tune or two. The walls were a patchwork of industrial insulation coverings, and were badly installed. Heat came from a potbelly stove in the center of the ground floor. The front of the old stove showed an odd resemblance to the face of Peter Lorre.

The wooden walls of the house were so old and dry, electromagnetic forces holding the molecules in place had long since vacated. The only illumination was three kerosene lamps and a few candles. We carried drinking water up from a mountain stream, which started at the top of the next mountain and made its way past our road on the way to the bay. The locals said it was naturally filtered and good to drink. Naturally filtered means any bird or cow shit making its way to the stream, as a drop-in or run-off, would be ceremoniously passed through the gills and waste track of the trout population. I don't want to think about what the fish and assorted humans deposited in this sluice of mountain swill. The water kept us alive for the time being.

Besides the guitar and amp, my possessions amounted to nothing more than some winter clothing and a box of books, among which was *Death of a Salesman, Tarantula* by Bob Dylan, and a well-worn copy of Roger Sessions' *Harmonic Practice,* a traditional classical harmony and theory book from 1951, given to me by a college girl who lived in the Village.

The Sessions book was like a Bible. I went through it with a red grease pencil making every possible note and mark in an attempt to learn exactly what was behind the mysterious power of tonal gravity. My underlines and annotations in the margins resembled something between a treasure map and NORAD launch codes. I had no frame of reference for the terms and concepts. I did my best to figure it out on my own, and with little success. There was no internet in those days, so it was all on me, and I couldn't imagine a more exasperating and challenging endeavor. I felt like a dandelion tasked with learning calculus.

We survived in this ascetic hermitage from September of 1972 until June of 1973. It was the coldest winter of my life. Loneliness and isolation permeated the environment. The space between the space Barry and I occupied was an extra chamber of empty, but we got along fine. There was a brotherly bond reinforced with my respect for his self-sufficient nature. He was slow to anger, which I found comforting. Through my manic energy, he saw a loyal friend and companion who was the best he had to rely on for musical support and guidance.

The biggest challenge we faced was no electricity, which meant I couldn't use my amp. Barry played drums for hours and I would listen, then I would play guitar for hours and he would listen. That was our practice routine for many months—raw and concentrated listening—not for entertainment, but the kind where you get deep inside how another musician processes and makes sense of what they are hearing; how it's brought forth and made to set the air moving. I enjoyed the real-time abstraction of one of those parts of the whole. For the first time, I was inside the instrument which represents the infrasonic world of rhythm and pulse, the birthplace of all pitch; an invaluable learning experience.

Earlier in Rockville, Barry and I discovered John McLaughlin, Weather Report, Return To Forever, and the one who made all of these groups possible, Miles Davis. The Columbia years with his Second Quintet, followed by the seminal recordings of *A Tribute to Jack Johnson, In A Quiet Way,* and the gold standard for everything jazz at the end of the tumultuous 1960s, *Bitches Brew,* were groundbreaking recordings.

So began my official transition from rock, blues, and R&B to the rarified world of jazz. From the odd-meter, hyper-active world of jazz/rock fusion, I started my journey back through jazz history—post-bop, hard bop, the modal period, bebop, swing, big bands…anything jazz. In an interview, John McLaughlin happened to mention an early jazz guitar influence, Tal Farlow. He believed Farlow was an underrated genius who impacted a great number of aspiring guitarists in England in the 1950s, many of whom went on to become major influences in their own right. Once again, there was that name, Tal Farlow.

Staying in the schoolhouse cost us nothing, but we needed supplies. Brief trips back to the D.C. area brought us work to buy several months of food and then head back to the hills. Barry hung wallpaper while I worked with Dad in his glass business. Dad and I reached an understanding that I, like he, chose to live moment-to-moment. For the time being, I was the one replacing those wavy, distorted panes of glass recalled so vividly from my childhood—the slow, amorphous solid, losing the long battle against gravity, pooling after 25 to 30 years in the short, 10-inch journey from top to bottom.

The freezing, wet mountain weather was constant. Before long, the van became immovable until March. We were now completely isolated from the modern world. The impending spring would long hold its first breath against a slow winter's end.

⸺

I chose to stay behind when Barry left for a prolonged period to find work. This was my first isolated opportunity to confront the fears I encased in silence for far too long. I was now alone to let them out and face them head-on. Nighttime was most difficult. I broke up the short days by taking walks, but the dead of night was always unwelcome when the relative silence was deafening. At times, I thought I could hear my circulatory system pounding in my ears. The external sounds of animals foraging, or the sound of air compressors attached to moonshine stills, emanated from around the mountain. At times, I believed I could hear the mountain breathing.

This was a time of exceptional change. My inclinations toward self-examination worked constantly. I suppressed so much pain and fear in the short time of little more than a decade. All of my weighted feelings and thoughts accumulated like centuries of sediment on the bottom of a stream. Forces of nature freed the sediment and sent it floating to the surface to sort out and prioritize that which demanded my attention. The rest I could banish back to the bottom, as I continued navigating the currents through the narrows and the switchbacks. I allowed no external intrusions to sideline my primary objectives. I had become increasingly difficult for people to be around. My lashing out with humor, sarcasm, and insularity was the face of fear, defensiveness, and the worst: lack of trust. Fear wears many faces, but always with the same troubled eyes.

By the end of May, the time had arrived to abandon the schoolhouse. The last thing I looked at was an epigraph, which stood out against everything else I abstracted from reading a small part of Aristotle's *Politics*. To pass the time, I chiseled it into the dead, desiccated wood above the front window. I worked on it nearly every day from the day I arrived. It read,

"…The object at which they aim is a low one…"

Aristotle's epigraph encapsulated my intentions. The age of 19 was an emotionally equivocating time, but I was certain of one thing: my path to succeed was clear in its direction. In the grand scheme, the Sonic was its own purpose. It existed for its own sake, independent of human response or intervention or participation, just like any other force of nature. I was nothing more than an apprentice translator of waveforms within a limited compass of frequencies in the entire energy spectrum of the known universe.

My greatest revelation during this time came several paragraphs later in Aristotle's writing. I discovered another epigraph by the great and ancient: "…but, there are two objects to aim at—the possible as well as the suitable."

That was the reveal. The possible was for those who had to do it, and the suitable was for those who only wanted to do it. The door of the schoolhouse closed one final time without a sound, as my tracks transitioned from endless snow to the soft, thawing ground. I felt the mountain exhale....

...Whichever Comes First

THE TIME HAD COME FOR me to seek formal study to help me decipher the launch codes I struggled to understand in Sessions' big red harmony book. A friend told me about the music department at Prince George's Community College. This modest facility staffed a small but substantial faculty who moonlighted from their duties as musicians in the military jazz bands and combos stationed in the Washington, D.C. area. PGCC would be my next landing.

JOANNE AND I NEEDED A place to live and a job, so I contacted Marilyn, who was still living in the Village in the Woods. For $15 a week, she rented us her spare bedroom. We reported for work at Bowie Race Track at five o'clock the next morning. Joanne landed a groom spot and I became a lowly hot walker. I paraded exercised thoroughbreds around the shed row for 20 minutes to cool down, then off to their stalls with the grooms waiting to finish the morning care routine.

When Dad heard that I was working for the legendary Richard Dutrow, one of the highest winning thoroughbred trainers of all time, he started digging for tips on the stake horses. To my surprise, I had been passing him bad information, because I was given bad information by the grooms and exercise boys. There must have been some unwritten code among the professionals who worked for the trainer to deceive those looking for a quick tip.

On a late August morning in 1973, I arrived at PGCC to sign up for harmony and ear training classes. The following two years I spent learning theory, notational concepts, and the basics of functional harmony by way of J.S. Bach, through voice leading and analyzing his chorales and, my favorite, ear training, were joyful times. I felt alive and energized and full of purpose. Many motivations going back years came to a perfect convergence fulfilling whatever promise they held. I switched from the solid body Telecaster, brought to me by the still mysterious actions of Larry Miller, to a 1960 cherry red Gibson ES-335 owned by another music student interested in going to a solid body. Five years had passed since I paid cash for a guitar—another even swap with mutual satisfaction.

I soon left the race track slog and took on a 5 a.m. janitorial job at a department store across from the Village. My reward for the short trip from removing equine bodily functions to cleaning the aftermath of human bodily functions was to spend two or three days a week out at the campus.

After Joanne and I moved to a basement apartment near the race track, our relationship started to disintegrate. At the heart of our collapse was my strange, false solitary existence. I created unjustified expectations of Joanne to bundle and stash her desires, in exchange for some kind of bullshit bestowed privilege for joining my solitary life of lofty creative pursuits protected by an insular interior world. I was churning out low-grade narcissism. It didn't take us long to recognize our strange and conflicted duality. Accepting the conflict was made slightly more tolerable with the assistance of the emotionally validating orgasm—everything comes with a price. When you tie that down with the basic fear of losing and separating from one another, it makes for great complications, often deflected with extreme actions and choices. Square one romance was always such an exciting, but short-lived place to be—so much promise and so much to look forward to. Such powerful demands these limitations brought to bear on us.

I FELT MOST AT EASE with the other students in this small theatre-turned-music department, because we all loved what we did far more than any non-musician could imagine. The most unique characteristic of this place was the presence of many jazz players amidst the prevailing traditional conservatory curriculum; that didn't seem to matter. Here was a place where my extreme penchant for details would be well-served. I treated every activity and event as being equally important to the next. I wasted nothing in my constant state of observation and listening.

There were two standout instructors, both as musicians and personalities. One was Jay Chattaway and the other was Fred Chapin. Chattaway taught ear training and was brilliant at it. He had a twisted sense of humor and was demanding to the point where he adapted some of Nicholas Slonimsky's techniques of polymetric conducting into his approach. Imagine the control it would take if you were tap dancing while drawing a portrait on a board with one hand, as you balanced your checkbook on the same board with the other hand. I couldn't nail the polymetric quadridexterity, but I certainly enjoyed the effort. Seeing the entire class reduced to the chaotic spasms of a marionette struggling to be free of their strings brought an added dimension of comic relief. Jay eventually went on to become a highly successful arranger and composer working for many years in Hollywood.

Fred was unique. He claimed to play in excess of 25 instruments equally well. His primary instruments were tenor sax and guitar. Fred always wore his ego on his sleeve. If he believed you were serious, he took time to mentor you. I learned a lot of useful things in the short time I knew him. In grand Spiral fashion, he and I had already crossed paths: it was about a year and a half earlier, at the Rockville Chord Quarry. Fredda had been taking private lessons from none other than Fred. He appeared one night playing guitar in her basement. Not only could he play, but what he played was incomprehensible to everyone in the room. Once I recovered, I asked him what that was and he said it was "The Dance of Maya" by John McLaughlin.

My re-acquaintance with Fred was another glorious Spiral moment, popping open like a Jack-in-the-box in space and time. I was now being formally mentored by the musician who, on that fateful night in Fredda's basement, introduced me to my new world of jazz.

One afternoon, Fred brought in jazz guitarist Herb Ellis to do a clinic for a select handful of the jazz heads. For an hour, Herb played tunes and then took questions about his approach to jazz guitar. Someone asked him who was his favorite jazz guitarist. He answered by first attempting to play some outrageous phrase and then he said, "The guy who created that lick lives on the Jersey Shore where he paints signs for a living. His name is Tal Farlow, and he's probably the best among all of us." I've been hearing that name for years, and I still hadn't heard his music. Herb mentioned Tal would occasionally take on private students. Someone with that level of musical command and influence choosing to make a living doing something else was puzzling.

1974 WAS MY YEAR FOR tattoo removal. My tribal stains represented a time from which I wanted few memories. If it meant exchanging one type of a scar for another, so be it. A dermatologist on the West Coast created a new and less scarring method for tattoo removal. He used coarse kosher salt to abrade about seven layers of skin. Joanne's mom approached the head of the dermatology department at Washington Hospital Center and he had heard about the new process. I became his beta patient and was the first ever on the East Coast to experience this technique. Rubbing salt into a wound is more than just a metaphorical cliché, once again proving the tribal values of manhood-equals-pain-equals-imputable character. By the way, less abrasive is a relative term. The one I most wanted removed was the one he couldn't treat with this method. It was my first mark from 1967, a Cross of Malta. It still lives as a constant and unblinking reminder of the futility of making a choice for the sake of validation by those who only appear to be stronger than you.

After Granddaddy moved from his little cold water flat around the corner from Catholic University, Joanne and I often stopped by to share a laugh or two and take him shopping. I knew he didn't understand why I made such an unexpected change in my appearance, but he never passed judgment. The old man turned his new home upside down and on its ear with his antics. He was always giving the old ladies a fit, especially the ones who lived by social pretense and other superficial agendas. His attitude was simple: what the fuck is so wonderful in their lives that would cause them to come across as better than me? They were all in the same boat—eating bad community food, living one stacked on top of the other, waiting to die with some shred of dignity and self-respect, while they rattled around in a one-room efficiency watching *Let's Make A Deal* all the while waiting in vain for a loved one to call, or stop by just because. Granddaddy was a complex man of extremes and little middle ground, but his oddities never compromised his loving and generous soul.

In October, I got the dreaded call from Dad. This larger-than-life and indestructible man was in the Veterans Hospital in Charles Town, West Virginia, and close to dying. Dad and I would soon reposition in time and space, like game pieces moving one step closer to our own mortalities. Joanne and I drove to Charles Town that same day with a dark and looming expectation he would be gone by the time we arrived. During the drive, I remembered an indelible moment in time:

Granddaddy and I went on a long vacation to a remote part of southern Maryland, a place called Point Lookout, where the Chesapeake Bay and the Potomac River became one body of water at the edge of the earth, seeking the Atlantic. He rented a cottage and all we did was fish, crab, and sit around and laugh. They were long days for a little boy without a television, but I read a lot and went off on my own to explore. A lot of the time we would sit on the porch and stare out at the ocean, the smell of honeysuckle coming from everywhere, carried by the salted and soothing winds coming in from this ancient body of water. The same cicada choir I remember from Nanny's cedar trees followed us to sing their lullaby and mating calls, with the same unpredictable crescendos and decrescendos. I never felt more cared for.

Two weeks slowly passed and we headed home. We soon came upon a small boy about my age, dressed in tattered clothes and barefoot, walking up the dusty and rock-strewn shoulder of the small backwater road. The temperature must have been 100 degrees. The dust in the air was so thick, you could bump your head on it if the car stopped short.

The boy struggled with walking on the rocks and stones. As we passed by, Granddaddy glanced in the rearview mirror and a look came over his face I never before saw. He pulled off to the shoulder, got out, and went into the backseat to retrieve a grocery bag along with a pair of flip-flops he bought for me to wear at the beach.

I turned to lean against the seat and watched out of the back window. He didn't wait for this child to approach him. While the two of them spoke, I could tell he was asking the boy where he lived, because Granddaddy was pointing in one direction and the boy was pointing elsewhere. He handed him the flip-flops, which the boy immediately put on his feet. He then handed him the grocery bag with food leftover from our stay. Finally, he gave him several dollars. After the child accepted the bag, Granddaddy gave him a soft and assuring touch on his shoulder, and sent him on his way. Granddaddy returned to the car and said nothing for the longest time because nothing needed saying. I learned many life lessons in that brief respite from the harshness of this halfway world.

This child, most likely born of poor parents, possibly sharecroppers, and probably with other siblings at home, received not only relief from the pain caused by the shards beneath his feet, but also the uncertainty of what could be another night of a questionable family meal. He also received an intangible lasting memory of knowing that this man, whose skin color represented something he learned to fear, was the exception, or hopefully, the rule—a conclusion he would need a lifetime to reach.

I believe fear, if for only this moment, found its way out of his young and unassuming mind and heart and settled on the dust of eons swirling about him from the hot, late summer wind—carried to parts unknown and lost forever. What he would remember was this kindly old white man with his grandson, a boy who lived with his own secrets and fears, showing him a spark of love and kindness forever frozen in the middle of a scorching August day in the middle of an obscure Maryland backwater. In 1964, this was a place with a culture still thriving on fear and prejudice, brought about by people who lived a deluded irony, within their collectivist mindset, that all people who are different than they must all be the same, and all who are the same as they deserve consideration as individuals. And, believing the different are their lessors, a mentality informing a self-proclaimed superiority, they wrapped themselves in the antithetical ideal of individual liberty colliding with their brand of groupthink.

The supreme irony was that they believed their groupthink was different, and more justified than the collectivism of aggressive foreign oppressors who were vanquished in our recent wars in far-off lands—oppressors most likely defeated by these very people or family members, as the veterans who bravely served their country.

The gift for me on that day was what I have come to see as a moment of true perfection in human interaction, when the barriers of age, skin color, class distinctions, and any other self-imposed limitations in the human condition, fell into a roadside ditch without pretense or expectation on the part of the child or the old man. It was a moment of objective clarity for a 64 year old man who knew just how hard life was for everybody because he lived life hard so many times over. He saw the same value in this child he always saw in himself and in me. Granddaddy did what came naturally to him, and without judgment or some hazy sense of moral obligation shrouded by a desire for approval from others.

Granddaddy loved to call many times a week, or sometimes stopped in unannounced. What was an annoyance to my parents was always my joy: the rides in the old Plymouth with only the two of us, when he spoke to me as if I were his equal; his unflagging commitment to seeing that Karen, Ronnie, and I always found something under the Christmas tree; and financial support, which Mom gladly accepted through the hypocrisy of her gnashing teeth and transparent derision. "Here comes the old man…he's such a liar; what a bullshitter…Is that him on the phone? Tell him I'm not here…"

He loved taking me out of school in the middle of the day to go shopping for clothes with his ASCAP check burning a hole in his pocket. He was as excited to have this day with me as I was to be with him, and he always gave what he spent on me to spend on Karen. And the guitars…Granddaddy saw something in me he believed needed protection and encouragement. I shudder to think how he would have been impacted had he known of the sexual assaults and subsequent fear and trembling I kept so deeply secret.

It would be easy to dismiss his attention on me as compensation for the failure of Mom and Dad's marriage, or not handling his relationship with his son's young star athlete days as well as he could have, or even his own failed marriage…maybe a dose of Catholic guilt? It's all rank speculation, and what does it matter? Even if he was motivated by any of those circumstances, I don't believe for a moment that he loved me any less than what I know he felt. He could have chosen to become estranged from all of us, but he chose differently.

Joanne and I arrived at the hospital and were taken into a common ward, the likes of which I recall seeing only in old war movies. As we approached Granddaddy's bedside, he looked up at me, took my hand, and said with a half-smile, "I'm really in a fix this time." I didn't want him to see my tears, although he believed there was no shame in a man crying. I saw him do it every time he dropped to his knees to pray, whether in my living room or on the slate floor in front of statues ringing the walls of the catacombs under the Shrine of the Immaculate Conception. His tears of faith I never understood because they were solely between this man and his God. He ceased to be my grandfather in those moments, and became a man falling to his knees, driven by mystery, reverence, and most and worst of all, fear.

We stayed by his side until visiting hours were over. I kissed him and assured him we would soon return. The doctor told us his prognosis was tentative and he was doing everything he could to help Granddaddy through this difficult wait-and-see period.

The following day, Saturday, October 20th, 1974, Granddaddy went his separate way. He was only two months into his 74th year. Dad's grief was long and difficult; mine was buried in disbelief. The era of the first 20 years of my life ended and another began. What lay ahead for me was going to happen whether or not Granddaddy was alive to share in it. He knew he wouldn't be around to see the outcome of the choices I would make, from extended adolescence into the long trap-laden trails in search of real manhood. He knew if I continued believing in myself the way he believed in me, I would be okay.

In Granddaddy's timeless awakening, he coiled at the speed of light on every split second of his life, with the untold memories of all that he loved. He changed into whatever he was to become with this conviction as his provenance: he did all that he could do for all that mattered to him. Granddaddy took his quarter turn and embraced a long and deserved rest.

After the funeral, Dad mentioned an incident between Granddaddy and a priest called in to administer his last rites. The priest appeared to be fresh out of the seminary, and this kind of hospital duty was probably one way this probationer would have to pay some Earthly dues. When the doctor and priest approached his bedside, Granddaddy appeared to have taken his last breath. The priest started the ritual and during the course of his Latin prayers, he leaned over to administer extreme unction. Granddaddy, from out of the blue, bolted upright, did a self-blessing, and then finished the prayer in Latin. Once the blood returned to the priest's head and he could find words to express his shock, the only question he could ask was whether Granddaddy was ever a member of the priesthood. Dad's answer was an unqualified no, although he liked to play one in real life, among so many other roles and characters. Even on death's door, the old man couldn't resist fucking with someone's mind one last time. He went out the way he came in—laughing—and he never missed answering the caul. "Some joke, eh boss?" The man just couldn't resist.

KENNY AND I HAD A falling out. Actually, it was I who fell, for he was still standing. We didn't see one another for well over a year and then one night at Larry's, we reconnected. We both lived with regrets, and there were no hard feelings. He was still playing bass guitar, but he left the graphic design field for a time. He worked with a few of the crew from Norman's camp at the ABC/Dunhill regional record and tape warehouse.

By now, my two-year stint in the music program at PGCC was over. Kenny and his wife Gail were living in Riverdale. Joanne and I were still playing house in Hyattsville. I was looking for work, so Kenny got me on at the record warehouse. One of the company's major perks was allowing employees to take home three albums a week at no cost—an idealistic, if not naïve attempt to keep pilfering down to a minimum. I raided the *Impulse!* aisle, where John Coltrane recorded his greatest body of work. Among other jazz artists, I collected everything Coltrane recorded with the intention of wearing them down to an oily smudge. During this time, Kenny fell in with a good Annapolis-based regional cover band with a lot of gigs.

Kenny invited me to tag along to one of their rehearsals. Besides the standard guitar, bass, drums, keyboard, and singer set-up, they also had a sax player. I got to play a bit and helped them learn some new tunes off of the records. Because of the skills I developed at PGCC, I was able to write out sax parts with the correct transposition, and my chops in hearing the tune and writing down the chord changes, without my instrument in hand, had increased to higher levels of speed and accuracy.

This band was expanding their repertoire to include more of Steely Dan's music, so this was an opportunity to add a much-needed second guitar and someone who could write out the horn lines. I gratefully accepted their offer to join and I started with them in the middle of a week-long engagement at one of the most notorious bars in the District.

The Butterfly was located in the legendary 14th Street Northwest corridor known as "the strip," where every skin and drug trade imaginable was alive and thriving, with stiff competition coming from places such as Benny's Home of the Porno Stars, Casino Royal, and the Cocoon.

The business model of the Butterfly was to show hard-core stag films on a rickety screen set up on the stage, which enticed the foot traffic to drink and hangout until the band began at 7 p.m. All during our load-in and set-up, we worked behind the movie screen as the films played on and on. Our wives and girlfriends would either have to hang out on the sidewalk in front of the club and risk being propositioned, or sit in the club within eye and earshot of the festivities on the screen. Faced with either choice, the ladies' heads would most certainly have melted, but, they chose the lesser of two evils and stayed inside, struggling to keep their heads and wits intact.

At exactly 7 p.m., the screen went down and the band was on. During our sets, all of the movie action transferred to the second floor, where the canopied booths were always full. There was a band room, a green room of sorts, as they say in the industry. We went up there only to smoke a joint. There was a locked door from inside the band room, which led to a top floor. Kenny asked a waitress aat was the big secret behind the green door. She said it was one of several locations around town where the films they showed in-house were made—a lovely little self-contained enterprise with relatively little overhead.

The crowds were typically good during the sets. There was one unusual attraction who was a regular—the One-Legged Dancer. He was arguably the best dancer out there simply because he had to be. One minor detail Kenny and I learned 40 years too late was that all during our sets, we performed the function of being a live juke box for two topless go-go dancers in recessed cages well past each end of the stage. No one in the band knew of this added attraction because the moment we stopped, so did they, and the cages went dark until our next set. Yeah, baby, welcome to the gig.

With gigs running the gamut from Capitol Hill congressional parties, to Baltimore yacht clubs, to Georgetown bars, to the shithole drug dens of East Baltimore, the band eventually drew to a close with one memorable final appearance in a roadhouse on the interstate between Frederick and Baltimore called the Cross Keys. This joint was one of the more sublime Environmental Protection Agency effluvium sites I ever had the pleasure to work. Besides the predictable time-warp décor from circa 1850 Oregon Badlands, its most fetching characteristic was the house hoard of outlaw bikers. The upstairs belonged to several members and over time, others showed up and claimed squatter's rights and took the place over. Fortunately, this was a one-night event. We kicked off the first number and the place filled up quickly with some of the most tweaked-out meth heads and killer weed PCP addicts I have ever seen this side of Spring Grove mental institution—an ugly combination of chemicals that even the engineers at Monsanto would have feared. Once the clientele sized us up, the mood changed quickly:

"*Hey!* Y'all know 'Sweet Home Alabama?'"

"Sure, we'll play it when we start the next set."

"*Hey!* I wanna hear it *now*."

"*Okay*, let's play it. Kick it off, Jeff."

After we ended the tune, a shout from a different corner says, "*Hey!* Y'all know 'Sweet Home Alabama?'"

"We just played it."

"Well, *play it again!*"

For the next two and half hours, we played this national anthem of the south in an eternal loop. In addition to my hand cramps, at the end of the night I developed a sonic allergic reaction to an open D major chord. It would be literally decades before I ever chose to play another one.

The lead singer eventually quit fronting the band. Another member took off for Maine to become a lumberjack and was never heard from again. Another stayed on in Annapolis and became a junkie. He eventually died from AIDS, while another left his wife and lived out his days as a homeless drunk on the streets of Annapolis. Kenny kept on doing what he did in the world of graphic arts. Once the band ended, I had to find work. A private school had an opening for a bus driver. I could have the job provided I got a Class C license.

———

FOLLOWING ALL OF THE PERSONAL upheaval, Joanne and I gave up the apartment in Hyattsville and moved in with her father in Wheaton. Her mother finally left him and undoubtedly for good reason. It was also during this time, after years of no contact, that Barry resurfaced at various jam sessions and jazz joints in town. He lived out of his van on whatever unattended property in the upper county he landed in to claim squatter's rights. In spite of his attempt at a second marriage with more children, and a shift to born-again Christianity, a vagabond woodsman was his life's calling, ringed with intermittent court appearances for various misdemeanors.

Barry was the most ephemeral of the influences in my life. The time we spent surviving in Star Tannery was more a test of my resolve to remain committed to my life's work, regardless of the compromises I made in quality of life. Barry's insularity never influenced me; my insularity was well established before I ever knew him. Our brief time together was a Doppler echo from one life in constant motion against the static nature of another.

———

Hollywood studio legend and jazz guitar master Howard Roberts became a major influence on me. I knew from his monthly columns in *Guitar Player* magazine that he could read any part put before him (affectionately described in studio musician parlance as "reading fly-shit"), as well as his mastery of styles; the essential skills for an A-list studio player to possess. Howard was also one of the original members of the famed Wrecking Crew, an elite group of studio musicians who were the band behind countless pop and rock hits from the 1960s.

Howard possessed a prodigious gift for teaching. He understood the psychology of performance in general, and specifically as it related to the guitar and the challenges of sight-reading on this complex instrument. From his monthly workshop columns in *Guitar Player* magazine, he developed reams of master class materials and traveled the country presenting intense three-day, never-let-up-except-for-air-food-and-water workshops. I couldn't pass up an opportunity to spend three days, eight hours a day, with one of my first musical heroes and jazz influences.

In April of 1976, I paid the $75 fee and showed up at the Holiday Inn function room in suburban Virginia with my guitar, along with 74 other guitar players with all levels of ability. When Howard entered the room, he quietly picked up his guitar. The first thing he said to the crowd of eager guitarists was, "We're all little nuts so we better stick together." Then he played some ridiculous shit that left everyone stunned and silent.

To be in the accessible presence of such a master musician transported me to an infective moment: his confidence became my confidence. I began to listen, focus, and refine what I was doing with content and, most importantly, creative intention. It all seemed familiar and right, as if someone left a light on, illuminating a spot reserved for me to land. Plateaus waited for my landing and as long as I kept pushing on—motivated to fill the emptiness, which followed the settling of what I worked to master—there was always room for more.

Howard appeared again in October for several nights at the Showboat Lounge in Silver Spring. During the day, he held another master class. On the first day, he offered a challenge to anyone willing to accept it: go up on the stage and play something you have never before played. So, a local player named

Paul Wingo and I went up and did exactly that—pure, spontaneous creativity with no stylistic agenda. That was a first for me—entirely new and unchartered territory that demanded I trust myself and those in the room. I expected what I was about to do would be heard objectively, without judgement. No one else got up there and stripped away all practiced pretenses and contrivances; to make the music they heard in their head, unpracticed and in the moment.

Pulling music from out of thin air, hearing it as the messenger and the one who is hearing the message, brought an unsettling, empirical awareness of not being in control of what was played. Yet, I was aware that I was the one through whom the music was being transported. I wanted more than anything else to recreate this rare and elusive exploit, to forever live the experience.

The two days with Howard ended with Kenny, Gail, Joanne, and me attending Howard's final evening performance. This was their first time hearing live jazz, and they came away with a new appreciation of the level of musicianship it takes to create this most extemporary of styles. During his break, Howard came over to our table to say hello and before he departed, he put his hands on my shoulders and leaned in to whisper, "What you did up there was really good; you have a lot to say." Imagine all of the ways a hungry and cynical 22 year old could interpret such praise, from "Is he just blowing Hollywood smoke up my ass?" all the way to, "If I move out to Los Angeles, maybe I can work with him?" The truth may be somewhere in between.

————

The relationship Joanne and I struggled to keep alive and moving forward was reaching its end. As her mother confessed to me decades later, we were both two needy kids who believed they had only each other. That pretty much sums it up from a mother's perspective with love and wisdom. We were both on emotional life support and the tanks were running on fumes. I was still driving for the private school and for the first time, I enjoyed a stable income, at least for a kid barely in his twenties with no car, but a future that was still navigable. I had to find another place to live and end four years of playing house. I answered an ad for a roommate in Kensington.

Someone I never before saw in my circle of musician friends appeared one day at a jam session. She played guitar and sang quite well in a folk and country style. There was something in her face of 19, especially her eyes, that was evocative and hauntingly familiar. She looked like an older version of someone I knew or saw when I was a small child. Her name was Candy Carpenter. As we were leaving, the bassist told me her father was Scott Carpenter, one of the original seven Mercury astronauts—yes, of course, that's where the eyes came from. I was remembering those *Life* magazine pictures from the early 1960s, especially the one where she was laying on her dad at the edge of a swimming pool, grinning toward the camera. Her photographs were all over those pages. She was the youngest of the four with the unique eyes. My, how the Spiral loves to romance.

After five years of so much back and forth, Joanne and I were, once and for all, finished.

I conceded to the truth that we had grown together in experience, but not necessarily in wisdom. In the end, her mother was right—two needy kids who believed they mattered only to each other. Then, with the entrance of Candace Carpenter into my life, my proclivity for relationship rebounding became set and clear. I was a slow learner in understanding the most abundant commodity everyone is so generous in sharing, and most willing to receive in romantic relationships, is complications—and many more complications still lay ahead for me.

———

HOWARD ROBERTS WAS PLANNING TO open an innovative trade school in L.A. called the Guitar Institute of Technology. The program was developed from all of his seminar materials, in addition to new technologies specifically developed for training guitarists to perform at a studio level. This was a perfect time for me to start a new phase in my life. The challenge in relocating to the West Coast was money; not only the expense of buying a vehicle and the resources to move 3,000 miles away, but the tuition for Howard's school was steep.

Driving for a private school didn't pay enough for me to save for much of anything. I recalled Fred Chapin's glowing praise of Berklee College of Music.

The more I investigated the school, the more the place and the prospect of relocating to Boston appealed to me. I put in an application to this storied music college, and to my great surprise, a letter of acceptance arrived with the starting semester of fall, 1977.

With summer drawing to a close, I began saying many goodbyes. Joanne reached out to me to say that she was also making a change in her life. She was moving to Brookline, New Hampshire to study equestrian arts while living with her aunt and uncle. She offered to drive me to Boston before she continued on to her final destination, which I gratefully accepted. Candy and I assured one another we would stay as close as possible in our distance. There was talk of her applying to Berklee for the coming fall of 1978 semester. All of her attempts at college in the D.C. area derailed for one reason or another, so why not try something new and distant? She could play and sing and would probably do well at Berklee.

I finished my farewells to my family, including Karen, who had been on her own and living off the rails for several years. Despite the drugs, the dubious men she attracted, and living pillar-to-post, I welcomed and appreciated her good wishes. Karen always knew right from wrong, and her sense of free will was clearly intact. One choice she made was to marry one of those ubiquitous bad boys from Palmer Park. Only time would tell the direction her life would end up going.

———

JOANNE AND I HEADED UP the Baltimore-Washington Parkway, soon passing the exit to Greenbelt. This time, unlike my return trip from New York City six years before, my mind focused on where this change I was about to undertake would take me, and if I would ever return to this area. I felt no desire or expectations to come back because it held many painful memories.

Six years or 52,560 hours—whichever comes first is the winner, but, it can only be a tie—a marker of indifference; it's always a new game. It took me more than 188,400,000 of every imaginable kind of heartbeat—happy, lost, broken, chained, skipped, fluttered, heavy, and strained—to start once again at a finish line as the next level of the inner-soul spiral pole events in space and time awaited me. After returning the heartbeats to the back of the line, I reloaded the next half-billion, sat back, closed my eyes, and relived a recent and astonishing marker event:

The early summer sun and heat of 1976 was on full burn when a friend invited me over to her parents' pool to cool off. After we swam, she retreated into the house. I sat alone on the edge of the pool, my mind blank as my legs and feet obeyed my brain's subconscious demands. I created small, spiraling pools as the sun crested and began its slow descent to the horizon, to once again saturate the other half of the Stone with its ancient and unapologetic energy.

The moment I stopped agitating the water, a ladybug landed between my ankles. I sat watching this creature struggle to save itself, thinking, *At this very instant, how many more times did this happen in all of the bodies of water where ladybugs inhabit the planet?* Without breaking tempo, I instinctively started to recite the abstract rhyme we all knew as kids: "Ladybug, ladybug, fly away home…"

Unless I played God using divine intervention to rescue it, the rest of the rhyme would be meaningless. After her legs stopped moving, I raised her out of the water with my right index finger. The ladybug perched motionless for several minutes. I presumed I hadn't made the rescue in time. I raised her to eye level and began to gently blow a stream of air at her…still nothing. I continued doing this, and then…she began to stir.

As I persisted in expelling a gentle stream of air, the ladybug slowly rose on her legs and turned with her back to me. In another moment, this tiny speckled aphid eater spread her fiery elytra adorned with seven black moons as far apart as they would expand, exposing her beautiful, diaphanous wings. Slowly and seductively, the soddened bug raised her hind section, as if falling onto whatever functioned as beetle knees. There was no turning back for us—I was in this until either I passed out from hyperventilating and we both went into the water, or the lady flew off once my service was no longer needed.

I continued drying her wings. The sun shined through her complex network of membranes forming the underside of her protective covering. I stared in absolute awe at colors I could never describe in Earthly terms. The hues began to disperse. As if perched atop a prism, I watched from above as colors danced and oscillated. I imagined hearing the corresponding pitches from each waveform of color represented in the sonic spectrum— from the deepest fundamental bass tones in the absolute infrared, to the seraphic harmonics at the high-end threshold of human perception pitched in the absolute ur-violet—blending into what must have been the Last Chord—the 479,001,600th and final combination of every pitch in the 12-tone, equal-tempered chromatic scale all sounding in succession and then all at once.

Stories were told about how the resonance of this chord held the power to simultaneously evoke every possible emotion and feeling known to humanity into a composite feeling of pneutralalia, the final and most obscure of all of the joys and sorrows. Before long, I was standing inside one of the panels of the wing. The ceiling of the Sistine Chapel would, by comparison, look like the incoherent scrawling of a mad man's graffiti on a blind alley wall.

I could see everything that ever was, in all of its glorious and varied repetition, and everything that ever would be, but with no indication where or when in time. The clarity of what I saw and why was so overpowering, I reached the point where the intensity of the pneutralalia released its grip on my soul. Then I understood: the passive observation of greatness required only an act of submission, but the creation of greatness first requires one to submit to a perpetual state of observation. Then…off she flew. She passed through the split infinity, between here and there, without hesitation, and never looked back.

A long time passed before I wiped away tears of the overwhelmed. I glanced at my right index finger. On the tip where the lady came back to life, an image appeared: (12!)—the symbol of the factorial representing all possible distinct sequences in the equal-tempered chromatic scale. Then, it slowly faded.

Berklee

Joanne and I spent our final night together in the Sheraton near Berklee. It was a sad moment of departure, despite our failures. This was a good way to say farewell and give some long overdue acknowledgement to the significance, if not the success, of the five years we shared. The outcome of this relationship was predictable, and maybe even a foregone conclusion, but the hurt and disappointment that dominated our lives along the way was less foreseeable. When you are too far in the feelings, thinking clearly becomes an afterthought.

When I think of the myriad girls and women who came into my life up to then, Joanne possessed a core of common sense and all-around decency that was rare for such a conflicted young woman. An inaccessible father and a mother who was stuck in the middle of a textbook 20th century Jewish suburban dysfunctional family informed much of her neediness. Regardless of their formal education, culture, and high-level professional careers, her parents had much in common with mine.

The next morning, we said our poignant goodbyes. She was continuing on to relocate only an hour north of Boston, to live with relatives in New Hampshire in hope of starting a new life that was certain to include horses. We knew that we'd never see each other again.

———

The buildings in two blocks of Boston's Back Bay that contained Berklee were repurposed hotels—cramped and old, with one too many ad hoc paint jobs. I was closing in on 24—several years older and many lifetimes more experienced than the freshmen pollywogs, 18 and fresh off the bus from whatever small pond they happened to tearfully leave behind. Because the bulk of my money was already in the hands of the college, I carried about $200 to hold me over until I could find work. I would have to settle, for now, with living in the dorms among so many inexperienced teenagers; a huge playpen with an Alighieri day camp intensity.

Berklee's location wasn't your typical New England college setting with green, rolling hills and quads lined with students in their most earnest mindset of soft study and hard play. In September of 1977, Berklee was still a college to study the art of jazz and jazz-related products. The college used its sketchy, streetwalker-strewn location, at the Fenway edge of Back Bay, as a selling point for the urban energy commonly associated with the jazz musician. No matter how they spun it, the sound from the street below of a hooker and pimp beating the living shit out of a john wasn't conducive to the goals for the students in the dorms. I didn't care what happened on the street. It was tame in comparison to what I lived through on the streets of my hometown. I was in Boston, the home of baked beans, the Red Sox, and a psychotic rapist/strangler named for the city in which he struck terror, and I was far from the tendrils of my mother.

During my time at Berklee, I wrang out every jot of information and knowledge. I was under no pressure to come away with a formal degree. I focused on as much harmony, arranging, ear training, and performance as I could fit into a full-time schedule. I wanted only to play and write. If I wanted to study academics, I could read books.

One of the first people I met was Paul. Both of his parents and his stepfather were A-list Hollywood actors with international household names. Armed with a trust fund, he loved to offer impressionable freshman girls all-expense paid voyages to the family estate in Switzerland during holidays and spring break—impressive resources, but being the heir to such a powerful showbiz legacy was no guarantee for success in the ways of female conquests.

I was eager to graduate from my semi-hollow body Gibson, and Paul was looking for the opposite, so we swapped guitars after spending a day playing each other's instruments. He got my classic 1960 cherry red Gibson ES-335 with a Bixby tailpiece, and I got his 1956 Sunburst tobacco brown Gibson ES-175, a vintage classic. It was a good swap at the time, but as it later turned out, Paul got the better of the deal.

One day, while looking over a bulletin board, a notice caught my attention. A grad student at Harvard was advertising for male musicians, between the ages of 18 and 30, to take part in a study she was conducting in partial fulfillment for her master's degree. Her thesis was an age-old conjecture that there is a fine line between psychosis and creative genius. She wanted to settle the argument once and for all by conducting a series of eye tests. For three hours of my time, at the 1977 Harvard human lab rat flat rate of $10, I'd be contributing to this important and groundbreaking study. I was low on cash, and besides, I always wanted to visit Harvard to see what all the fuss was about. Who knows, maybe she would settle the question about genius and insanity once and for all—I was betting on insane.

I walked down the buffed and narrow Harvard hallway to a lone open door. Harsh white fluorescent ceiling fixtures threw the only available light into the hallway, along with their incessant electro-vocalized charms of the 60-cycle hum.

I tentatively entered the room and a woman in her mid-thirties was sitting at a small, cluttered desk going over some papers. On her desk was a small sign that read, "If you don't see it, don't ask." Without looking up, she intoned in her best Miss Jane officiousness, "Hello Steve. Please have a seat. I'll be with you in a moment." She explained in great detail what she was hoping to prove in her study. Despite my lack of experience in matters such as these, the whole proposition seemed pretty fantastic. Nevertheless, $10 would go a long way in keeping me in cigarettes and other notions. After filling out a brief questionnaire, she gave me a new $10 bill and off we went.

All of the tests involved perception of information using only the eyes. After three long and tedious hours, the final testing room was cold and dim. Near a wall was a low wooden table with a bench. To one side was a tangled bank of imposing electronics; a familiar-looking contraption, but I couldn't quite place it. She instructed me to sit in the middle of the bench, with feet flat on the floor and hands palms-down on the table. Directly in front of me, suspended by a string, was a bright green tennis ball. Behind the ball was a large red dot.

I nervously asked if she used red dots in any other colors—I got nothing back on that one. To the left of center, near the end of the wall, was another red dot, and again, to the right of center, near the other end of the wall was another red dot. She glued several electrodes to my forehead and told me to follow the ball with only my eyes, without moving my head. Within a minute, something went terribly wrong.

In a scene reminiscent from a Stooges short, the researcher stood there with her face and hands covered in black ink. Reams of paper, scrawled with sine waves of all shapes and sizes, were uncontrollably piling on the floor. The machine to which I was still wired must have been a surplus polygraph from the psychology department. My eye movements were so unrelenting and rapid, the pens of the old polygraph crossed paths and became inextricably entangled. Instead of stopping the machine, she attempted to unhook them while it was still in motion.

After she cleaned up and calmed down, she declared the entire study compromised. The noble machine, even in its crippled state, continued to register the muscle tremors still occurring behind my unmoving eyes. I offered to give her back the $10, but she refused. I don't know if the project came to some reasonable conclusion about any correlation between artistic genius and mental illness. Ten more dollars living in my pocket was all I cared about.

I learned two things from the experience. As an introduction to the excesses of academia, the entire event verified the truth behind the allegation that academia, by and large, exists for its own entertainment. As a freshman about to start a life at Berklee, I saw no indication that the agenda-driven, rarefied world of Harvard, and the pragmatic, hammer-and-nails, music-as-vocation nature of Berklee, would ever become two sides of the same coin in the higher education industry. Sadly, that reality was going to change, but it would take decades and a radical shift in leadership at Berklee, for it had begun in 1945 as a family operation turning out journeymen musicians and eventually became a platform for personal legacy-building within the post-modern Cult of Personality and identity politics.

The experience also made me think about how misused and overly-romanticized the term genius has become in our world, especially in the way this young grad student attempted to make her case, by creating a head-on collision between Freud and pseudo-neuroscience.

Putting aside the romance of the psychotic ideal, someone once said the difference between talent and genius is that talent is the ability to hit a target no one else can hit, and genius is the ability to hit a target no one else can see. Genius or not—insane or not, after my Harvard eye experience—I never again saw things quite the same way.

———

Soon after the spring semester of 1978 started, I reached the age of 24. A couple of weeks into January, a major blizzard decimated the area and closed down the city for a solid week. Visions of William Golding were not far behind. What we survived in the first week was nothing more than a dress rehearsal.

Two weeks later, on February 5th, a devastating nor'easter slammed New England with over 27 inches of snow in 24 hours and hurricane-force winds. The Massachusetts of Governor Michael Dukakis was closed under martial law. Unless you wore skis or drove a team of huskies, movement on foot was the beginning, middle, and end of transportation. From the looks of things, to get Berklee up and running was going to take longer than the first disruption. I reached my breaking point. I called Candace to announce I was getting a refund on my tuition and catching the next train out of there for Washington. She agreed with reluctance—not a good sign.

I brought all of the books and materials to continue my second semester studies and used the tuition refund to pay bills until I needed to find work. My plan was to return to Berklee in September and do credit-by-exam for all of my missed courses. I expected to test into my third semester without missing a beat—an ambitious plan, but very doable. After staying for a month in the small and crowded house with Candace and her roommates, I found my own roommate flop.

Having no furniture, Candace's mom, Rene, helped me by designating me the keeper of the monkey pod table. This was no ordinary table. During the time she and Scott lived in Hawaii, in the middle of his third deployment during the Korean War, Rene took up a creative project to distract her from boredom and loneliness. She spent 50 hours sanding down a slab of indigenous monkey pod wood to a surface ready to take a good finish coat of varnish. After they transferred to the Patuxent Naval Base in Maryland, Scott found a piece of driftwood and attached it as a base to create this beloved and venerable family keepsake. The slab was a free-form shape, like a gigantic but well-loved amber amoeba, with an ever-so-slight downward tilt on the base. It was an honor to place it next to the bed. To this day, the whereabouts of that table are unknown.

My motivation to encourage Candace to apply to Berklee was purely selfish. I hated the disquiet that came with a lonely, long-distance relationship. This was a solution that solved some problems for both of us. However, I never thought to examine the dis-ease I felt due to the distance; I believed it was love.

Separation anxiety had not yet made its way into the general lexicon of self-help books. I accepted the anxiety as a stain on a corner of my soul, calling on a debt I never created. I assuaged feelings of helplessness in times of separation by retreating to my single-minded purpose, but old fears and feelings were never resolved, only deflected, tamped, and buried. Feelings isolated over a long period smolder and loom, changing their shape without losing their essence, only to return to their original form whenever called upon. My fear was like a virus lying dormant until the conditions were perfect and natural resistance reached its lowest point, eventually summoned after my inevitable banishment beyond the canopy and drip line of a woman. Candace arrived in late August to register for the fall of 1978 semester. We would have to make it up as we went along.

———

As MY GOOD FORTUNE WOULD have it, the college notified me that my financial aid for the next academic year included work-study. College work-study jobs are legendary for being dull and boring. Instead of being assigned to work the checkout desk in the library or the mailroom, I reported to the Berklee Performance Center.

The reclaimed Fenway Theater, built in 1912, became the BPC or The Berklee. It owned the acoustical reputation of being a sow's ear turned into a gunnysack. The theater was the staging area for Berklee student and faculty concerts, along with the occasional outside professional show. The entire color scheme was more in line with Alma Berk's taste in finished basement decorations than a standard professional performance venue—grainy wood tones with green and beige accents.

The characteristics of the hall were not nearly as interesting as the people hired to run it; in particular, a North Shore native named Dave Pelletier. I met Dave the day I reported to the theater manager's office to start as a janitor, which was less confining than being an usher. After a short grilling, Dave signed off. Working no more than 15 hours a week was my limit, but that restriction was soon going to change.

I showed up and quietly did my work. My days of cleaning horse stalls and bathrooms and floors at Woodward and Lothrop echoed in the Spiral. The following week, I met the rest of the work-study crew. McHale was the designated lighting director. He was a few years older and possessed a detached coolness, which at first was hard to penetrate. He and Pelletier, who were about the same age, locked horns from time to time over staging and lighting details.

Pelletier held the work-study help with a reasonable amount of contempt, until you otherwise proved yourself. McHale was the only one who was Pelletier's equal when it came to experience in theatrical matters. I, among others, cleaned the place from top to bottom—from the green room to the stage and all the way to the front of the house and onto the sidewalk. I didn't complain because I took the same pride in this shit work that I took in all of my prior shit jobs.

Two weeks into the gig, Pelletier called me into the office. He offered to make me a stage manager and gave me a key to the front door. I was clueless about what a stage manager does, but it sounded better than scrubbing dirty toilets and scraping calcified chewing gum from the ugly green carpet in the lobby. The stage job, at least at this very modest level, involved standing in the wings with a headset and communicating with McHale at the master lighting board. From there, I would tell whoever was standing next to me to hit the mark. The task would be easy because I'd be working with students and the occasional faculty member. Wrong.

The next night I reported to work and donned my headset. The person waiting to go on was a famous Hollywood director, one of the most influential of his generation. After I called the house lights, he stood there stoic and statuesque, hands folded in front, with his chin slightly elevated, and his trademark grey Van Dyke beard and high hairline. "Okay, Mr. Altman." Without looking at me, he took off in a relaxed and leisurely gait and greeted a standing ovation.

The best moment of his presentation was hearing him excoriate the television show *M*A*S*H*. He said he despised it because it wasn't true to his vision that formed the movie. Standing next to such an accomplished individual, who exuded purpose and confidence as if he invented the concepts, was impressive. After about 10 minutes, the romance for me wore off, and I went up to the office to hang out in the land of the cynical and the indifferent.

———

OTHER WORK-STUDY STUDENTS ARRIVED AND Pelletier put them through the same Navy-inspired tests as everyone else: clean the living shit out of the place for about two weeks, and if you were still standing, you could move to the stage crew. Their names were Jay, Aldo, Ray, Dave, Harvey, Dennis, Havlice, and Bobby.

Bobby was our resident Czech, one of the nicest and bravest men I ever knew. He exemplified the power of the human soul and spirit yearning to live freely through the power of music. Bobby left Czechoslovakia illegally while it was still under the repressive yoke of Communist rule, and came to Boston to make a new life. Until the fall of Communism 1989, he could never return home without the possibility of imprisonment or death. I never knew anyone who was a prisoner in their home country from such a long distance away.

Harvey was peculiar. An older Jewish man, right out of central casting for a Neil Simon play, he was a Vietnam vet living with his mother. He was desperate for meaningful female companionship. Harvey also took one too many hits of

LSD with a cannabis chaser. He was the most poignant of characters—part anarchist, part subversive poet, part comic relief, part disc jockey at WMFO, and a big-hearted man whose gentleness was often veiled by bouts with his suicidal demons. His very invisible friend was someone he named Pilkew C. Dorlipp, who often dropped in on Harvey's waking moments unannounced and stayed way past his welcome. Harvey was a Level 5 acid casualty who never gave know as an answer.

The stage was set for the unleashing of one of the most famed and wildest stage crews to ever exist in Boston, and Pelletier was the mastermind behind it all.

———

PELLETIER'S PROFESSIONAL BACKGROUND STARTED IN the early '70s doing live sound and set-up tech work for many of the major rock bands of the day. He came out of the Navy in 1970 and found his way to Elton John's first concert in Los Angeles and then started working for Tycobrahe during Joe Cocker's *Mad Dogs & Englishmen* tour. In a brief slice of whirlwind time, he was part of the sound and tech crew for nearly every major rock act of the day, including The Rolling Stones and The Who, during their two most ambitious world tours at that time.

Dave eventually returned to the area in the mid-1970s and was hired as the assistant manager of the Berklee. This was Dave's fiefdom, and as long as we took care of business, met his very high professional standards, and towed the line, we enjoyed free run of the place. And run we did. Sometimes it was a stampede. For me, at times, it was somewhere in the cracks of a saunter or a mosey.

The commitment and work ethic of this crew gave Pelletier a lot of time to sit in the front office and think up shit to do for his own entertainment. The man loved a challenge, especially if it meant tweaking a few suits on Beacon Hill. One characteristic he and I shared was our penchant for being in a perpetual state of observation—he was more likely to share his observations and ideas, whereas I kept things to myself.

I remember the night he invited me to join him at the Brattle Theatre in Cambridge to attend a limited showing of a movie called *Bonaparte*. I figured it would last maybe two hours, tops. At about the four-hour mark, I asked him how long was this fucking epic? He said we were coming up to a half-hour intermission, and then the second half would take up the remaining four hours—an eight-hour slice of a day I'll never get back. It brought an entire new meaning to the word captivating. It's fair to say this guy was growing on me as a personality. Dave began focusing his attention on bicycles and professional bike racing by creating the first annual Witches Cup Bike Race. My involvement in the race would culminate in one of the funniest and most bizarre experiences of my life.

During some down time in August of 1979, Pelletier conscripted several of us on the crew to temporarily relocate to the city of Salem, 30 miles north of Boston. The purpose of our little hobo trek was to help Pelletier realize his goal of setting up the racecourse for the first-ever professional bike race in New England. We were all up for getting out of Boston for a few days of working hard and playing even harder. Our pay was coming from a single source, bike race hats, 2,000 of them donated by one of the sponsors. It was up to Aldo to wander through the crowd for two days muttering a monotoned and metronomic, "Hat, buck, hat, buck…"

The Hawthorn Inn, located on the edge of the common, comped the crew several rooms. I was the last to arrive in Salem. My priorities were to put my original goal of coming to Berklee above all else, so my commitment to this life of the professional stage-tech-in-training was, for the long-term, nonexistent. (With the exception of McHale, Ray, Bobby, and me, the other crew members abandoned music and went into various fields in theatrical arts.)

I stepped off the MBTA commuter train into a sunny, hot, and humid day in Salem, the home of anything having to do with witchery—from the dark history of the hanging trials to the modern-day tchotchke shops and museums with witchy women and witchy warlocks selling witchy paperweights, pentagrams, brooms, costumes, and books on dark magic.

I can envision one of the witches holding a séance to conjure up the spirit of H.L. Mencken, and his first words recorded from the afterlife are, "No one ever went broke underestimating the American public's fascination with imaginary forces beyond nature."

I made the short walk to the inn lugging my guitar and bag. I could feel the electricity of excitement and anticipation around the appearance of professional two-wheelers. There were throngs of people and bikes stretched far and wide. I walked into a side door leading into a ballroom and saw Dennis on the other side of the room playing his guitar, with someone on piano. The pianist saw me, stopped playing, and started walking toward me. He was a short and wiry older gentleman, with a huge smile, and dressed like a member of the backup band for Hank Williams. As he got closer, I could see his hands in both front pockets of his jeans, enabling his shoulders and elbows to flap back and forth while he was hissing a laugh, accompanied by a huge grin. He extended his hand to shake mine as he said, "Howdy there, my name is Bobby Hebb and I'm pleased to meet ya. What's yours?" As I processed this unexpected greeting, he said, "Why don't juh take out your *git*-tar and join us?" I explained that I just arrived and wanted to sort out my accommodations, but I'd return and we'd do some playing.

When I came back, they were gone. I saw Dennis later and asked him if that guy was bullshitting me about being Bobby Hebb, the singer-songwriter who penned "Sunny," one of the most covered and enduring R&B hits of the 20th century. I fell in love with the tune when it first appeared on the radio in 1966. Dennis said no bullshit—he is *the* Bobby Hebb. Pelletier also verified the claim and explained that Mr. Hebb paid a hefty bail for shooting his wife. While awaiting trial for attempted murder, his lawyer recommended he take up residence for about six months in the most expensive suite in the inn—more than sufficient time to establish a pattern of odd and erratic public behavior as part of an insanity defense. "Sunny" made a fortune for Mr. Hebb, so he could afford a six-month stay with constant room service and other top-shelf amenities the inn offered to a deep-pocketed guest.

I headed down later in the evening for a dinner break, and amidst much noise and clamor in the lobby, I noticed a crowd gathered around what appeared to be a Saudi oil sheikh holding forth with anyone who happened by. There was no context or reason for such an appearance. From the keffiyeh atop his head down to the sandals on his feet, this cat was the real deal. I got closer to hear the conversation, and when I came face-to-face with the sheikh, I saw it was none other than Bobby Hebb. He gave no indication he remembered me from our earlier introduction. He played it straight and cool, and believed he was what he pretended to be. I left in disbelief, smirking under my breath at the surrealistic absurdity of this abstract moment.

On the final day of the race, the crowd grew to around 50,000. As I headed out the front door, I noticed a minor car accident in front of the inn. The entire crowded town was an accident waiting to happen. This was nothing more than a fender-bender without injuries, but there was a small police presence controlling traffic and talking to the two drivers. Entangled in a loud disagreement with a man of the cloth leaning in way too far, hovering with arms flailing, was an elderly woman seated in the front. She appeared to be fighting him off in an attempt to push him away and out of her space. It was Bobby Hebb, dressed as a Catholic priest, attempting to administer last rights to an otherwise perfectly fine and pissed-off nonagenarian.

The gigantic hand of Winsor McCay came down once again from the clouds, with pen in hand, and drew another artful dodge for Mr. Hebb. The final outcome of Mr. Hebb's expensive charade was a two-year stint in prison. Upon his release, the first to greet him was the IRS.

Sunny…the bright days are gone and the dark days are here…

THE PROFESSIONAL OUTSIDE SHOWS BOOKED into the BPC continued to increase. The New England Emmy Awards scheduled their five-day takeover of the hall to broadcast their show. Among many showbiz luminaries appearing was Dinah Shore. I watched her television show in the late 1950s, with her trademark "See the U.S.A. in a Chevrolet" jingle. I loved her signature sign-off with that big kiss she always blew toward the camera. She seemed like a delightful and gentle woman, and was a fine singer who came up as a star in the big band era. On broadcast night, I got the onstage headset assignment.

For 10 memorable minutes, she and I stood shoulder to shoulder. She watched and waited patiently for her cue to go on. This radiant star could see I was making furtive glances toward her, taking in her gracious and upright presence and perfectly quaffed beauty. She was reading over a handful of three-by-five cards and the pre-written patter clearly wasn't to her liking. Instead of pulling some prima donna fit by throwing them in the air, followed by a dramatic, "I can't work like this," she saw Gene Shalit nearby and asked him for a pen so that she could clean up the patter.

The big band down in front was playing the theme song for the station break, which happened to be a tune titled "Four Brothers." I knew the melody and absentmindedly began singing along. She immediately turned to me with her legendary smile and wide-open eyes and joined in. A little scat duet with Dinah Shore…man, how much better could these few moments be? Once I got the cue to send her onstage, she thanked me and headed out to hit her mark.

Dinah Shore epitomized Southern charm and gentle grace, and for a brief moment, I enjoyed the privilege of the experience up close and a little personal. I never forgot her demeanor as a lifelong example of professional presentation.

The Boston Globe Jazz Festival always favored the BPC as its main stage. It was a nine-day event that generated more padded overtime than we knew what to do with. The jazz greats I saw are too numerous to mention, but two stood out above all others for very different reasons. First was Stephane Grappelli, the legendary French jazz violinist, who finished off a brilliant set with a solo piano rendition of "Autumn In New York." When he came offstage, he toweled off, sidled up next to me, and whispered a breathy proposition for me to go back with him to his hotel room. "No thank you, sir. The enjoyment of your music is where I draw the line. By the way, I think you may have dropped your bow rosin near the piano."

Next was the immortal Dizzy Gillespie, who was always guaranteed to put asses in the seats. I saw him on two occasions. The first time, I again had the privilege to observe up close how a seasoned and secure professional handled a minor annoyance simply with the power of legend and patience. This involved a logistical problem: the sound checks were over, and the stage was finally dressed to open the house. There was a strict-to-anal policy that no one other than a tech person was to be onstage—no exceptions.

I was alone in the hall, sitting in the front row catching a break, when the curtain from stage right opened and out strolled Mr. Gillespie to take a seat at the piano. The master was stealing a few quiet minutes to enjoy pushing around some chords. One of the promoter's underlings peeked out from the curtain and asked him to clear the stage. The legend's response was to simply look up as he kept playing, and stare straight ahead. He returned his gaze downward to the keyboard and continued playing. A minute later, the man returned and in a more insistent tone of voice, asked Mr. Gillespie to please clear the stage. He stopped playing, slowly raised his head, then slowly raised his hands, keeping them hovering slightly above the keys. He turned his head slowly and barely to his left, never saying a word. He held his position for a few seconds before the man slowly backed out of his field of vision, closed the curtain, never to return—the power of the "half-glance guilt pivot swivel" was on full burn and only someone with Mr. Gillespie's juice could pull it off.

He returned his hands to the keys to play a few more bars, got up, closed the lid, and disappeared the way he came in. His lesson was something at which I always marveled: silence, followed by a well-placed turn, could be louder than words when confronting an annoyance of the human kind. So few can pull it off because doing so would require a vault full of clout that one would have to dynamite to access.

The final time I saw Mr. Gillespie was backstage after a show he did sharing the bill with guitarist Kenny Burrell. The audience cleared out and most of the backstage people were finishing their jobs. I stood nearby, well within earshot of Mr. Gillespie, Mr. Burrell, and the great big band era drummer "Papa" Joe Jones. Mr. Jones stood there alternatively bouncing a rubber ball, then grabbing his genitals, as Mr. Gillespie held forth for several minutes by extolling the comparative effects of various laxatives. How the other two could keep a straight face through his MIT-style descriptions, with visual effects, was beyond my comprehension. As it turned out, his favorite was Swiss Kriss, an herbal remedy long touted by his friend, Louis Armstrong. "Leave it all behind ya," as Mr. Armstrong's grinning ad used to say.

IN THE WINTER OF 1979, jazz pianist Bill Evans did a two-hour set with his trio. During the last half of the set, I joined Aldo at the BPC backstage door for a few games of chess. He was an above average chess player, and I was attempting to recapture some average skills. As we hovered over the board, my position turned tenuous.

The door to the backstage opened and out walked Mr. Evans, dressed in a long tweed coat, smoking a non-filtered cigarette, with his longish hair slicked back in its most characteristic fashion. Because of the narrow hallway, he stood against the opposite wall and watched this game with focused interest while he waited for his transportation. In my nervousness, with this jazz legend staring at my desperate endgame position, I turned to him and asked, "Do you have any suggestions?" Without hesitation, he approached and leaned in over my right shoulder, the same way he leaned over the keyboard when he was deep in the stream of a tune. He closely examined my losing position. After about 10 seconds, he slowly backed away, stood upright, and with his dark, junkie eyes, looked directly into mine and said, "The surest way to lose is to convince yourself that you are playing brilliantly."

As if DeMille gave a cue for action, a cab pulled up and Mr. Evans, with all of his emotional wounds and demons and timeless musical brilliance, sprinted out the door and careered into the night. In less than a year, he was dead at the all-too-young age of 51. Under the guise of my losing position on the board of an ancient game of strategy and conquest, his parting words to me carried the weight of a thousand dead stars.

He summarized the entirety of how he saw his life by sharing wisdom and advice with a 25 year old kid. His testimony never whispered humility, false or otherwise—it was simple and objective honesty from an extremely self-examining man. Mr. Evans gave me one of the special private lessons in my life.

Developing stage presence and a professional attitude was my takeaway from nearly two years I spent working as one of the original members of the BPC's stage crew. While the majority of my friends were honing their new professional skills as electricians, lighting riggers, designers, and the like, I was constantly observing the entire spectrum of musical artistry—from the mediocre flash-in-the-pan acts, to the timeless legends of their genres—learning how to take control on a stage; learning how to communicate with an audience; learning how to treat the ones working around you—those in the shadows of the curtains and lights whose job is to make sure your show goes off without any technical problems.

One final observation I took away from the experience was, with a few exceptions, the bigger the name and talent, the more secure the individual, and the more secure the individual, the easier to work with and the more approachable and appreciative they were. This was especially true of the old jazz giants.

An important time-marking-in-the-Spiral event unfolded one Monday evening, when Pelletier, Ray, and I went to Central Square to a movie house. Based on my experience with Pelletier and the eight-hour epic on Napoleon, I considered packing a sandwich, a change of clothes, and forwarding my mail. This time, the show was a double feature on the history of cartoons, followed by the Elvin Jones biopic, *A Different Drummer.*

After the movies, we headed back to Berklee in Dave's car. When we arrived at the midway point of the Mass Avenue Bridge separating Boston's Back Bay from Cambridge, hovering for a split eternity over the Charles River, a news bulletin interrupted the music on WBCN. A shooting had occurred outside of the Dakota in New York City…

Grains Of Random Synapse in the Half-Shell Bring Pearls Before Time

THE DAY BEFORE THE LENNON shooting, Sunday, December 7th, 1980, another day ending with a why, marked 39 years and one day before that fateful Monday, beginning an endless list of markers of singular events, with one unintended outcome: the pushback against a world, and specifically ourselves, so desperately seeking recovery since our entry into, and subsequent victory in World War II.

It started with a post-victory infection called the Cold War and the appearance of the pathogenic post-Stalin Sputnik; with NASA and its pilots being the first responders to create a 10-year cure against this existential threat to the emotional health of the body politic, followed by the appearance of a host of secondary infections—Vietnam; the killing of a Kennedy who got us into this second-rate war; a Johnson who was in it way over his head, to cultivate and culminate in his Great Society; followed by back-to-back killings of a King and a Brother; and the forced resignation of a second-rate president who lied to cover-up a third-rate burglary—all adding to a devastating and unrecoverable compromise to the immune system of a culture mired in a separation of values between us and our mothers and fathers who did their best to bring their children through the sacrifices and challenges of defeating the fascism of the Axis powers.

We, the kids, transformed our parents' legacy of Pervasive Cultural Uni-Conformity, as their natural reset to the traumas and losses from the three wars, into boredom and non-conformity, simply because it was the path of least resistance to us establishing what—our individuality? Sure, or so we thought, but we were never clear from exactly what? The belief that we, the people, never got it right from the beginning? Compared to what—the conceit that our boredom was somehow endowed with more importance than all of the boredom which preceded us in the entirety of human history? Did the concept of boredom even exist in the Stone Age? Iron Age? Dark Age? Or, was it born in Paris during the Age of Enlightenment? Yet, no one—no matter how noble their intentions to fix something for the greater good, to right the wrongs, to reinvent the past as a way to influence the future, to once and for all escape the tyranny of the innersole pole—was immune from the state of shock and recovery to changes for which no one was prepared, in a shattered world which no one Imagined.

The insipid brilliance of the Constant of Pervasive Cultural Uni-Conformity, which never pretended to be an end in itself, was rejected—before it ever evolved under its own internal weight and reasonably in its time. We sanctioned our denial of the legacy; denial justified in the ceaseless tattoo of the music we listened to, the clothes we wore, the books we read, the poems we wrote, the hair we grew, the food we ate, the drugs we took, the people we fucked, the excuses we embraced, and worst of all, the double standards we created.

No matter how you shear it, all we accomplished was bartering one conformity for another. Zappa got it right. We called it something else, but all we did was trade one omni-costume esprit de corps for another, one flag for another, one Age of Entanglement for another.

Why was it so difficult for us, the Boomers in Bloom, to understand and accept that we must step back and reset from square one? Where a unified cultural front, in all of its predictable, homogenized projection of moral, ethical, and material values and beyond, was the only way to create order out of the chaos of the emotional and physical rubble? How did we come to the audacious conclusion that we, the Youth, and only we, were both Stardust *and* Golden? We were certainly not unimpressed with ourselves. And then…for the time being…

Four boys from England arrived with a message no one chose to fully embrace and live up to, especially them. I suppose that's the downside of the responsibility of traversing the eternities where being the messengers becomes being the message. Did Marshall McLuhan ever have to flash his badge? The lesson here is you have to empty the vacuum before you can fill it. All of the shit we created for ourselves finally hit the fan—Speck, DeSalvo, the Chicago 7, Manson and his All-Girl Orchestra, and the culmination of Woodstock as the Beautiful People's rendition of "The hills are alive with the sound of mucus," warned us that this was the last opportunity to have our uniforms cleaned and pressed and our hats blocked before the Age of Accountability was to befall us. Equity equals assets minus liabilities…but only if you have your own skin in the game—otherwise, you're just another thief who digs it. Instead, we all hitch-hiked to Altamont for a Beggars Banquet to bear witness to the call of the bluff that the Angel guardians directed to Lucifer—Mr. Disturbance, a man of wealth and taste. Watch him now as he backs off from the bluff of his rickety stage. You didn't expect Jumpin' Jack to actually jump into the fray he helped to create, now did you?

Even the Grateful Dead knew to stay away from this death of and by a thousand contradictions. Someone dropped the fire curtain with not a second to spare, but it was still too late. No need to bring the house to full, because the flames more than lit the way…hey, don't forget to turn on the ghost light if you are the last to leave the stage. Meridith needs to find his way out.

If only Manson made it known on his resume that he did a stint as the house band in the Richard Speck Home for the Greedy…"I'm comin' down fast, but don't let me break you…" "And here's a little clue for you all…" Hell Trek Reset is Helter Skelter spelled inside out and sideways.

The death of a Jimi and a Janis, and Jim, the Doorman who never doffed his chapeau sealed the deal. Maybe they knew something we all knew but were too committed and cowed and refused to own because the most unbearable of punishments would be to not have the approval of the one to your left and the one to the other left, right?

Then, Monday, December 8th, 1980, 39 years and one day later…

The murder of Lennon, who helped write the mono-mythic soundtrack of the generation of the Boomers as Heroes-In-Waiting for any One of a Thousand Faces to wear. That wasn't the way it was supposed to go down, but hey, that's what happens when you build Utopia with Volution Slides. It's time for a Candy Land reset; time for a cartoon; time to change the bong water? Fuck it—take it back to tribal with benefits. But then, how do we figure out if the one with the ability to invent the benefits has any influence in who gets the benefits, and under what conditions will the bestowment of such beneficence become a reality? That's a tough one.

The murder of Lennon closed the lid on the casket of My Generation. The Grateful Dead waited in his shade for further instructions, while the duo America reached gold status on the back of "The heat was hot 'cause there ain't no one for to give you no pain La la la la la la la laaa." I'm still waiting for an explanation on *that* fucking line.

No one ever said living in a 20th century post-war world-in-recovery was going to be easy. Goddamn, how we have so undermined Man's conscious conceptual faculties.

2ND PARTIAL

Esse Quam Videri

"Never measure the outcome of an action before the action ends."
—Jake's Second Law of Physics

IN THE WINTER OF 1981, I again found myself alone with no home and no place to go and with little money. Boston held nothing more for me, especially since Candace and I were in the process of ending our involvement. We got along well in the first year of our three-year relationship, but after she came to Boston, she grew and we grew apart. The astronaut's daughter fell in love with a French pianist from Berklee and moved to Paris after I left town.

On the other hand, I squeezed all I could out of my relatively short time in Boston. Now 26 and accustomed to living entirely for myself, I allowed the distractions of the short-term to short-circuit my long-term plans. I was ready to move on to the next phase. I called on friends to crash land. I arrived at the band house in Wheaton, Maryland and the vice-stained floor of the basement rehearsal room was all my erstwhile friend Chuck Underwood could offer. I was happy to have it. I told him I wouldn't be there long; just enough time to find work, save some money, and move on.

I stopped in at a venerable old music store and applied for a job. The owner's daughter, who was close to my age, interviewed me and after about five minutes of a lot of boilerplate questions, hired me on the spot. As soon as the interview in her office was over, she pulled out a small marble slab and starting cutting long lines of coke. After she finished packing her pre-frontal cortex, she slid it toward me. I took off the top of my head and repositioned my brain toward magnetic north with about two or three long blasts. I thought to myself, *Sweetheart, this is going to be an expensive way for you to keep me from sleeping on the job*." I could see this was a unique situation and not a little spooky and outrageous. We sat grinding and bullshitting for a long time, and quite expeditiously. In between more lines and cognac, she was asking a lot of questions about my background, such as what have I been doing for the last several years, did I have a girlfriend, to which I said no. Without question, she was going to be one of the strangest women I ever knew.

In the brief month we kept company, a complicated situation developed. I had to be smart about this connection. A not unattractive redhead, fortunately, I harbored no designs or desires to get her in bed, which was unusual. I avoided one central and predictable pitfall as I found myself in the middle of an unexpected turn of events. In the wake of my sexual history, it would've been easy for me to turn to an oft-repeated exercise in the futile and silent pursuit of emotional and psychological compensation—one more chance with finding and keeping love. Maybe I was at the burnout phase of my life's mission to always be in the company of a woman; a quest, for reasons I believed were clear, but nevertheless mired in my emotional salvage operations. Looking beyond her attractiveness, as a hopeful sign of my healing and maturity, my platonic mindset was a welcome relief from the constant pressure to always be about sexual conquest.

After a month of eating sushi, drinking liquor, and snorting coke—all on her dime—I reached my absolute limits. I could feel the beginnings of at least three addictions setting in, the most troubling having been brought on by the near total purity of Old Chimalpopoca Electric Talc. She revealed that she was tentatively falling for me. Her reluctance stemmed from complications with having a sax playing, junkie, bisexual male prostitute boyfriend, with a revolving credit line in most of the jails on the East Coast, who was as unpredictable as he was versatile. That was reason enough for me to keep a respectable distance. I was a slow learner in understanding that the most abundant commodity everyone is so generous in sharing and most willing to receive, is complications. With all of this chemical plunder, I couldn't control my guitar, and that was a serious problem. The shit I was putting into my body was running me down and taking a toll on me, both physically and mentally.

One night, as I wafted in from another long night of tortious turpitude with Lady Bacchus, there was a phone message for me from Frank T. in Boston. Frank was one of the first-call guitar players in town and a mainstay with the Boston Pops. The next day I returned the call and he said, "I have a gig for you." The guitar player with the *Anthony Tillman Show* was leaving on short notice, during their engagement in Naples, Florida. It was an impending emergency for the band, and they needed someone who could read and play styles. The road manager mailed me a packet of the show charts along with some live recordings. If I wanted the gig, a plane ticket would be waiting for me at Baltimore to Fort Myers.

The music arrived and it was mostly illegible, with every hand-scrawled edit and scribbled cross out with an ad-hoc insertion imaginable, for last-minute changes in the shows. I listened to the tapes to get a feel for the routines. I decided to take the gig and scrambled to get a second guitar because my instrument was too limited for the many styles I was expected to play. The next day, I gave short notice at my job that I would be leaving in less than a week for Florida to take a gig with a show. Instead of disappointment, she wanted to celebrate in her usual overjoyed manner. I refused. This was my one chance to shake my impending addictions and get straight. She further expressed her generosity and gave me $600. I bought a second guitar and stocked up on vitamins of all sizes, kinds, and colors imaginable.

I told the guys at the house what was happening, and they gave me a good send-off. One of the other local guitar players was there, and when he asked me for details, I mentioned the name Anthony Tillman. He replied, "I saw him perform in Baltimore a few years ago. That mutha is a great entertainer. He's a little bit of Sammy Davis Jr., Ben Vereen, and Lou Rawls. He's been out there doing it for years." Tillman started out as one of the singers for the Baltimore-based group New Censation.

I knew this was a formidable A-list road band from the live recordings—a full rhythm section and four horns. The other added attraction in hitting the road was available women in city after city. The money was decent enough—starting at $200 a week in cash, plus travel and board was covered. Covering my food, clothes, and any habits I brought along for the ride was on me.

On the last day of February, I headed to the airport. What a pleasure to be getting away from both kinds of snow and the ice. My benefactress insisted that I stay in touch; if I needed anything, to call without hesitation. Her unconditional largess was unusual and not completely altruistic. I assured her I would repay her for everything—to her, it was all a gift. Okay, easy enough—a phone call here, a post card there, be sure to let her know when we do a local appearance. We pulled up to the Delta terminal, said a nice huggy goodbye… it was a real joy knowing her.

———

THE AIRLINE OVERBOOKED THE FLIGHT, so I volunteered to take the next one and received the customary full cash voucher. I called ahead to let the road manager know I'd be coming in two hours later than originally scheduled. I didn't know the full story about this band, so I believed I was justified in holding onto the extra cash from the refunded ticket as an emergency reserve. I wanted to make a fast exit in the event this turned out to be some jive-ass gig. Road bands were notorious for having bad leaders with bad habits. Musicians could be strung along for weeks without seeing any money.

After the blood returned to my knuckles at 35,000 feet, my mind wandered to Granddaddy. The old man was the only one who understood my drive and motivation, especially in my early years. He never stopped believing and I missed him dearly. This is a moment he would have loved to share.

The Latin motto on which Berklee based its entire identity, "*esse quam videri,*" which translates to "to be, rather than to seem," came to have the full force of its meaning as I started on my path to making my life as a professional musician.

Landing is Just Another Word
For Controlled Crash

THE SUDDEN CLEAR AIR TURBULENCE jolted me out of a sound sleep. It took me a moment to recognize that I was in a bus with wings, soaring six miles above the dirt, at close to 10 miles a minute, on my way to a gig in Naples. My fear of flying started me thinking back to the first time I ever flew—a short flight from Boston to D.C. with Candace for her sister Kris' wedding. The whole experience was way too surreal for my patience, but I did enjoy the mild irony of having an astronaut's daughter holding my hand during my maiden jet flight.

The final leg of my trip destined for Fort Myers was mercifully brief, and after a short wait at the baggage carousel, I dragged along an old suitcase packed with vitamins, the few threads of clothes I had to my name, two guitars, and a small amp. The van was waiting with two people, one of whom looked familiar. She introduced herself as Robin, the lead trumpet player and default road manager. The other person was a soft-spoken man, about my height and age, with a sartorial, men's shop manager Gentleman's Quarterly presentation. He was Michael, Tony's brother.

We pulled into the parking lot of Copperfield's, complete with a cheap outdoor sign in an attempt to connect the image to the classic Dickens character. This was the premier show room in Naples, home of 600 millionaires. The place was wall-to-wall covered with men and women across a wide range of ages, with everyone dressed in their finest Florida frippery. The energy in this place was like walking out into a hot and humid day after spending all night in air conditioning—it slammed against your entire body as you struggled to catch your breath. The air filled with pounds of secondhand cigarette smoke didn't help.

The band was cranking on an old rock and roll medley while a short, dark bundle of human high-watt incandescent illumination, dressed in a threadbare purple show suit, was on top of a table with four young blond women seated around the perimeter. The follow spot tightened all the way down on the left cheek of his ass, as he stood looking over his right shoulder, sweat pouring off him, his suit saturated along with the seam of his right underarm splitting while he forced his glute to spasm at an ungodly rate of blurred jiggle.

With each cymbal crash, Tony switched the jiggle from one glute to the next. The crowd went into a tribal delirium. One of the young women at the table of honor was quite spifflicated and took it upon herself to reach up and make a grab for a spot below his waist. In that instant, Tony cut off the drummer. He gave another cue to the band, and they entered for the last part of the song. He jumped from the table and landed into a split, where he stayed with his arms splayed and his head bowed, like a sculptured homage to James Brown.

The place couldn't have gotten any louder, but somehow all of those white, hot, sweaty drunks found a way to expel a little more air from their lungs. All I could do was laugh, and then laugh some more. Working with this outfit was going to be some serious shit. From the drummer came the final announcement: "Thank you ladies and gentleman. Mr. Anthony Tillman. Give it up for Anthony Tillman. Good night and don't forget to tip your waitress, o-vah."

Michael leaned over and mentioned that Tony had just finished his "B" show. I thought, *If this was his 'B' show, what could he possibly do for his 'A?'*

Home is Where the Road is, so Jus' Gimme Da' Beat

It all came back to me in one rushing memory—Robin was from Boston. She was the lead trumpet player for several of Berklee's elite ensembles. I approached the bandstand and realized I needed no introduction to several of them. The baritone sax player was Sue, a wafer-thin blond resembling one of Margaret Keane's big-eyed waifs. I briefly worked with her in Boston. The tenor sax player was Greg, a parsimonious, tobacco chewing Amish refugee from the Central Valley area of Pennsylvania. His playing style sounded like Boots Randolph doing a sarcastic impersonation of Coltrane—I never took him seriously. The bassist was Al, from the Wilmington area. I remembered him from Berklee as well. Al was the youngest, weighing in at the tender age of 20.

One of Tony's legendary skills was his ability to improvise tunes on the fly. He expected his band to be right there with him, no hesitation and without fail. On my first night, he put the band through such a challenge. The secret was to listen for a tune Tony was using as a point of departure for his improvisation. Another cue might come from the patter he was using to engage an audience member. He would then improvise a lyric based on some characteristic of the mark. His paraphrase of a familiar melody was all the band needed to work from. All of us had substantial repertoires, so we could jump on his clue and take it in a fresh, but familiar, direction. This was musicianship and performance at a high level, and the audiences loved it.

After the night was over, so was this three-week stand. We packed everything and loaded the equipment truck, ready to pull out early the next morning. We were due in Myrtle Beach the next night to start a one-week stand. I went back to the condo, without female accompaniment, and collapsed into a restless sleep.

Tony's agent kept him working for what felt like 58 weeks a year. The band in the Myrtle Beach showroom was held over, so the agent found us a fill-in spot in Atlanta, Georgia called "Carl's Vegas-Vegas." Gig red flag warning number one: be suspicious of any nightclub located in the middle of a parking lot of a shopping center off the interstate, especially one that refers to Vegas twice.

The description of the décor is best left to your imagination. I was only a few days into this gig, so I kept my head down and paid close attention to the routines, especially the one or two-word verbal cues from Tony. I focused on memorizing the music, which didn't take long. With my eyes off the page, I could watch Tony, and stay on the lookout for the real shows, which were in the seats.

After a short dance set, Tony arrived with two unfamiliar women. One was dark-skinned with long dark hair, possibly from South America. The other was a tall, lanky blond who could have come from any small town in the Midwest. Both dressed like he met them on Decatur Street. He and the two women disappeared into his dressing room.

Showtime arrived and Robin said this was going to be his "C" show, so we pulled up the Donna Summers hit "Bad Girls." The band launched and out came Tony in a blue sequined jump suit. As he worked to the center of the show floor, I noticed some of the sequins were hanging loose and in tatters. The man was hard-working and it showed.

Partway into the tune, two dancers in costumed full floozy flounce, came bouncing onto the floor; these were the two women with whom he arrived. The choreography required the dancers to move about the room and single out some guy to do their little double-team bad-girl bit in his lap. There were fewer people in the club than in the band, so the energy went nowhere. One dancer moved in on a guy down front. After 10 seconds in his lap, fussing with his hair, and stroking his face, his date reached over and dug her stiletto-like nails into the dancer's chest and pushed her off and onto the floor, but the show continued. The dark-haired dancer moved in again, and turned up the heat on this poor bastard. Again, his date reached in and made another move with her nails, but this time, she appeared to be doing open-heart surgery on the dancer. Instead of getting up and dancing off to finish the number, the dancer grabbed a drink and threw it into the woman's face and started in after her hair.

This show may have been the shortest in entertainment history. Tony and his brother, along with the bartender and a waitress, separated the women, but not without some residual damage. After restoring calm, Tony finished the show.

At the end of the night, there was some question about whether we would finish the week. A new written agreement specified cutting out any show requiring the dancers. The dancers were fine with it because they didn't have to dance. Their new assignment was to hustle drinks at the bar to help keep asses in the seats.

The next night brought a good crowd. By the end of the week, the place was filled wall-to-wall. The stint was considered a success, as far as Carl was concerned. This was the week I started to drink regularly between sets. I still carried my escape stash of cash from the plane ride, just in case....

...and the Band
Played On and On

THE DRAMATIC APPEARANCE AT VEGAS-VEGAS ended-ended with my first full week on the band. For such a class act, Tony endured his share of dives and shitholes, but it all balanced out. The dives were the exception. He put on all of his shows as if he was playing for kings and queens, regardless of the clientele or the condition of the venue. Tony upheld the celebrated tradition of the road bands, going back to the days of Duke Ellington, who worked for 50 years and rarely turned down a gig.

We moved on to Myrtle Beach for a week at a non-descript showroom in a Holiday Inn. The gig amounted to nightly paid rehearsals in preparation for one of Tony's major semi-annual appearances in Panama City Beach, Florida.

(Al eventually solved the mystery of the dancers in Atlanta. The dark-haired and shorter of the two was Tony's Puerto Rican wife. The other woman, who was blonde and taller, was a trained dancer from a small Ohio town. She and Tony carried on long after his wife was gone.)

Myrtle Beach didn't end without some tension. A redneck approached Tony and Michael on the last night and threatened to lynch them if he saw them leaving with the local white women. Despite the fact that Michael and Tony were in possession of a revolver, in the event such a confrontation elevated to another level, the calm and grace with which the brothers handled such a threat was impressive. This was the one I witnessed; who knows how many they chose to keep quiet.

We headed out the next morning for Panama City Beach, Florida. Something told me next month was going to be remarkable—whether that's to say the least, or the most, remained to be seen. The last thing I did before leaving was send off a post card to my coke-fried, vitamin-infused benefactress, as promised.

Hurricanes, Breakers, and Rip Tides

On at ten, off at four. Three shows, three dance sets, and no time off for four straight weeks—welcome to the gig. Tony and the band were the main attraction at the Breakers on the Beach in Panama City, Florida, during most of the month of March. Not only was the town overrun with every kind of college kid imaginable, but this was Tony's semi-annual appearance, so people planned their vacations around his arrival. They came in droves from as far away as eight hours in any direction. This part of the Panhandle bordered lower Alabama and Georgia, with Mississippi and Louisiana only a short drive to the west. Anything could happen.

The Breakers was a major income stream for Tony. He was pulling in $10,000 a week, a major haul for the year, and nearly twice what he would get in most other venues. One thing he always encouraged was for the band to circulate among the crowd, especially on the breaks before the show sets. The Hurricane was the featured low-budget ootsy-foo foo drink, and this place sold them by the gallons. Patrons always wanted to buy the band a drink, with most people budgeted to buy the cheapest drinks available. That shit was pancreatitis in a glass.

Females outnumbered males by at least three to one. As was often the case, at the end of the night, most of the men and women left not with one another, but the people with whom they arrived—too drunk to process their disappointment at the idea of waking up alone the next morning, and too inexperienced to know the better-than-even chances of a greater disappointment at what they would awaken to. It took skill to gracefully extricate oneself from the reality of the morning after—all within the brume and fume of liquor, cigarettes, drugs, and sex, tied up neatly in a plain brown paper bag giftwrapped, with a stick-on ribbon hangover.

The locals owned and operated many of the shoreline motels, restaurants, electronic game arcades, and beachwear variety stores. There were also seasonal migrant workers from nearby Georgia and Alabama, many of whom were women married to men who worked the oil rigs located out in the Gulf. These were lonely women who were desperately missing the loving arms of their off-shore heroes and were always up for some surrogate lover to hold them over, until the real men in their life would return after a long sequestered six-month tour of duty working on these man-made petro-islands. These derrick widows were more selective than one would think. The ideal pick-up was transient, younger, and presented something interesting and exciting in their experiences, standing them apart from the average local barkers and arcade backyard boys.

Enter the road musician. It was the perfect set-up for all involved—no messy break-up because there was no commitment in the first place. Such terms were easy for the musician, but deep down, the widows would often fall for their young paramours. The lure of the romance of the travelling musician created conflicts in who the women believed they were and who they wanted to be. It was also an easy ticket out of town with the hope they would never have to look back, regardless of the long-term outcome of their choice.

There was another sub-culture of women who came from long distances not to find employment, but to accomplish an iniquitous goal with severe long-term negative consequences. They usually traveled in pairs and relied on the dim lighting and other distractions in the nightclub, not the least of which was booze and raging testosterone, to hide the ugly truth of their intentions.

About two weeks into the engagement, I noticed two such women at a table who happened to be making a lot of eye contact with me—the age-old signal to come forth and say hello. I casually made my way over to their table where they offered me a Hurricane. They introduced themselves as sisters from Georgia. From what I could tell, the older sister was in her early thirties and the younger looked to be about 25. The older sister did most of the talking as the younger sat there, quietly sipping her drink and avoiding eye contact. As the night grew to a close, the older asked where the band was staying. I told her where and my room number. I encouraged them to stop by. I was rooming with Michael and he was guaranteed to be out until daybreak.

About an hour passed and nothing, so I figured they found something better to do. I thought, *Fuck it, no big deal.* A knock at the door startled me awake and there was the younger, standing alone. I invited her in and asked about her sister. She explained someone took her to a Waffle House for the 5 a.m. breakfast special.

With different lighting, I saw details in this woman I hadn't notice in the dimly lit club. I couldn't put my finger on it, but there was something about her eyes. She also wore too much makeup. It suddenly became clear when I asked her age—15! What? Fifteen? No, no—you're supposed to be 25 and here with your sister. Fifteen-year-old girls don't go to nightclubs, drink booze, and pick up men. Fifteen-year-old girls stay at home reading their favorite Nancy Drew mystery, or some *Teen Beat* fan magazine. Fifteen year old girls giggle on the phone with a girlfriend about the high school football star, or throw a slumber party—but not this.

Fifteen was the age of consent in this part of the world. That fact didn't make this any more acceptable. This girl needed to get herself together and get out of my room. I asked who was the woman pretending to be her sister. She said it was her 30 year old mother.

So, this woman had her child at 15 and now her child has reached this magical age of moving into conscripted womanhood. I unwittingly became entangled into this sub-culture ritual of female kids who have babies. When their daughters reached the age of consent, they'd bring them to Panama City Beach and make sacrificial virgins out of them by offering them exclusively to itinerant musicians, like the rare and exotic fruit of the pawpaw tree. I felt sick all over. My memories came flooding back in a wave of mass proportions and then, like a rip tide, it took me further and further out into my deepest fears of those dark and foreboding times 20 years before. I struggled to get back to the safety of emotional dry land. The returns on the Spiral are so unforgettable.

I went to sleep and got up around 2 p.m. the next afternoon. There was no one around. We scheduled a 5 p.m. rehearsal, so I thought it would do some good to get in a little swim time in the Gulf; maybe put the shock of the previous night behind me. With this slice of the Gulf to myself, I'd swim for a half-hour, then head across the street to a place where Al and I went for early dinners before heading to the club for the rehearsal.

The water was incomparable in its temperature and clarity. I thought, *Man, it doesn't really get much better than this.* What could my one-cell descendants have been thinking to leave this for dry land? Heading back to shore, I noticed some unusual resistance, with an undertow sucking sensation. I realized a rip tide had me in its grip and there was no one around to help me. Motherfucker! The adrenaline pounded unmercifully in my ears. The shore was getting further and further away. As panic started in, I remembered you should always swim parallel to the shore until you're out of it. And swim I did, exactly like my microbial ancestors taught me.

I made it about 200 yards away from where I started and got to the shore with no problem. As I walked back to my room, I couldn't resist my mind shifting to thoughts of the young girl and how her situation triggered the dark memories of how my childhood was torn from me. She and I now shared a bond, the one qualifying difference being her mother set her up, most likely with the girl's consent, but it didn't matter. We both lost something that was forever gone and irreplaceable: our childhood.

One Hundred Pounds of Trouble
and She's Headed Your Way

THE IMPERIOUS AUNT SHIRLEY—SEVERAL BAND members warned me about her, and their warnings were, to say the least, understatements. A mountain woman from one of the lower counties in Tennessee, she resembled a smaller, skinnier version of Phyllis Diller, with the central nervous system of a rabid least weasel. Shirley first met Tony when she and her extended brood were vacationing in Nashville. Ever since, they planned their vacations around any place he appeared within three states.

I first saw this sideshow during our month-long engagement at the Breakers. I thought they were hecklers down front—people ranging in age from 10 to 40. The excessive enthusiasm from the elders in the group was one distraction, but during the shows, their 10-year-old boy, who must have been 20 pounds overweight for his age and height, was shadowing every single move and line and song coming from Tony. This child saw every show so many times that he committed them to memory.

Shirley had a thing for Tony and he played it with great caution. It didn't take much alcohol for Shirley to get stupid, and if it weren't for the fact she was always strapped—a .38 in her purse and a .45 in the side pocket of her Cadillac—she would be just another lonely heart off the conjugal leash making every second count. She restrained herself for nearly three years, and now, it was high time to get some of Tony.

On this near-fatal night, Michael and I were sharing a room. Returning to the motel, he and I debated whether we had enough strength to head out to a Waffle House and eat about 5,000 calories representing the entire food chain. If you ever want to put on weight, this is the way to do it: drink a lot of alcohol over a six-hour period, top it off with the above-mentioned insulin onslaught, and then sleep on it until three o'clock the next afternoon. Rinse and repeat for eight months, and you're guaranteed to put on 30 pounds. I went from 125 pounds to 155, and a 28-inch waist to a 30-inch waist in no time.

There was an unexpected knock at the door. Michael answered and there swayed Shirley—ankle-biting drunk, with her cocked .38 pointing at his head. The only thing in my view was him holding onto the open door, stupefied and speechless. His silence was filled by strings of slurred racial invective from her, followed by, "Okay now Tony, you're coming with me 'cause I'm finally going to get some of your fine black ass."

Michael remained calm and softly reasoned with Shirley that he wasn't Tony. The standoff continued for another two or three minutes. Her sister finally arrived and calmly walked up from behind and gently took the gun, apologizing profusely for Shirley's behavior. He said he wouldn't press charges if she removed Shirley from the premises and not to bring her to the club for the remainder of their stay. Shirley's sister agreed without conditions. Panama City was the last time we saw them, until Cajun's Wharf in Nashville, toward the end of May.

The Nashville gig was moderately memorable. Again, Shirley and her brood were there every night. Tony's little shadow was in his rightful place in the front row doing his Marcel Marceau thing. One of Shirley's nieces, who looked like a 20-something Little Orphan Annie, was giving me the twice over, leaving me feeling uneasy in light of what happened the month before in Panama City Beach.

The Ice Capades also happened to be in town and on their last night, Dorothy Hamill and several of her principle skaters came over to catch the show and hang out. As the night wore on, Tony was getting the place fired up. Ms. Hamill and the skaters were quite loose, and Tony saw this as an opportunity to turn it up a few clicks. The man was brilliant at reading the mood of a room. During a percussion break, Tony grabbed one of the skaters and latched her onto his waist from behind. The rest of them fell into a conga line, like it was some kind of Ice Capades routine. I timed it so I would fall in directly behind Ms. Hamill and her famous haircut, holding onto her waist for dear something or other. At the end of the night, she invited the band as her guests to their closing show the next day. Afterward, we met her backstage to say thanks, and as chance would have it, her husband, Dean Martin Jr. was present. He stayed off in the background so that Dorothy could have some freedom to interact with her guests. Dean Jr. was the Dino of the 1960s teenage boy band Dino, Desi, and Billy. His father covered Granddaddy's tune in 1952, and that was the version that proved to be the most enduring.

———————

TONY WANTED TO CHANGE THINGS up, so he sent for Stefanie, a singer from Philadelphia, to do the dance sets and assist with some of the show shtick. Stef and I hit it off quite well. She was funny, with a great ear for street dialects; a natural stand-up comic in the making, which I believe she could have pursued with a good chance for success. She was also a very good singer, both out front and as a backup. Short, with blonde hair, she always had great energy and engaging personality. One night, after the last set, instead of the usual after-hours safari, I went back to my room and slept. Stef came back with me and soon left to meet someone from the gig.

The next morning Stef returned from her night out on the town and asked where my friend was. Perplexed and even more curious, I told her I didn't know what she was talking about. Strange shit happens in this world of the travelling musician.

She explained that shortly after leaving the room, she returned to retrieve something. When she quietly opened the door, it met some unexpected resistance. She peered around to see what was in the way, and there stood Aunt Shirley's 20-year-old niece. Her back was against the wall with the look of Boo Radley—eyes wide as saucers, erect, and statue-still, with a look of terror on her face. It scared the shit out Stef, but neither of them made a sound. Stef got out of there and assumed I knew what was going on. I knew nothing.

All I could figure is that she followed us back to the room and when the coast was clear, either got a passkey from the desk with a made-up story, or found the door unlocked. She never tried to wake me, and never made a sound—presumably she just stood there, looking at me in a darkened room for an indeterminate amount of time.

She could have had a knife or a gun, and in a moment of clarity, decided to not kill me, or worse yet, neuter me in my sleep. Maybe she thought it would be nice to come out to the room and do some straightening up—you know, clean the bathroom, bring in some fresh towels and sheets, like some Southern elf princess.

The next morning, I noticed an odd kitchen implement—an old-fashioned handheld food grater sitting in the vanity sink. The strange now became ridiculous. The only explanation for this mysterious utensil is that she thought it would be a good idea to follow me 35 miles out of the city, wait for the right moment to stand there and stare at me in the dark for hours, make some coleslaw, clean up, and then leave, all without a trace and without leaving me any slaw. Strange shit happens, indeed!

The Spit-Valve Capitol
of the World

WE WRAPPED UP THIS PART of the circuit and headed to a town in north central Indiana called Elkhart, a few miles east of South Bend. Elkhart was famous for four essential industries: brass and woodwind instrument manufacturers such as Conn and Selmer; Miles Laboratories; the recreational vehicle industry; and the Hacienda, a local Mexican restaurant which boasted the "wet burrito" and the slushy frozen margarita. Elkhart was a small, but industrious little urb of South Bend, with some of the nicest and hardest working people in the world, contrasted by some of the most static humans on either side of the Great Divide.

Our two-week stint was at a small showroom called Aldie's Lounge in the Best Western Lodge in downtown Elkhart, the first of two appearances for 1981. Our first gig was relatively calm, except for one episode. Steve, the keyboard player and musical director, along with his one-night-stand wife, just up and vanished. The only detail as to his whereabouts was a note he left at the front desk with a terse invitation: "Go fuck yourself, we're headed to Hawaii." Not only did he clear out all of his gear, but he also took all of the charts. If there was any written music, it was gone.

That night, Tony improvised a show by calling a string of oldies hits along with a few dance routines and audience participation bits. The small Midwest crowd ate it up. It also bought some time for him to track down Steve to send back the charts he didn't write. In Steve's absence, I became the default music director, arranger, and chord driver—and the band played on…

The Two-Year One Night Stand, Pt. 1

...AND ON. BY THE TIME August dropped into the Spiral, Tony had enough of the bullshit and petulant complaints, so he fired everyone—a crushing turn of events I took personally. I was never before fired from any job. Fortunately for me, Candace and I were still friends and available to help one another. She was in her last months of living in Brookline before she took off for Paris in what became an on-again, off-again relationship with her French beau. Multiple on-again, off-again relationships were all the rage among us of the urbane baby boomer 20-something set. All along, I had been sending her some of my weekly pay to put into my savings account. When I got back to Boston, I had squirreled away a grand.

A call from Michael came in early September. Tony was holed up in a motel off of the Southeast Expressway to reassemble a band and Robin was still at his side. Tony asked me to come back out because I knew the shows. As his music director, I'd also write charts. Instead of going with a keyboard player, he used two guitars and a new bass player. Greg was still in the band playing tenor. With this reconfigured group, we threw together two shows and some dance sets in order to get back on the road and finish out the year.

Our engagements took us to Richmond, Augusta, Nashville, Washington, D.C., Little Rock, St. Louis, and then back to Elkhart for a second go-around. Richmond was uneventful. We followed a ventriloquist act into the venue, and from all accounts, the help was glad to see this onslaught of dummies were the alive-and-breathing type.

Augusta was a bit of a train wreck because the club manager failed to do a thorough job advertising the engagement. This was a famous spot that James

Brown frequented. The owner of the club was an old friend of Burt Reynolds named Doc Carlucci. Carlucci's manager was a six-foot-two German expatriate named Trudy. It was rumored she had been a member of the Nazi Youth during World War II. After three days, it became obvious Trudy couldn't pay the band. After our third night, Tony told us to pack it in. Trudy was in a major bind because without any live music, the spotty clientele would disappear. Trudy could be heard barking over and over in her best Stalag 17 vocalese as she marched and stomped throughout the club, "You vill neva verk a-*goosta* a-*ghenn*," punctuated with a string of racial invective that would have made her Nazi forefathers blush.

During this time, we were told that we were booked to Saudi Arabia at the end of December and into the New Year. Tony was no stranger to the Islamic kingdom. The ARAMCO employees, many of whom were American expatriate geologists and chemical engineers, were starved for American entertainment. Tony was a huge hit among this crowd. Each of us received a nine-page pamphlet from the State Department, about four months in advance of the trip, about what you can and cannot do when travelling in an Islamic kingdom. Emblazoned at the top and bottom of each page was the admonition, "Do not bring drugs or alcohol!"

Washington, D.C. was our next port of call at the Sheraton International in Virginia, a huge complex located within the shadow of the Pentagon. On our last night of a three-week stand, the place filled to standing room capacity.

We began the first show when three familiar people sluiced in at the last minute and took their place standing by the back door. It was my redheaded, coked-out benefactress; her extremely versatile sax playing, junkie, bisexual male prostitute boyfriend; and a nebbish little subversive whom I met early on at a salon hosted by some member of the local radical intelligentsia. Seeing her reminded me I had dropped off of her radar for several months. It was nothing personal—I was caught up in the energy and distractions of the road life.

Tony was in the middle of a poignant moment with his "Mr. Bojangles" routine, with people sitting in reverential silence. The junkie boyfriend approached stage-right with a stealthy, stalking gait. His right hand was inside a paper bag, with his left hand poised to pull the bag away in an instant from whatever was hidden. Tony noticed this stranger and pointed to himself, as if to ask, "You want me?" The stranger shook his head no, and pointed to me in silence. Some serious shit was about to go down.

The band stopped playing and the crowd remained silent. I reluctantly walked over to the edge of the stage staring at my fate. He looked me in the eyes with a malevolent smirk while pulling away the bag with slow and deliberate drama. A sudden burst of paranoia overcame me. I believed this asshole was about to shoot me, a reasonable concern most normal people would allow to cross their mind. With my guitar still slung around my shoulder, I reached down to control his next action. I let him slowly pull away the bag. What he revealed created an odd combination of fear and relief. The entire room of spectators believed this was all a part of the act; Tony, I, and the rest of the band knew better. This was sabotage and I was the target.

He stood there holding his weapon and massaged his entire two minutes of fame. He was looking for thumbs up, which he received with deafening approval. All of those years watching Soupy Sales take countless pies to the face instilled in me a false sense of bravado. I dared him to do it by simply standing there. Then, it was over. He launched the pie with full force and fury.

The crowd became deranged with approval, completely clueless this wasn't part of the show. When we got back to the hotel, an angry Tony demanded an explanation. My coke-laced keeper had it in for me. It wasn't a matter of the money she gave me; that was a gift, but I gave her my word I would pay her back every penny. All of that changed when she sent her boyfriend up to the stage to sabotage Tony's show and ridicule me. Maybe I should have taken it as a compliment—she wanted to maintain regular contact with me, and as soon as I dropped the ball, she sought vengeance like a woman partially scorned. Her stunt turned out to be a $600 cream pie made with too much cream and too little sugar.

Little Rock was our next hit. Their big showroom was another Cajun's Wharf, owned by the same outfit in Nashville. The capital of Arkansas was surprisingly pleasant, with great Southern food and charm on full display. I hoped to find some female companionship; by now, it was my obsession.

The complications of emotional involvement with a fleeting hook-up were a common problem, and never easy to resolve. Having a regular companion was one way to create an illusion of emotional continuity that often came with a price for all involved. The only women who were insulated from such delicate barbed wire were the ones living in an open marriage.

When the shows ended and the lights went out, I returned to living a transient and isolated life until the next city, when we re-assembled and took our appointed places to once more start the show—same scenery with different characters and everyone had their time and place to hit their marks.

One enduring constant with road life was the like-minded souls who gathered to the energy in and for the moment, like moths to an unseen flame. Dedicated transients were a given, but what of the ones who lived settled and stable lives? They trifled with stepping outside of their predictable comfort zones for the experience of living in a compressed state of time and space, if for only a few hours on a weekend night in the shadows of those who represented a generic version of the world of show-biz glitz. All they needed was the template, and they could fill in the rest.

On rare occasion, a woman would appear trapped in a mundane nether-world, looking for liberation from the well-worn misery they were living. Their ambivalence was caused by being so close to freedom in the embrace of so much uncertainty. It all comes down to the age-old struggle between having security or freedom; choosing one over the other doesn't compare to the problem trying to have both can create. I happened upon such a person one night at Cajun's—another marker in my long-term quest to manifest the image of "Mother and Child," as I wended my way through the Spiral.

She was the perfect personification of Mom, had Mom acted upon her countless threats to become among the missing. She was 28, Mom's age at the time of my birth. The entire backseat of her car contained all of her worldly possessions—various clothing piled high and deep among some scattered framed photos of young kids and a velveteen painting of a black stallion, like the ones sold at the corner of a gas station parking lot on a thousand corners of any intersection in any city in the South. She was from Fort Smith and on the run from her husband and kids.

After the band finished, she and I left, and I took control of the keys. The waitress who introduced us saw her get into the passenger side with a man she thought looked like her friend's husband. She feared her husband tracked her down and abducted her from the parking lot. We went to my motel room where we stayed through the night.

She confessed wanting to drop everything at home to take off and never return. She had a boy and a girl she left with her mother. The parallels between her and my mother were astonishing. So many scenes from my childhood came rushing forth: the statue; Mom's affair; interminable summer days staying with Nanny while Mom went off to New Jersey beach resorts with Willie as I counted every car, every day, until she returned. I never trusted that she would come back.

For the first time, I saw from the other side what could have been the outcome of my mother's follow-through on her threats. Through a drunken haze, this stranger lamented how she married badly and had kids at too young an age. With no means to be self-sufficient, she wasn't able to survive on her own—she was too young and too uneducated.

Before long, my feelings of lust turned to feelings of dismay. By the time I awoke, she was long gone. The only remnant of my encounter with my mother's proximate was the velveteen picture she left leaning against the outside door—an abstraction wrapped in mystery. Maybe some things don't deserve an explanation.

———

FOLLOWING LITTLE ROCK, WE HEADED to St. Louis to do three weeks at the Playboy Club—that citadel of male virility requiring a special key to gain exclusive access for any man who wanted to take a trip down Mammary Lane. Behind the stencil facades, the waitresses worked for below-average wages, served average drinks with above-average prices, in above-average costumes for average tips. The price of the special key in the form of a plastic card was no bargain either. The cost to the married couple who opened the franchise, tucked away in a Holiday Inn on the edge of an industrial park off Interstate 55 in lovely South County, was on the order of outrageous.

St. Louis brought us our first union shakedown in the guise of three menacing enforcers sent from the local chapter of the American Federation of Musicians (AFM) to collect travel dues and check union cards. The two kids who joined the band in Boston didn't have their AFM cards. "No problem. In fact, Robin, don't sweat the cards. Let's step into this office for a few moments and discuss a solution." I don't know how much cash they extorted, but from the color and look on her face it must have been four figures out of Tony's till.

For three torturous weeks, Michael and I circled one cotton-tailed waitress like two ravenous hyenas waiting for a rabbit to die. In the end, it was I who ran off into the underbrush with this willingly captured young fugitive from the Warren of Iniquity.

On the final night, after the band headed to Nashville, she and I got a room reserved for employees. At sunrise, which came knocking and burning much too soon, she told me it would be in my best interest to quickly get a move-on. She said her jealous boyfriend, who was a starting defensive guard for the St. Louis Cardinals, was due to arrive any moment for their regular dirty weekend. The irony board unfolded. Now it was I who was reduced to a warm-up act. Okay, fair enough. With my rental car packed and fueled, I set land speed records heading south on Interstate 55 toward Memphis, then on to Nashville for another week, then back to Elkhart for a second go at Aldie's Lounge.

———

THE EVENTS AWAITING ME ON our return to the spit valve capital of the world scouted me through the next two years. My impending choices left a defining and indelible impact on my life, starting with the night I met a local girl named Lisa—23, with a sweet, simple, and fun-loving personality. She looked like a third-place finish in a Knights of Columbus Cher look-alike contest.

If a moment of intervention by a bespectacled guy in a white lab coat, and a thick Austrian accent, was ever needed, it was now: "Don't you think it's time you stop perpetuating this desperately endless cycle seeking maternal love and attention so lacking in your childhood, with every female you happen to lay your eyes on? In the end, these encounters always leave you backsliding to more hurt and disappointment than from the previous experience. Maybe confront your mother about having been afraid, alone, and emotionally abandoned by her, all the while dying by the hands of a sexually perplexed babysitter, and an evil sexual predator."

What a clarifying moment that could have been for me. But, I was 27, and too deep into finding comfort the only way I knew how—by confusing earnestness with thoughtfulness following on the heels of confusing sex for love. I was slow to learn, quick to burn, and still willing to receive complications.

Lisa and I spent the night at a local fleabag and hung out during the days for the duration of the gig. After meeting her family, I concluded her mom, divorced and bitter, didn't care much for me. She was wise enough to know my transience would spell trouble for her daughter. Her favorite word was surreptitious, overused and always pronounced with a lispy hiss, accompanied by a glower fired in my direction.

The Elkhart gig was coming to a close and the holiday season was only a week away. Immediately after Christmas, the band was to meet at JFK Airport to depart for the much-anticipated 10-day tour of Saudi Arabia. Lisa and I had connected under the most predictable and superficial reasons—the age-old fiction that living in the moment with a total stranger magically translates into a stable foundation for a healthy long-term relationship.

The stage was set for my two-year one-night stand, in the hinterland of Hoosierland, on the storied plains of Northern Indiana.

The Two-Year One Night Stand, Pt. 2:

Do Not Bring Alcohol or Drugs!

THE OFFICIAL ADMONISHMENT FROM THE Saudi kingdom was an unending loop. Who in their right mind would travel halfway around the world to perform for multiple generations of ex-patriated American geologists and petrochemical workers and their families, and *not* want to bring alcohol or drugs?

Some of the employees had been there from the beginning, when in 1944, the Arabian-American Oil Company turned deposits of dinosaur glurp and goo into black gold. Without the expertise of American petrochemical minds, Saudi Arabia would have been awash in a paleo-shit storm of an unimaginable magnitude, without a clue about what to do with it. A mutually beneficial relationship emerged that would wobble and lurch on the center high-wire of geo-politics for decades to come.

Several of the band members played this gig before and knew the drill when it came to how an American should act when going through Saudi customs. We would be a tolerated, but unwelcome guest in this ancient tribal land of the falcon and the one-handed thief. Since Robin's last trip, she had converted to Judaism and became quite Zionistic. She believed it was time to take a stand against a culture that was never ambiguous about its destructive attitude toward Israel.

Robin put Tony on notice that she was going to wear the Cross of David around her neck as she walked through the customs gate in Riyadh. Tony, in a rare, not-so-gentle fashion, reminded her if she did such a stupid thing, he wouldn't have to fire her, because several of the uniformed armed militia Tony and I took to calling "Brutha Burp," a constant presence with burp guns worn with peremptory cool, would swarm her like falcons on a newborn camel. He wasn't bullshitting—busty Western blonds fetched the prettiest penny in the international sex slave market.

The Pan Am flight from JFK to Heathrow was uneventful. Saudi Air was our next carrier with a seven-hour nonstop to Riyadh. The flight arrived from Miami and was full when we boarded. The prevailing gender of the passengers was male, but the oddity only began there. With few exceptions, they were all dressed in designer jeans, black lambskin leather jackets, and strands of gold chains draped and dangling into the area where the open shirt awaited. The saturated, over-compensating bouquet of Halston Z-14 cologne and Marlboros was particularly retching. Tray tables lined with airline alcohol replayed row after row.

There must have been some explanation: maybe a Jordache commercial was being filmed somewhere in the Middle East, or maybe a world summit for the international guild of Sylvester Stallone look-alikes? I settled back with my pre-whitened knuckles and prepared for takeoff. For the next couple of weeks, I'd be living in a vice-free zone, so I figured I better get it all in before we entered Saudi air space. After several drinks, I dozed off. The only thing shaking me out of my boozy stupor was the constant clear-air turbulence.

From my calculations, nearly 24 hours had passed since I left Elkhart. Since leaving New York, we had been in the air nearly 10 hours. Saudi airspace was fast approaching. Then I saw a most fascinating transformation: the multitude of Miami beach poster boys for the land of pleasant Western debauchery and American sin changed into their thawbs and keffiyehs. I last saw this garb when Bobby Hebb was pretending to be a Saudi oil royal attempting to beat an attempted murder charge.

The booze and cigarettes were gone. Several men were in deep prayer. The lure of the great Satan offered so much to the impious, and ladling from the Forbidden Honey Pot would leave no incriminating residue, as long as these young Saudi nationals changed out of one uniform and into another before they reached the shores of Makkah.

We touched down in Riyadh in the dark, early hours of the morning. A short rain had ended, leaving the tarmac glistening with a slick, reflective quality from a combination of water and jet fuel, mixed with a fine, lingering mist of steam and sand from the desert. As we walked across the runway to board another plane for the final short flight northeast to Dhahran, I noticed our road cases were being diverted to the main cargo building. The equipment was under a mandatory quarantine and assiduously searched for bombs and illegal contraband. It's no exaggeration to presume contraband would qualify as anything, including the American air trapped in the cases when we sealed them in New York.

WE ARRIVED IN DHAHRAN AND went straight to the hotel. This modern oasis was nothing less than palatal. The lobby was a sweeping, cavernous space, adorned with solid gold fixtures and figurines, both ancient and modern. Crystal chandeliers twice the diameter of a pitcher's mound hung one after another for as far as the eyes could see. The entire place was immaculate. The only missing presence was Brutha Burp. However, the men standing around dressed in stylish, Western three-piece suits, with their arms hanging confidently and held at their wrists, were most likely packing some serious heat.

My fatigue was intense. I was beyond sleep. The bass player and I paired up to share a room. The moment I had walked into the room, I looked inside the closet and noticed a bottle lying on its side. This was no ordinary bottle, but Black and White Scotch containing about an inch of whisky—motherfucker. This had to be a set-up to snare the decadent American musicians and their sinful ways. There was no other explanation for what would have otherwise been a random and arbitrary occurrence, and the random and arbitrary didn't occur in Islamic kingdoms.

The undisturbed dust on the bottle was our only defense. I called Tony's room and told him the situation. He said to leave it alone, and in a matter of moments, Tony and four security agents were at the door. The head agent asked in a respectful tone to explain the situation. I told him the exact sequence of events—we hadn't been in the room more than five minutes, when I opened the door and saw the bottle.

All four agents examined the bottle, speaking in Arabic. The look on Tony's face was one of, "You motherfuckers better not have smuggled that in here, because you'll end up going to prison and there's not a goddamn thing I, or anyone else, can do about it."

The agent said, "The dust on the bottle shows it has been in the closet and undisturbed for quite some time. Thank you for bringing this to our attention." They turned with military precision and left. Yeah, welcome to the land of Layla, magic lamps, magic carpets, and bottles of forbidden magic water magically appearing and then disappearing.

The band was due for a breakfast meeting with the ARAMCO representative. The meeting dragged on with an affable gentleman who'd been there since the early 1950s. He reviewed in excruciating detail all of the restrictions on our behavior in an Islamic kingdom, as outlined in our State Department pamphlet. I went back to the room to attempt some sleep, but it was futile; I was up for the foreseeable future.

The camp that housed all of the Western workers was close to the hotel. Upon entering the gates, the landscape instantly changed from an empty desert littered with crushed and crumpled Corvettes on the side of the road, to any street in a Miami suburb, including beautifully kept one-story houses in Bermudian pastels, with gas grills and swing sets. We approached a large building next to a U.S. post office, complete with an American flag hanging out front. This was the community dining hall where we would be eating all of our meals while in Dhahran. Segregation at mealtime by gender, regardless of marital status, religion, or nationality, was non-negotiable because that's the way God planned it. The next day, our impounded road cases magically appeared with our amps and other equipment. One of the Bruthas decided to search the interior of some of my pedals and boxes. A simple visual check of such a shallow cavity containing the small battery and wires wasn't sufficient, so they yanked out wires and reduced several of my devices to shit.

The first day shows ended early. The next day, we took a shuttle limo into the city of Al Khobar, the main shopping and tourist area. Tony was focused on one thing: gold. This was the city to buy as much as you could afford. We were told to meet back at the drop-off spot in one hour, and by all means, do not look at any women. No problem—the women were covered head to toe; there was nothing to see. We left the main drag and headed down dark and narrow side streets. Filth and litter were everywhere. Everyone from shopkeepers to shoppers simply threw all of their shit in the street and no one thought anything of it. On each corner, there was a brutha dressed in fatigues and a matching beret, with the burp gun slung over his shoulder. I had walked into a George Orwell novel. These people were living under the constant yoke of martial law and were okay with it.

We were the aliens on the street, dressed as the paragons of immodesty in designer jeans and outlandishly colored shoes and shirts. Robin and Stef had to wear scarves according to Islamic traditions, no exceptions. As the streets narrowed, I began to notice for every small, greasy, open-front electric motor shop, there were four jewelry stores. The only description of the value of the contents of these cramped jewelry shops is in excess of the GDP of most second and third world countries. On the Western retail market, an absolute value of the combined merchandise would be hard to calculate because in this land, workmanship was not calculated into the value—precious gems of all types, in all combinations, emblazoned solid gold statuary, which were exclusively animal figures. Tony got what he came for—a solid gold double-braided bracelet.

We took a different path back to the waiting bus. As we passed one of the many disheveled electric motor shops, at least six men dressed in draping, grease-stained garments gestured with eagerness for me to come into the shop. I resisted their invitation on general principles. However, from the partially toothless grins and glint in their eyes, I don't think they wanted to discuss Ohm's law or the pros and cons of alternating current.

I mentioned this odd encounter to the guide, and he said because of my Western blondish complexion and designer jeaned, 28-inch waist, I aroused some kind of sexual intrigue in them. He explained that homosexuality was a constant clandestine activity among many single Arab men, due to Islamic restrictions on consensual premarital sexual activity. I can't imagine the punishment for homoerotic activity being met with a less severe punishment than hetero activity outside of marriage, but then again, I was so deep in this rabbit hole, nothing made sense in this land of gold and oil and air-conditioned shanty shacks. An old Arabic saying came to mind: "There's a willing and waiting Layla behind every tree in the desert." Now I understood.

Other than the disconcerting call to prayers five times a day, our remaining time in Dhahran was uneventful and the performances were boilerplate. The entire trip was starting to drag out longer than the original excitement. The constant suffocating presence of watchful eyes was no help.

The next jaunt piled the band and the road cases in an old twin prop plane to fly south into the Empty Quarter; a new oil camp was about to come on line. The scheduled performance was for a New Year's party. Single-wide trailers set up on the fringe on the refinery awaited our arrival. We had only a day to relax. We took a brief tour of the camp, which consisted of several gigantic sand dunes overlooking cul-de-sacs with only the blacktop roads, the sidewalks, and driveways next to a space for a non-existent house. It had the eerie look of a civilization wiped out, and the only thing was a road to get from one spot to the next, except there was no one and nothing there to greet you.

Towering stacks, with flames 60 feet high spewing from the tops like gigantic trick birthday candles, framed the dystopian landscape for many miles. They were burn-off towers, eliminating the unending stream of the natural gas by-product coming from deep inside the wells. Those towers burned nonstop for over 40 years—the eternal flames of commemoration where East meets West, oil meets water.

The last part of this nickel tour showed the ingenuity of the engineers in solving a serious and long-standing problem: there was no place to play a round of golf, because grass doesn't grow in a desert. Their solution was to oil the sand. This unusual approach in design wasn't without its limitations—all of the fairways had the same texture as the putting surfaces. The entire course was tantamount to being the largest mini-golf course on the planet, coming in at over 7,000 sand yards, complete with putting browns minus the windmills, waterfalls, and loop-de-loops. I think they were all set in the sand trap department.

Any golfer's paradise is whatever you make it to be, one tee and stroke at a time, as long as there's a hole and a ball and distance that will increasingly shrink the closer you get to your goal. I think a golfer's hell would be to play a round with Zeno of Elea on a par infinity one-hole course, but then again, I never really liked golf because it is too much like yardwork.

WE SET UP FOR THE New Year's performance in a large metal Quonset hut. According to Tony, this gig was the major showcase for which he was always brought in to perform. Only his "A" show would do. This crowd was quite worldly and discerning in their musical tastes, and he always made time for wowing them with improvised routines. This was where we earned our salaries.

Stef approached me on a break holding a tall vessel of liquid, offering a taste. This desert swill was, in fact, moonshine. The chemical engineers created it as a natural by-product of petroleum distillation. To create the illusion of gin, they flavored it with juniper berries. Stef swigged it for the rest of the night, and paid dearly over the next three days.

Someone explained that the government understood the need for Westerners to tipple and imbibe. As long as the booze was unavailable to the locals, they would turn another blind eye for an eye. And remember kids, no alcohol or drugs! If we follow the pious far enough, they will eventually intersect with the pragmatic. At this nexus, we learn one irrefutable fact: every price has its cost.

The time arrived to return to the home of the free. The pilot announcing that we were leaving Saudi airspace couldn't have come a moment too soon. We would be in London in about seven hours. I was awake this time to witness the transformation—one by one, each of the Saudi men dressed in their homeland garb carried a small suitcase to the lavatory. Each emerged like a runway model, dressed in the same Western party clothes on the flight east. The winds of Halston Z-14 cologne preceded their exit from the lavatory, announcing their grand entrance into the Western world. Airline alcohol lined the tray tables like the soon-to-be executed, and chain-smoked Marlboros were not far behind, creating a grey-blue haze rivaling the busiest refinery in the Empty Quarter. I thought, *Such self-imposed cultural schizophrenia has to have an eventual downside—only time would tell.* Heigh-ho, heigh-ho, it's off to Miami they go.

The Two-Year One Night Stand, Conclusion

THE TIME ARRIVED FOR ME to drop into another round of playing house with a girl I barely knew. Lisa's father beamed while her mother seethed. There were already early signs this wasn't going to work in any way, shape, or form. I was much too serious. I was an acerbic elitist—a no-deposit three-pack of defense mechanisms a long time in the making. She was a sheltered girl from Northern Indiana who lived to please her mother. I was a street kid without a permanent home, who happened to make my living in a travelling band. Our worldviews, however naïve, were too divergent for either of us to have the confidence and patience to arrive at a workable understanding. One true thing we held in common was our sexual appetite. All other facets of a mature committed relationship took the cheap seats, as all of the action played out in the center ring.

Upon returning from the Middle East in January of 1982, I went out again for another Florida and Southern Midwest circuit before returning to Elkhart. My time off from Tony was going to outlast my savings, so I had to find work. I met Pat Harbison, who was living in Elkhart on a National Endowment of the Arts Jazz Artist-in-Residence grant funding his work with secondary school stage bands. Through Pat, I met the elder statesman of the northern Indiana jazz scene, a tenor player named Al Ricci, and a drummer named Russ Hunt. Al was a mainstay in the area going back to the 1930s, and had mentored many well-known jazz musicians. Russ was a long-standing presence on the regional jazz scene.

I soon began playing regularly in Al's rehearsal bands. In an area with such an odd combination of farms and factories, many outstanding musicians worked in the brass and woodwind instrument factories. Their stories we typically the same: as young instrumental phenoms, word about their skills spread and eventually the top bandleaders would come looking for them. With offer after offer, they respectfully declined because the idea of road life wasn't appealing. Instead, they worked for these companies and enjoyed the best of both worlds: a steady paycheck to raise a family with a good pension at retirement, and weekend gigs with whomever and wherever they wanted. There were two living legends of trumpet who enjoyed such an ideal life, named Dino Foccosi and Julius Siri—the greatest four-man-sound-in-a-two-man trumpet section I ever had the pleasure to work with. Al's band was made up of these guys and others like them.

Word on me spread and I was playing more jazz than anything else. To my surprise, there were actually good paying jazz gigs in the far northern reaches of the Midwest, while many big city players scrambled for shit money door gigs. Pat, Russ, and I were doing a lot of playing, along with another local legend, a bassist named Rudy Williams. Rudy was an older man and very old school. He had a great, intuitive musical ear along with an aversion to reading music. According to legend, Rudy had taken a high profile one-nighter requiring a good sight-reading bassist. He showed up to the rehearsal and opened the bass book to the first chart, and noticed a chord symbol which read "C13," short-hand notation for a complex chord structure. He whispered to the drummer, "Hey man, does C13 mean I have to play a C 13 times?" The drummer whispered to Rudy, "Fuck reading the music; just listen and play, because you know these tunes." Sarah Vaughn and her music director never knew the difference.

At this junction of the Spiral, I was 28 and on and off the road. As long as I was musically active, I was stable. In April of 1982, I got a call to play in a local rhythm section with Pete and Conte Candoli. Al, who mentored the Candoli brothers from the time they were kids in Mishawaka, hired me to do the four-night stand with these two trumpet legends. I remembered them from the movie, *Bell, Book, and Candle*. Conte was a decades-long mainstay in the trumpet section of *The Tonight Show* band. Pete was one of the first-call lead players in Hollywood and he did small acting roles, which included *Peter Gunn*.

This was my once-in-a-lifetime opportunity to begin my jazz career as a short-hit sideman with these two major league jazz heavies—the Spiral is benevolent, and never forgets.

When I arrived at the rehearsal, Conte was wearing a shirt with a large, exact reproduction of Ernie Kovacs' California driver's license. Shortly after the great comic genius died in a car accident, Pete Candoli married Kovacs' widow, Edie Adams. That shit with the shirt was way too inside for my comfort.

The brothers had their entire show worked out and arranged, and they gave generous solo time to the rhythm section. Conte was the stronger improviser of the two, but they both possessed extreme lead chops. The rehearsal went fine. The only non-local was the drummer, Tony Papa, who toured with the Artie Shaw orchestra in the mid-1950s and was a friend and manager of the brothers. Rudy "Play C 13 Times" Williams was the bassist on the gig. With all of the players over the age of 50, I was the anomaly; the baby in the band.

By the last night of the gig, the group was hitting its deepest groove and poppin'. I was hoping for them to take this on the road for an extended tour, but that was never in the cards. Conte returned to his second chair position in Doc Severinsen's trumpet section, and Pete went on to other engagements. After the final set, both men thanked me for doing the gig. Pete surprised me when he took a moment to step out of his insular mood and said, "If you're ever on the coast, be sure to look us up. You really have something to say, and you'd do well out there." I remembered similar words coming from Howard Roberts in 1976. Was this more bullshit Hollywood platitudes?

The brothers played this kind of pick-up gig so many times in their storied careers, the entire event and the people playing their supporting roles became boilerplate. I was just another sideman, in spite of my relatively young age and lack of experience playing at this major league level. The brothers could have done their shows without me, in spite of specifically written parts for guitar, and the guitar would have never been missed. I was the most expendable. Nevertheless, I proved that I could piss with the tall dogs.

The quality of my improvisation skills in the beginning of the week, compared to what they became by the end of the week, leaped over several plateaus.

My rapid transformation was because, like the one-legged dancer, I had to at least be good or else I'd fall over. Responding in kind to the musicianship surrounding me was a matter of survival, or I'd face serious disapproval, especially from myself. It's a matter of rising to the occasion, and one must always seek opportunities to work with those who are better, because that is the only way to grow.

Somewhere in the mix and swirl of my first several months settling into Northern Indiana, Lisa introduced me to her assistant manager at the Hacienda. She talked me up to this guy, because he too was a musician. One evening, as I waited in the bar for her to finish, Lisa brought this gentleman in and introduced him as Rick Kress. The first thing I noticed was his Atlas-esque physique. He looked like he spent half his life bench-pressing the world. He was personable and very articulate, but there was an undercurrent of reticence, maybe shyness or maybe a threadbare aloofness, fringed with indifference. I could have dismissed him as an apology for simply existing, but there was something about him that inspired my persistence, hoping that he would allow a friendship to develop between us. As we sat across from each other, eye contact was far down on his list of positive body language.

I told him I was hitting the road again after recently performing several nights with the Candoli brothers. He claimed to be a drummer. There was something familiar about his face. I saw this face before, but couldn't quite place where. Then, it came back to me. It was an album cover in a record store on Connecticut Avenue in Washington, D.C. in 1976, except it wasn't him; it was someone who could have been his father.

I asked if he knew Carl Kress, one of the earliest and highly influential jazz guitarists of the 20th century. He confirmed that Carl was his father. The only thought to enter my mind was, *No shit! Here I am, a transplanted vagabond itinerant musician, waiting for the next flight out of the Hoosier state, and now, I'm sitting next to the son of the great Carl Kress.* The next thought to enter my mind was, *What the fuck are you doing working in this place, on the shoulder of old Interstate 20, at the edge of the spit valve capital of the world?*

This was a perfect moment of monachopsis, an obscure sorrow brought on by feeling clustered in the presence of another misfit.

I asked what brought him here and he told an old, familiar story: he fell in love and married. After moving between the Midwest and the East Coast, they eventually returned to his wife's native Indiana, where she became ill, followed by her desire for a divorce. He wandered about and landed in South Bend and Elkhart, waiting for his next major life event. Little did either of us know that the man who would marshal him into several major life events over the next 35 years was sitting across from him, 10 years his junior, getting drunk on margaritas and looking forward to getting back out on the road.

———

THE CALL CAME TO SUIT up and head out to Florida to start another extended tour. Al was back playing bass, and the horn section was reduced to trumpet and bass trombone. In addition to Robin, who came back on the band to help break in the new tour, was Rule, a trumpet player from Panama City, Florida who looked like a good ol' boy version of Sebastian Cabot. John, a bone player from Bradenton, Florida, was a nice Irish kid who stood six-five, and made Rule look like a fire hydrant standing next to a red-headed telephone pole. Their appetites for booze, drugs, and women were as big as the sound they got from those two horns. Much to their frustration, the appeasement of their appetites never exceeded their desires.

This installment of the band was especially poppin' because Tony hired Greg Phillips, a drummer on hiatus from a recording and touring R&B outfit called Starpoint. Greg was a natural, much like drumming legend Buddy Rich, in that he had no sight-reading skills, but if heard an arrangement played through once, he could remember every last hit and kick.

Our after-hours social activities were as out of control as ever. My first extended bouts with separation anxiety came front and center. I had justified suspicious that Lisa was sleeping around, even as I continued sending her money each month to help with the bills and rent. My fear and lack of trust added to my anxiety, which in turn fueled my choosing to pursue as many willing women as possible. I was doing a lot of drinking, although I had long ago stopped doing drugs. The combinations of those influences made for a rocky and emotionally unstable road life; more so than it was on its own terms. All I wanted to do was go back to Elkhart, and for no good reason other than to assuage my insecurities; there was never any let up.

Several months out in Melbourne, Florida, I reached the limits of my patience and gave Tony a month's notice. I did my best to leave amicably, but Tony disliked mercurial instability in his players, and who could blame him? This was his life and livelihood, and it was his name on the marquee. The departure was difficult for both of us. Tony's next goal was to land a steady house gig in Harrah's Casino in Atlantic City. Not many months after my departure, he got the call for Harrah's.

The band eventually scattered. Al and Louie returned to their homes in the Philadelphia area. Rule and John went to work playing for Ringling Brothers, living in an old railroad boxcar outfitted for the circus band and clowns. Robin left to live indefinitely on a kibbutz in Israel while Michael stayed in the lower Jersey area. Greg went back to Baltimore to resume working with his siblings in Starpoint. (Tony followed the trail that started in Atlantic City with doing an opening act for Bill Cosby. This brought Tony to the attention of David Cassidy, which paved the way for him to start working in Vegas, portraying Sammy Davis Jr., in a show called *The Rat Pack*. The Vegas exposure led to him develop a new show, with the blessing of Mr. Davis' widow, called *Simply Sammy*. Tony eventually moved into a new creative phase as a burgeoning playwright, while he maintained his work as a first-class entertainer on the high seas of the world.)

EXISTING IN ELKHART WAS FEAST or famine. Rick Kress and I played in Al Ricci's rehearsal big band, and with Pat Harbison on the local Musicians' Union green sheet trust fund concerts. I still carried my Musicians' Union Local 161-710 card from D.C. to take advantage of the few dollars the gig would bring to my wallet. It was inevitable I would have to seek work out of music until the next gig came along. As timing and fate would have it, Rick left his job managing the finer points of wet burrito production shortly after I went to work in a local factory. Assembling aluminum storm door frames for trailers and RVs, with a 30-pieces-an-hour minimum quota, was about as far from music as I could imagine. Rick also applied to this outfit and worked in the wooden door department, drilling holes for hours on end. Due to our rank incompetence, there was a lot of wasted raw material.

Aside from our daily grind in a Midwest factory, we jumped at any opportunity to perform and drink heavily. I found work in one more factory which was more miserable than the first. It's nothing short of dumb luck that I didn't lose a valuable appendage operating a badly modified automobile exhaust pipe bending machine, but I sure came close.

The unresolved personal wreckage I brought into this new reality was nothing more than a vague and formless mass, which served to add more confusion of an indefinable shape and quality, much like most of the shit that passes for modern art. The music was slowly being consumed by compounded torment.

There was still time for me to reverse my downward trajectory, even as I held to the belief that I was somehow still moving upward on the innersole pole. My Escher-esque existence had come to life. The currency of many pain-filled decades would have to be spent before I would fully understand why I made the choices to continue my descent into wreckage.

I BEGAN TO SEE IT for what it was: hope fueled by desperation, desire in finding some peace and happiness through the love of another to heal uncounted wounds; to find the value in trust and confidence in another; and to manifest the indelible childhood image of the stone carved "Mother and Child." For the time being, all I could do was to hold on for dear life.

By October of 1983, Rick was no longer able to tread water in his own catch basin of emotional run-off. He packed his car and was driving back to Long Island to see if there was actually something called Square One; if there was room to place his playing piece one more time. I took this opportunity to head back to Maryland and scope out any options for Lisa and me to justify tearing her away from her mother and Hoosier family life. Her strident pressure for me to find work increased day by day. I had reached my saturation point.

I packed my guitar and suitcase into Rick's car and we headed out of town on a rail of our own making partly as a response to an unabated and noisy mockery from the two women in our life, and partly as our escape plan to recover whatever was left of our self-esteem. The situation with his smitten-riddled significant other was dead in the water.

My situation was fast rotting on the ground, clinging to the belief I could take Lisa out of her element, and change both of our lives for the better. She talked a good game about wanting to be released from her Midwest legacy, but talk would be the beginning, middle, and end of her actions.

OUR DRIVE EAST BEGAN AND ended in awkward silence, exhausted from the beating we took from the choices we made. No one but us was responsible for this outcome. Rick and I knew that the time spent in Elkhart was gone for good; good energy spent chasing after bad. We wasted a lot of time alleging and cursing the boring and vacuous lifestyle of a factory town, smug in our mutual admiration for one another's excessive hipness and elitist attitude. We ignored one inarguable fact: aptitude and intelligence are not always one and the same. So much for the smartest dogs in the room.

All that it got us was a self-imposed exile from two women we had no clue in understanding, and run out of town on our own hubris. I still had professional options to develop. Rick believed he had nothing more than a concerned mother back on Long Island. The fact that he had 10 years on me maybe added to his sense of failure, in light of what I had been able to accomplish in a relatively short period of time. I never stopped believing that he had something to offer the music world.

Eight very long hours later, we arrived at my mother's third floor, one room apartment next to the Center in Greenbelt, with those casement windows and the lone air conditioner running nearly nonstop from May to mid-September.

Here was one of those raw, full-circle events that the Spiral loves to throw at us—exposed, un-nuanced, and in full view. I felt like I had been on an emotional bender for years and the hangover was lasting longer than the bender itself. The irony-filled shame I felt was four-dimensional. As the three of us sat silently in her living room with nothing to say, a weird thought entered my mind: *When someone has fallen and there's no one around to hear it, do they make a sound?*

Rick left the next morning. The chances of seeing him again were slim to none, but we'd stay in touch. I concluded that I was nothing more than his Murphy-friend, hidden in the wall and taken down should the need arise. My time on the Northern Indiana border left me feeling helpless with a foreboding belief that I wasn't quite finished with Elkhart.

I had no good reason for being back in Greenbelt and Washington, D.C. in general. Why here and not Boston? In my heart was a secret admission that I held no real interest for this Indiana girl. I was once again trapped in a vicious cycle of playing past relationships starring new characters. The fever of exact repetition expecting a different outcome each time is the premise on which this halfway world operates. Of all the sarcasms I have experienced, the musician's reliance on repetition to hold the listeners' interest is at the top of my list, with one important exception: unlike the repetition living at the center of insanity, the repetition of the musician is disguised as a succession of contrasts—or is it insanity disguised as genius?

A DAY OF MONUMENTAL IMPORTANCE arrived when I summoned the courage to take the short walk down to the Center. More than 20 years and a couple of lifetimes passed since this location played such an essential part of my life. One thing I knew for certain was that the older you become, the magnitudes of the world around you, first experienced as child, will diminish into a new and less substantial reality where permanent memories collide with the unstoppable, ephemeral nature of time as growth and change.

My original perceptions of this larger-than-life place of young wonder and certitude dissolved like a desert mirage. To my surprise, little had changed in the material heart of the Center. Some of the stores were gone, but the co-op still stood, as did the Greenbelt Theatre. It was now a run-down community playhouse featuring bad local rock bands and drug deals several nights a week.

The one constant I hoped for, the unfading and immutable statue of "Mother and Child," was where it always lived since 1939. The years of wind and rain were reasonably kind to the original soft, gentle lines of the centerpiece. I was now older and taller.

I stood above the plinth looking near the top of the head. It seemed smaller, but its message of pathos never loomed larger. I was alone here and now, in this former place and time, with nothing more than a life interrupted. Now, standing before it one more time, it taunted me with its unblinking, idyllic message. I turned away and started back to the apartment—and then the first pure, truthful thought in a long time entered my mind: *I have to learn to live my life, not as the fearful and disappointed child, but as the parent who holds the child with all of the love and understanding he deserves.* That learning curve would be the steepest and most challenging of my entire life.

I called Lisa the next day and announced that I was returning. My belongings were still there, so I had to retrieve them. Her words of contempt rang loud and clear. She expected and wanted me to be gone for good when I left Elkhart with Rick.

We agreed I would sleep on the couch and find quick work to save enough money to buy a car and head out for better times and recovery. Many parts of my soul would have to die in order to make a change in my life. All that I lived and worked for was about to come crashing down around me.

———

UPON MY RETURN, ON A cold and windy late December night, I wandered into Casey's in the center of Elkhart, and drank until every nerve ending rendered numbness exhausted. Emotional neuropathy finally said goodnight before it left me sitting there alone, paralyzed from my head all the way down to the bottom of the legs of the barstool. I gazed down into the half-glass of Old Overholt and the ice began to shape-shift the same way clouds do if you stare at them long enough. The ice started out as abstract geometric figures before taking on the appearance of amorphous images, changing into clearly defined pictures. Before too long, I was scrying the ice, like a crystal ball, while slipping further into a liquor-induced hypnogogic state.

I couldn't decide if what I was looking at was images from my past, present, or future, or possibly some nether region between any two timelines. I was unable to drive Lisa's car back to the apartment, but that didn't stop me. She was waiting to make her big declaration of independence from this broken-down man-child, who, under the cover of her willful choices, turned a brief sexual encounter into a two-year one-night stand. There was nothing for me to gain and everything to lose. There was nothing for her to gain or lose by putting an end to the entire charade. It's called cutting one's losses.

Everything Lisa's mother feared, from that first day we met with the skeptical glower she fired across my bow, had now come to bear down on all of us. I believed I was some golden boy who magically appeared—poof! I was going shake things up and sweep this lady-child off her feet. I was in full-blown living-the-legacy-with-women my father and his father created. The curtain was coming down as I sank into a shoal of my own creation.

A wise woman once said that you can avoid reality, but you can't avoid the consequences of avoiding reality. My reality was about to paint a self-portrait for which I had no other option than to sit absolutely still. When I walked into the apartment, we exchanged harsh words. I grabbed my guitar by the neck and in the slowest motion possible, slung it over my shoulder, and like the newly liberated rusted Tinman who longed for a heart, hovered it over my road locker.

The next morning…

…I awoke alone in a strange single bed, in a strange room, in a strange building, dressed in strange clothes, among strange smells and unfamiliar sounds…

3RD PARTIAL

The Flight to the End of the Funnel

"The passive observation of greatness requires only an act of submission. The creation of greatness first requires one to submit to a
perpetual state of observation."
—Aristotle's landscaper, "Anonymous" Euonymus of Dichotomous

THE DOCTORS AND NURSES DISASSEMBLED my state of mind to the limits of their
secondhand textbook theories. I might as well have been some alien life-form
who took a wrong turn at the Seven Sisters carrying a loaded Messier 45. My
two-week stay on Elkhart General's A-Ward was drawing to a close. My stead-
fast denials of alcohol being a permanent problem for me wore them down to
conceding my point. From the beginning of my incarceration, I argued that my
problem was the result of self-imposed exile in Indiana.

Maybe I should have done the gig and moved on, but that would have
introduced an entirely new wrinkle with the time-space continuum. I had to
put this nightmare behind me, get out of this town, and return to the life of a
working road musician. They all agreed and were willing to sign off on my release
on one condition: I must have a viable destination and the means to get there.

I told Rutt and the Headknockers that my plan was to move to L.A., and
call on my professional connections. I needed money to make this move, so my
grandmother Mary reluctantly offered to send me $500. She made it clear this

was her only legacy and bid me farewell and good luck. There was a coldness in her voice that sent a chill through me…how Dad must have felt when she left him and Granddaddy all of those years before.

On the 30th anniversary of my arrival into this world through Doctor O'Donnell's cut and tug, I said a final farewell to the land of industrial waste footwear. I knew that my experience in this place of forgotten time was my choice and no one else's—bittersweet and loaded with irony. On one hand, I failed to secure lasting female companionship and love. However, for the first time, I worked with some of the best jazz musicians anywhere in the world. In my avidity to heal wounds not of my making, I created new ones. I presented myself as a sullen, inaccessible loner with little to no capacity for being alone. Buried deep in these contradictions were the conflicting premises of their creation. I had to identify and eliminate the false premises.

A drive-away car took me by way of Route 66, from South Bend, Indiana to Los Angeles, with a brief "hello rabbit" stop at the Playboy Club in St. Louis, hoping to see the bunny from a few years before—no such fortune. After dropping off the car in Indio, I took a bus to North Hollywood to hole up with my old road companion, the honky-honk sax player. The best he could offer in his cramped, one-bedroom flat was the hall closet and I happily took it.

What little money I had wasn't going to last. I found a day job at a start-up magazine for the nascent personal computer market. The work was mindless and consisted of spending the entire day in the mailroom placing address labels on magazines. The unease of the situation fed into my increasing separation anxiety from Lisa. More accurately, my anxiety fed more on the idea of a Lisa and not so much the actual person. She represented my last known emotional address, but it could have been any one of myriad women who graced my life. Where the fuck was that realization when I needed it?

I didn't waste time looking up the few professional connections from which I had any chance of getting work. The first call I made was to a pianist who was a connection through Al Ricci. Al assured me this guy would have work and would be able to reconnect me with Pete and Conte Candoli. I knew Conte's number, but I wanted to first test the water through this contact. It was a matter of ego preservation; I'd rather receive rejection from someone in the capacity of this lesser-known contact than someone of Candoli's gravity. In the end, what difference would it have made who turned me away? All I was to Conte was a young, skilled, but still green jazz player who needed to log in many more miles before I could compete with his well-established circle of first-call guitarists such as Howard Roberts and Joe DiOrio.

Howard was busy with his performing schedule and getting the Guitar Institute of Technology up and running. Besides, like the Candoli brothers, I didn't entirely trust his sincerity when he made those praising comments to me all those years ago. It's the Hollywood put-on bullshit, which I believe was at the center of any accolades or approval I received—you know, put the kid's mind at ease, leave 'em feeling better than when they walked in.

I turned to contacting Joe Dougherty, one of the drummers I knew from my Kensington days. He was about to become the new and permanent drummer for the Grass Roots. It was an amicable reunion, and he took me to sit in on a gig he regularly played with a local singer. I was in no state of mind to play even the most basic standard tunes. Without a car to get around and make it to jam sessions and gigs, I was at a great disadvantage. After a month of going nowhere, I surrendered. I sold my amp, took the cash, and with my remaining money, bought a one-way plane ride to Chicago.

I landed at midnight in the Windy City, as the snowstorm increased to whiteout conditions. I caught the last shuttle van of the night to South Bend. I was the last passenger to arrive at the terminal point with several miles to go before arriving in Elkhart. The van driver was reluctant to keep going, but shaking hands with Andrew Jackson was enough of an enticement for him to continue driving. I began improvising my next decision as we slipped and skid along Route 20. I was desperately searching for some place to crash, and it would be a hard crash; the lack of sleep over the past 36 hours combined with unimaginable amounts of anxiety-produced adrenaline and jet lag created chaos in every nerve and cell in my body.

We arrived at the run-down roadside motel across from the Mexican restaurant where Rick and Lisa once worked. I unloaded my belongings and waved off the driver. I watched as the tail lights and the exhaust faded from sight. The space between the snowflakes filled in with the snow dancing in the slipstream of the van, creating a blanket of white. For a moment, I stood like an immobile figurine inside a paperweight, at the mercy of an outside force, which let the flurried matter settle for a moment, before once again agitating the contents.

There were no signs of life, lighted or otherwise. The one holdout showing electrical activity was the neon sign at the edge of the road for Route 20 Motor Inn. The glass tube in the shape of the number two refused to accept any further influence from the noble gas; a taunting hopelessness, because the sign portrayed the bleak poetic claim of Route 0—just another road to nowhere. After several jabs at the buzzer, a disheveled innkeeper appeared. She fought back reluctance to dress for business and agreed to open a room. From the looks of the place, $21 was the most money she had seen in a long time.

Stepping into the room was like walking onto a diorama stage in the museum of timecicles, 1950. The room smelled like grime which had festered since mid-century. The stained, pink candlewick chenille bedspread covering the sagging single bed complemented the lamp with a yellowed Lone Ranger shade sitting on top of a small, three drawer oak chest. With two of its pulls missing and random graffiti carvings on the top surface, the four walls of pitch-stained pine boards presented the perfect backdrop for this charnel house showpiece. The only sign of hope was the black rotary Ma Bell phone on the fleur-de-lis stenciled TV tray pretending to be a bedside table. The wind-driven snow against the rattling single-paned windows removed what minimum heat was weeping from the rusty electric baseboard fixture—I was fortunate to have the shelter.

Tentative daylight appeared. I sat at the edge of the bed staring at the phone for a long time. I knew I had to call Lisa because my next choice was too egregious to consider. After she answered with a dusky hello, I let the pregnant pause go from false labor into an unplanned C-section. An agitated sound came through the handset. I struggled to say nothing more than, "I'm back."

Her lime green Datsun hatchback arrived with a heavy halt. I loaded my shit and the moment the door closed, I heard an unrelenting, high-decibel diatribe, covering all of the bases for her screeching disapproval of my return. She made it clear I could have the couch for only one night. I had 24 hours to find a place to live.

Purgation Manor
(No Epiphanies Allowed)

THE ADDRESS OF THE ROOMING house was familiar because it occupied the upper floors of a joke and magic shop at the intersection of South Second and West Lexington in downtown Elkhart. If there was ever a time in my life when I needed the combined intervening forces of humor and magic, it was now. My sense of irony was intact, but the time-tested art of illusory deflection never held much of an attraction for me. I purchased a pack of three multi-colored, hard rubber juggling balls. The picture of W.C. Fields on the wrapper made it the perfect combination of humor and magic in one little easy-to-open package. I heard somewhere that learning to juggle was a skill to help sharpen focus and concentration—two personal attributes in low supply.

The rooming house was undergoing renovation. The occupied rooms on the second floor and the single room in the basement left the only available room on the first floor, the least expensive, at $15 a week.

The room was the most preserved from when the building was erected in the mid-1800s—the original bare and well-worn wooden floors, window sashes, and a doorway with a skeleton key lock. A single old dresser, the ugly cousin of the one at the Route 0 Motor Inn, stood in the far corner with a bare, well-meaning light bulb hanging from the middle of the ceiling. A cast-iron radiator stood ready to hiss, spew, and bang its happy little percussion sonata to chase away the brutal February Indiana cold. This place had been a whorehouse for men on cattle drives making their way from the South to Chicago. If these walls could talk, I would've insisted they instead listen and learn. The double bed near the door had seen better days. Located up one floor was the shared bathroom, with the original pedestal sink and claw foot iron bathtub and no shower, which promised a modest form of torture for me, as one who detests soaking in my own filth.

Lisa brought by a set of sheets, a pillow, and a wet burrito. She left quickly, leaving behind very few words. The next morning I walked a short block to a lawn and garden center that was hiring a driver. The owner asked if I could lift a minimum of 80 pounds at a time. My driving record was good, so I could start on Monday. The job paid five dollars an hour.

That night, I made my way through the burn and sting of a 10-below wind chill to Casey's for dinner and as much alcohol as I could consume. I awoke the next morning on death's door. My fever must have been over 100 and the chills and total body aches kept me incapacitated for days. There was no way to call for help. Dehydration may have reached critical mass. When I wasn't sleeping, I could only lie there and stare at the paint peeling on the wall. A calm eventually draped over me. I believed this was where and how I was going to leave this world. There were no visions of family members, living or departed—no visions of friends, no lights at the end of tunnels. It was more like a flight to the end of the funnel.

After missing the starting date for my job by over a week, the owner assured me the job was still mine. The work was very labor-intensive, with fixed weekly schedules to keep. Every Wednesday, I drove to the regional Purina distribution center to load, by myself, in increments of 25- and 50-pound bags, four tons of various animal chow. Such regular tonnage created in me a ripped and buffed specimen of 30 years young in the short period of a month. I was never in better physical shape in my life. More importantly, the daily work routines also help change my dark mood to something lighter and more balanced.

I eventually came to terms with this as a temporary setback from which I would emerge better and stronger than ever before. The beginnings of a new maturity were greeted by my sense of responsibility for helping the wounded child—a follow-through to the learning curve with my realization on that final day in Greenbelt several months before, when I turned away from the statue for the last time and assumed the role as the parent embracing the child, with the child becoming stronger each day.

I hadn't taken my guitar out of the case for nearly six weeks. The time to return to my instrument was upon me.

A room opened on the renovated third floor, so I took it over for an extra five dollars a week. It was roomier, with more natural light than the chamber I occupied in the first month. Winter was starting to loosen its grip on the region, and I planned to be out of this proverbial single man cage flop no later than June.

Down the hall from me was a young man who presented a menacing countenance since the day I arrived. He never offered so much as an obligatory nod hello. I was in enough of a compromised state of emotional equilibrium and I didn't want a hostile presence keeping me awake at night. That was about to change in a very harsh and violent way.

One evening, while practicing my juggling, I heard what sounded like a wounded animal in the hallway. The young man down the hall was sitting on the floor, sobbing from a bloody beating about his head and face. His clothes were torn to shreds and covered in blood. He looked like someone hitched him to the back of a tractor and dragged him across a cornfield. His threatening posture quickly vanished behind his injuries. I sat and cradled him to help bring calm, and after several minutes, I helped him to his feet. We went around the corner to a tavern for beers and some food. After a long time eating in all forms of silence, he finally spoke up.

Two guys abducted him from his job site and drove him to a remote spot across the Michigan border. They held him captive for more than a day until he was able to convince his brother to come and answer to his captor's demands. His brother was who they wanted.

Once his brother arrived, they returned the kid, bound and gagged in the trunk and tossed him by the side of the road outside of Elkhart. He freed himself and made the long walk back to his room and collapsed in front of his door. A few days later, he got a call that his brother was found dead. His abductors warned him to not notify the police or he would face the same fate. From that day forward, the rooming house took on an even darker stillness with its stranded souls.

Transom Ransom

As June arrived, so had the end of my patience. I pulled through as much as I was going to in the limits of my environment. Any further time in this House of the Ineluctable was going to start me on an irreversible backslide. I made a call to Boston and arranged to take a sublet.

The Friday before the Monday I was leaving, one last challenge demanded my attention. I was awakened by an obnoxious alarm clock coming from the room across from mine. The tenant was gone for the weekend and the landlord was out of town, so there was no way to gain access to the room to stop this sonic torture. For two days and nights, the alarm blared in endless futility. I did everything I could to make this a positive musical experience. However, my option of playing along with it as a pedal point ostinato accompaniment soon ran its course. To save what little sanity was left, I set up a chair outside the door and pushed on the transom, which, to my good fortune, was unlocked. I climbed over and down by curling my body over, around, and through an opening smaller than half my height. Having been born caesarian, this was probably as close to the experience of normal childbirth as I would experience.

The split second before my hand touched the clock, the alarm stopped— dead silent. I hit the off button and stood there in disbelief and anger. I turned to open the door and discovered it was locked from the outside cylinder. I had only two choices for escape—splinter the door, or go back out through the transom. Drained of anger and frustration, my only remaining emotions were laughing or crying—and not restrained, polite dinner party chortle or weepy, silent tears, but level 10 Stanislavsky outbursts.

I chose laughter, which to the trained ear, may have sounded like Ornette Coleman attempting to play, "Stairway to the Stars" through the blowhole of a bottle-nosed dolphin. I pushed and dragged the heavy dresser up against the door to go out the way I came in, effectively creating a retrograded, born yet again momentous miracle. If Merton can have his Epiphany at 4th and Walnut, I can have my South Second and West Lexington Miracle.

As I left the next morning, the occupant of the room was arriving. My heartfelt good morning passed a half-assed grunt and a nod. From the floor below, I stopped and listened to the sound of nonstop attempts with bashing his door against the back of an immovable dresser, accompanied by nonstop swearing based on an imprecatory prelude and fugue of, "What the fuck…? Who the fuck…? How the fuck…?"

The negligent roomer discovered someone accomplished the impossible and much to his expense. If he stayed quiet for a moment, he would have heard someone else mutter under his breath, "I'm sure gonna miss this fucking place."

Another Story Moving East

No good, bad, or indifferent byes were offered—just a quick slide to the Elkhart Amtrak station. The Lake Shore Limited from Chicago arrived on time. I saw this as a hopeful sign that I would soon be no longer in medias res; no longer neither here nor there. I could finally answer the question, real or imagined, "Where were you as the train headed east?"

"I was in it, sitting facing the direction in which we were headed, with my back to the west."

The train was scheduled to arrive at Boston's South Station in 20 hours. Returning one final glance up Main Street, I reflected on my enigmatic existence in the Spit Valve Capitol of the World, where I played some of the best and worst gigs.

I learned that the limits of a one-night stand pick-up in a nightclub was like entering a Hoosier state fair pie-eating contest intending the impossible task of squaring the circle. I met some of the nicest, hardest working people you'd find anywhere in the world. Indiana was also the birthplace of some of the most important and influential musicians in the world of 20th century popular and jazz music. I felt a modest historical connection to the state. The train departed on time, and very likely startled countless frogs along the way.

I awoke from a deep and dreamless sleep about 20 minutes from South Station. It was marvelous seeing all of the familiar landscapes of Metro West and the ride that paralleled the Mass Pike as it headed into Back Bay. I saw Fenway Park flash by to my right. I recalled being in the bleachers that September night when Yaz got his 2,998th hit. Just before we entered the Pru tunnel at the Mass

Avenue Bridge, I caught a quick glance at Berklee at the Boylston Street corner. Until that moment, I didn't know just how much I missed being in Boston.

Aldo met me at South Station. On the ride to his Mission Hill room, he caught me up on who was still around, who was gone, who would like to be gone. He was among the latter. The band house was exactly like the crash pad I knew at the house in Wheaton, where I landed in 1981: dirty, shit furniture, everyone living day-to-day, hand-to-mouth, overdue utility bills, and the rent months in arrears. The occasional mugging outside my window completed this post-beat utopian bohemian brew, but these were my friends, and we were all bound by our love for the moment and music. It was good to be back.

I considered reaching out to Tony Tillman. I was ready to resume road life, but with a better perspective on living more wisely. However, he was now settled at Harrah's Casino with a stable band, so that option was off the table. None of the other territory bands were working as steadily, and many were looking to settle down in a fixed location, as Tony did in Atlantic City. I began working with the old BPC stage crew, who were now professional stagehands for the Boston Opera Company. For the time being, it was all I had.

Four-Way Close

I ARRIVED AT BERKLEE TO wander around, hoping to run into a former instructor and say hello, and to see what kind of changes were taking hold; to bask in the comfort of the nostalgia and affection I felt for the place. The first familiar face I came upon was Larry Monroe, who was now a top floor administrator. The subject of the upcoming fall 1984 semester came up. They were scrambling to fill 30 full-time faculty openings. Was I interested in doing some teaching? I, a kid who never made it past 11th grade because of "you won't go to school, so you can't go to school," was being offered a position as a Berklee faculty member? The Spiral loves its irony. I could hang with it for a year or two, save some money, pay off my student loan, and hit the road again with another territory band. I accepted Monroe's offer. He put me in touch with my first-ever Berklee instructor, Barrie Nettles, who was now in charge of the Core Music department.

Fred Lipsius, the alto saxophonist and arranger, and one of the original members of Blood, Sweat, and Tears, was among the 30 new hires I connected with. Tim Hagans, a trumpet player from Dayton, Ohio, who did time on the road with Stan Kenton, was another. Fred's story and what brought him to Boston and Berklee was of great interest, especially our mutual connection with a pianist named Eddie Sears I worked with in South Bend, but Tim and I hit it off immediately. Tim was the assistant chair of the jazz studies department at the University of Cincinnati. When he and his wife left Ohio, and headed to New England, my friend Pat Harbison left Elkhart to take over his position at UC.

My biggest concern was with how the demands of working a full-time schedule at Berklee could have a negative impact on staying professionally viable. I didn't want to risk the walls of the college closing in around me as my ultimate identity. I knew if I succeeded in juggling Howard Roberts' working trinity of play your instrument, write your music, teach someone what you know, then I would be able to resist the stasis of academia for academia's sake.

Drop 2, Drop 3, Drop 2 & 4

MONDAY, SEPTEMBER 10TH, 1984, AT 9 a.m.: freshman ear training class. It was my first time ever standing before a group of college freshmen who aspired to become professional musicians. My central nervous system told me I had been doing this far longer than this first day. I centered my approach on the concept of teaching as if I was teaching myself, and the students were a natural extension of me. With this new gig came the need to relocate out of the ghetto of Mission Hill. A room opened in a big, blue triple-decker across from the state pathology lab, just on the edge of the Arnold Arboretum. Maybe stability was possible after all.

———

EQUATING SUPPRESSION WITH RESOLUTION HAS been a problem in my quest to purge my demons. My suppressed emotions were like a sidewalk buckling upward, caused by the subterranean pressure of the root system of a tree, where two worlds collide, both of which have their purpose, but without considering the inherent biases between nature and man's need and desire to control it. The force of nature wins, because it can; suppressed energy seeks to fulfill its purpose through resolution.

Music, the sonic fruit of growing waveforms, is the perfect expression of a kind suppressed energy—from the seed comes the tree comes the stem and the blossom, and finally the fruit. Once you finished with the pulp and rind, all that remains is the smell—the essence reduced to the molecular—and from there, all that remains is the memory.

It's always about the memory—the only time travel machine in existence—except for one fundamental flaw in its design: you can return to only the present—or is it the present? Maybe the present to which you return is the future, measured from the moment in the present you left to remember the past. Could the avenoir, John Koenig's concept defined as the desire to see memories in advance, be a possibility? One thing is certain: without change, there would be no basis for memory. To see memories in advance would require something beyond change, which is ultimately timeless. No matter where we land, the uprooted requites the seed of its creation.

———

IN OCTOBER OF 1984, THE chairman of the guitar department advertised a clinic featuring Tal Farlow—the name that was an intermittent echo throughout my life. By now, I had heard enough of his recordings to conclude that he was a serious musical force. His early recordings were far more representative of his talent as a jazz improviser. After nearly 20 years of hearing all of the references and explanations of his influence on so many important guitarists, I finally had an opportunity to see and hear this legend.

Out strolled a tall, slightly stooped at the shoulders gentleman, who could have been a body double for Gary Cooper. He sat at center stage of the performance center and after saying a quick thank you in a soft-spoken North Carolina drawl, he picked up his guitar and played some tunes. I left with an impression that maybe this great musician had seen better days, and yet, flashes of brilliance penetrated the air. I wanted to hear more from this gentleman, and before long, he would hear from me.

Added Tension Spreads

ONCE AGAIN, I WAS ROMANCING an older woman who had six years on me. There must be something to the number six. In music, it represents the sixth partial and the completion of the major triad, the basis of all tonal systems. There are two ways to reach the number six: 1 + 2 + 3, but if you spin the + sign 1/8 turn in either direction, you get there with 1 x 2 x 3.

My first 30 years exhausted the limits of the plus. The next 30 would be spent exhausting the limits of the times.

LAURIE WAS A 37 YEAR old reading and speech specialist and she was well suited for the student counseling gig at Berklee. I, on the other hand, was 31 and starting my second year as a full-time faculty member at the most prestigious contemporary music school in the world. Road life still called to me, but I wanted to hang onto this gig and establish a base of operations in Boston, and network to take distant playing opportunities.

I was exhausted from indiscriminately chasing after the chimeric fantasy of short-lived female companionship. I preferred monogamy, but I didn't know how to develop and sustain a relationship based first on real love; I had the room, but nothing to furnish it. Ephemeral romance left me feeling hollow, especially during my road days; emptied of sexual energy, waiting for the next build-up, and no objective comparison to gauge whether I was giving love, or only taking love, or if love was even in the room.

Giving affection and expecting it returned in kind is not a measure of true and objective love. Affection is a cagey swindler. Sexual conquest is simply that: conquest. It is an ascent to harvest and seize the low-hanging affections of another and love is left behind on the bough to go it alone, only to wither and die, falling to barren and desiccated ground. It would take me many years to learn from another that love is a currency—a return for the happiness one receives from the goodness of another.

In late 1985, I dispatched the models of a past that always stood against me, looming as self-destructing markers. There was much to learn about how to live life well. I never expected I would have learned so fast at such a young age, always on my own, always under a cloud of fear. It was time to settle down and bring much needed and much deserved rest to my heart and soul. I had to start somewhere, so I turned to confront the pain inside the scars.

I believed that filling old furrows with the choices of marriage and children was a step in the right direction—ultimately, with no resolution of the original pain, that belief was betrayed by reality. On a bench in the Park Street subway station, I proposed marriage to Laurie. With her trust and belief in what I knew to be the most honest presentation of what I was—a man-in-waiting—she said yes.

Trusting those around me was always difficult and would likely remain so for all of my remaining days. I made a heartfelt commitment to both marriage and the goal of parenthood. I believed that turning trust inward, and choosing to live my life as someone who would never betray the belief and confidence of those around me was my only solution for success. And so began my journey toward true manhood.

Quartals, Clusters, and U.S.T.

On May 24th, 1986, we tied the knot in our Brookline home that she bought in January from the liquidation of assets from her first marriage. Tim Hagans stood by as my best man. The only capital I owned was my commitment to the marriage, an unquenchable work ethic, and determination to turn the tide of my dark and destructive legacy. We settled down into starting our life. My surprising desire to have children was a primary motivation. One persistent refrain I couldn't shake: was all of this really mine? What did I do to deserve this?

Tim approached me with the idea for Laurie and me to relocate down to the New York City area, along with him and his family. He suggested that we could work together to establish ourselves in the New York scene, by playing every general business gig that came along, and going into town to play the jazz club jam sessions as often as possible. The rush of energy I got from Tim's idea was palpable. It seemed like a natural progression for how my career would grow. I put in a good and honest two years at Berklee, so I had that experience to add to my skills. The problem was how to approach Laurie with the idea.

She was a born and bred Jersey girl who enjoyed her childhood and family life growing up in Middletown. The last thing she would ever do is relocate to where she spent time and energy escaping, although her sister and brother-in-law lived a good, full life on the Jersey Shore. So goes her non-negotiable stand on Tim's proposal—end of story.

The only way I was going to live in New York was without her. There was not much room to work things out. Brookline was where we were going to live and raise a family. Berklee, for the next 30 years, was my chosen world.

The resentment I felt toward her was surprisingly easy to repress. Such ease came too readily—not a good sign. My feelings germinated into contempt with an irreparable breach in our relationship. This was the first time I felt negativity in our marriage and I feared it wouldn't be the last. I was beginning to understand what Emerson meant when he said limitations have their limits. My determination to make the best of my choice would start with the birth of Anna.

Someone said becoming a parent is a person's entry in joining the human race. For all of the romantic sentiment in this platitude, it always comes down to a person's choice, which in turn, impacts the questionable absoluteness of such an utterance. My parents bought into fulfilling the traditional pressures surrounding marriage and children. Below the surface, their choices came at great expense to their own shortfalls in who they were, and what they aspired to be as individuals.

Laurie and I faced no such pressures. We had children because we wanted children. We were ready to take on the mysteries and responsibilities of parenthood. Several influences inspired my desire, one being the most basic in all of humanity: procreation. Of course, this opens the suspicion of doing something for its own sake, simply because you can.

I wanted to heal and undo my damage. I wanted to enjoy the presence of untrammeled innocence once again. I wanted to watch the face of a child when they experience something wonderful for the first time. I wanted to be there for their first of countless tears and smiles and laughter, and watch them build their lives toward confident independence, one setback and two triumphs at a time. I thought:

I would rebuild my childhood to prove that if trusting others was going to be a lifetime struggle for me, then I would become the most trustworthy person I knew. I had to create a balance; I had to get it right, once and for all...

...and in September of 1987, I witnessed the birth of my daughter, Anna. A little more than two years later, in October of 1989, I witnessed the birth of my son, Alex. In both wondrous moments, as I stood between our eternities, I too was again born. This time, there was no cut-and-tug, no rooftop eviction from the womb, because this time, they were as ready as their mother to make the final transition to their worldly destination. The short time they spent in her embrace—for the time being neither here nor there in this eternal passage—would inscribe on their souls the indelible imprint of their mother's love.

Anna and Alex side-slipped and skidded their way headfirst into the deep-end of a halfway world which held the power to splinter their humanity. I waited on the other side for their arrival as if my life depended on it—a young man who was clueless about parenting, having lived the darkness of the lives of so many others, before I learned to live mine in the lightness of what I always believed to be true.

Once they bonded with their mother, I took them in my arms and looked into their beautiful, blue infant eyes—wide, unblinking, aiming to focus, bridging the ages—making us forever one with the other. Their eyes radiated a silent invitation into their neonate world, to honor me with being the very first to inscribe their soul. Under the harsh glare of medical white light, I bestowed them with the kiss and tear of fatherhood. My silent vow promised each of them that when we wandered off the path for a short time, it would be to play hide and seek in each other's heart.

Protection from the monsters, both real and imagined, was my responsibility, until such a time when they could distinguish the difference and take the steps to protect themselves, especially from demons of their own making. Anna and Alex would learn my love for their mother would be one of the greatest gifts I could give to them. I wanted to teach them, with gentle words and deeds, everything I learned about the good and bad in people. I would do everything in my power to shield them from my fallout. They would always have a center of love's gravity called home, whether it was the one in which they were born and raised, or one of their own making.

For Anna and Alex to think for themselves, to come to their own conclusions, and to always be ready to offer proof of their convictions, was our priority. We would always hold them to a higher standard than any friend or acquaintance passing momentarily through their lives.

My children would learn that a strong work ethic was more than simply getting out of bed every morning and showing up on time. Completing the job, and doing it better than anyone else, whether it was cleaning someone's bathroom, writing a story, or composing a song, was the goal. After all, if it held no value for them, why should it be of value to anyone else?

The given in their lives is each other representing the atavistic landscape of their parents, but siblings are really the perfect echo of each other's creation. I wanted to raise a brother and sister who would trust, honor, and love each other in ways Karen and I were never taught and never could.

We wanted to leave behind a best friend for Alex and Anna in each other; to share in living the values informed from their earliest memories and enjoy reaching the same conclusions, as they embraced their journeys from youth to adulthood to middle and old age. I had to take many cues and lessons from their mother. I was a nervous and hyper-vigilant father, because I was a nervous and hyper-vigilant child. My sole objective was to shower them with laughter and lightness and love.

They never heard a harsh word or my raised voice, yet sometimes my fallout would insist on running interference, but I was always at the ready to neutralize it. The gauntlets I faced growing up were enough for several lifetimes. I did everything in my power to create the conditions for a new and better reality for all of us.

Tal

I HAD MADE IT THIS far as a self-taught guitarist with whatever mastery of my instrument I could claim; there was so much more to conquer. Howard Roberts had an enormous impact by setting me on the path. For me to continue with him would mean relocating to the West Coast. By now, Howard was sick and in less than two years, he would be dead from prostate cancer.

The name Tal Farlow was a load-bearing beam on which I bumped my head many times over many years; a sonic thread weaving its way through my life, all along the Spiral, from the time I was a kid, repeatedly hearing his name, to the day I saw him on stage at the BPC. I remembered Herb Ellis saying that Tal lived on the Jersey Shore and took on private students. Coincidentally, Tal's home in Sea Bright was very close to where Laurie was raised.

One summer day during a family visit, the thought crossed my mind to call Tal. He listed his number in the local phone book and halfway through dialing, I put the phone back in its cradle because I got nervous about calling. Oddly, I felt less so about meeting him face to face, so I drove to Sea Bright and found his home. I was not the first to walk up unannounced and knock on his door. It was something he was used to.

From the approach over the Shrewsbury River Bridge, I could see his small, quiet town. Looking 30 miles to my left, through a slight haze, was the skyline of Midtown Manhattan—it took no more than a fleeting glance to send me back with so much wistful nostalgia. It was more than 20 years since I first set foot on the Island of Envision with Crazy Eileen. My romance for that city was as three-dimensional as the skyscrapers defining its skyline, and it refused to wither and die.

I pulled into Tal's driveway crossing the point of no return. His beloved one-and-a half story, blue-shingled bungalow graced the bank of the Shrewsbury River. After a long hesitation, I approached the side door entering the kitchen and gave a polite knock. A tall, slim, bespectacled man appeared at the door. His clothes looked as if he had just crawled from deep inside a furnace. Standing before me was a living jazz guitar legend. After all the years of hearing his name, I finally stood before him.

In his gentle, soft-spoken North Carolina drawl, he asked if he could help me. I introduced myself and apologized for appearing unannounced at his home. I explained I was in the area and was interested in studying with him. I reminded him that I had sent a recording demonstrating my playing. He acknowledged receiving the tape and thanked me. He apologized for not inviting me in because his wife was ill. I apologized once again for my impertinence and we agreed the next time I was in the area, I'd call and set up a lesson appointment.

In my first lesson, for $50, Tal sat knee to knee with me in his living room for four straight hours. At $12.50 an hour, he wasn't doing this for the money. Tal loved to play, and I got to enjoy the unique privilege of sitting and absorbing every chord and melody note he spun. Like a master weaver sitting at his sonic loom, he created every imaginable harmonic dressing and attire on a song form. Everything he played entered my ears as confident, roaring whispers. He mastered the ability to make traversing the sonic landscape, through the neck of his beloved blond prototype Gibson Tal Farlow model, seem as though he was always exploring new ground.

I noticed that he was using a limited number of devices. Resolving this startling contradiction happened when I figured this must be the whole secret to creating your own artistic voice—self-imposed limitations on what you use to create the greatest number of variations in what you want to say. This is the essence of the artistic voice, the path by which you separate yourself from the multitude of improvising musicians to create a singular identity that is quickly identified and remembered to be styled as a player. Tal presented himself as a gentle giant who chose to cast light instead of shadow.

The drive home from the lesson was rain-soaked and wind-driven. It was a perfect metaphor for the jazz cleansing I received in Tal's living room—baptism by bebop. I took my time to process and reflect on this transformative event. I concluded this day as the culmination of every instance of reference to the name Tal Farlow I ever experienced over my life.

I prepared for what awaited me and the commitment to follow through. Yeah, the follow-through: probably the most useful lesson my father ever imparted to me. When Dad introduced me to the golf swing at the age of five, he made damn sure I understood the importance of the follow-through. His advice always stayed with me as a quality-of-life lesson reaching well beyond the limits of its original intent. Sadly, Dad never followed his own advice through to the end.

The challenge of the work that lay ahead came easy. I never felt more justified or alive. Tal laid his gifts before me in the purest possible way—firsthand wisdom, with a second chance for me to return, and no expectations.

Spin Cycle

In the five years from 1993 to 1998, like the 52,560 hours between 1971 and 1975, I took on hyper-drive permutations in the Spiral. Alex and Anna continued growing into their pre-teen lives with relatively little turmoil. My marriage to Laurie seemed more or less stable, although, after several years of marriage, I still faced a difficult time accepting any claim, beyond our children, to what we created. It always felt like I was stacking one emotional stilt on top of another in order to find the center to justify believing, not merely assuming such a self-conscious belief.

The bond with my children grew in ways I could never imagine and the quality of our time spent together never faltered. I had no expectation for them to take on more than they could handle, and I kept a sizable part of my mind and heart clear for them to find shelter whenever they needed it.

In 1992, the National Endowment of the Arts awarded me the honor of a Jazz Fellowship grant to continue my private studies with Tal. One of the outcomes of my lessons was a book I wrote called, *The Jazz Style of Tal Farlow*. Tal was one of those players who brought a lot of wonder and not a little mystery in his approach to the instrument. In fact, no one ever published an in-depth examination of his style. Here was a running vacuum, so I filled it.

Tal later told me that someone from *Guitar Player* magazine attempted to do this but the entire project came to a grinding halt. The writer they sent to his house, after watching Tal play up close for a few minutes, sat back and with a look of total stupefaction, said, "You can't do that on the guitar." Tal politely stood up, shook his hand, and told him the meeting and the project was over. I imagine this guy took a very long flight back to California.

Following my initial proposal to Hal Leonard Publishing, their new product development rep set up a conference call in one hour. After a short time on the phone, we agreed on a very nice deal that made Tal, me, and Hal Leonard very pleased. I had nine months to deliver the finished product. There was one small problem: I also had nine months to deliver a finished Harmony 4 textbook to Berklee. Problem solved: write and deliver both books in nine months. If a human female can handle the complexities of conceiving, carrying, and delivering twins in nine months, then I can do the same on paper with far less discomfort.

With my first album in the can, a new textbook for Berklee, and my first major book publication, my network continued expanding. Pat Harbison, from my days in Elkhart, suggested I contact a guitar player in Louisville named Jeff Sherman, who was in charge of the jazz studies program at Bellarmine College. Jeff launched an annual jazz guitar clinic and concert. He was in the process of booking the featured players for 1993. This was a perfect opportunity to reunite Tal with his friend Jimmy Raney, who was still living in Louisville, and Attila Zoller, who was also very good friends with Tal, Jimmy, and Jeff.

Jeff graciously invited me to round out a fourth slot for the clinic and concert. He also represented the closing of a small tangent on the Spiral. He had long ago befriended Howard Roberts and enjoyed a close relationship with him.

This impending appearance was my second rubber-meets-the-road opportunity. I poured all of my energies into making sure I was worthy to share the stage with these three giants.

Tal and I arrived in Louisville a few days past his 72nd birthday. He still possessed the uprightness and energy few men half his age could claim. No one, not even Tal, knew that a microscopic renegade cell in Tal's esophagus was growing.

After resting from the trip, Tal contacted Jimmy and awaited his arrival. Many years passed since these two greats had seen one another. This was their reunion. The last thing I wanted to be was an interloper, but he assured me it was fine to stay. With a knock at the door, a surge of nervous energy went through me. I was about to meet face to face someone whose playing I always admired but, like Tal, was shrouded in mystery.

In walked Jimmy, carrying a guitar case. He stood five-nine, but next to Tal's Lincoln-esque frame, he looked shorter. They gave one another a very heartfelt hello old friend embrace. I had no business being there, but before I could act on it, Jimmy introduced himself with a very warm and solid handshake. Hearing Jimmy speak for the first time, his voice had a slight rough-hewn edge that contained a distant echo of his Kentucky upbringing, likely influenced by years of smoking and heavy drinking. Voices rarely sound like what one imagines. Jimmy used his to express clear thoughts, a quick and dry sense of humor, and a very articulate quality, which proved how well-read he was.

Jimmy got down to business and took the guitar from its case. He dove into a re-harmonization on the Gershwin standard, "Someone To Watch Over Me," which he learned from their old boss, the venerable New York pianist Jimmy Lyon. Tal and Jimmy felt a lot of love and admiration for one another and too much time had passed with little to no contact.

After a quick dinner, Jimmy invited us to his solo gig. We settled into Jimmy's car with the collected remnants of everything he consumed in the past three months. Jimmy gave us fair warning that he had the worst sense of direction of any human. It took us five minutes to get out of the hotel parking lot. From my vantage point in the backseat, surrounded by ankle-deep debris and clutter, this was looking to be a fascinating evening.

It's remarkable a master musician such as Jimmy, who never met a set of chord changes that could derail him, would have such a terrible time behind the wheel of a car. Highly skilled people can compartmentalize their strengths and weaknesses. It's probably a defense mechanism the mind creates to protect the purity of the strengths; Jimmy Raney was no exception.

We arrived late to Jimmy's gig in a local bookstore, complete with harsh, florescent retail lighting, in a small, non-descript strip mall on the outskirts of downtown Louisville. Jimmy played there once a month. The owner was a huge jazz guitar fan, and when he saw Tal walk in with Jimmy, the look on his face is how I would imagine a kid would react if two favorite comic book heroes stepped off the page and came to life.

The gig was brief. Jimmy set up a stool and a small amp in a space between the fiction and philosophy aisles. Here were two of the most important jazz guitarists in the entire 20th century, creating a once-in-a-lifetime combined presence in the middle of the day—a crystalizing moment for me where the limitations of surprise surrendered in its collision with the lingering, sideswiping impact of the unreal; a surreality in its most imposing and irresponsible allure. It was enough to make my head spin.

We made our way back to the Holiday Inn for a mid-evening dinner. Jimmy did most of the talking, as he was wont to do. Without warning, a boisterous laugh followed by a gentle bear hug received by Tal and Jimmy, appeared Attila Zoller. I was in the presence of someone who lived life the way he entered a room. His broken Hungarian-accented English was going to take some getting used to. Physically, he appeared to be indestructible.

The two-day clinic finished with a public concert at Bellarmine's performance hall. The place was filled to capacity with the help of local press and TV coverage. It was obvious everyone came out to hear Tal. The set developed around each of us playing a couple of tunes with the rhythm section, and then the four of us came out and played a jam session feature. The highlight of the evening was Tal's solo version of the immortal ballad, "Stardust." The audience sat transfixed as Jimmy stood by weeping in the wings

After the concert, I spent a lot of time talking with Jimmy. Among many topics of discussion, we got around to music and specifically improvisation. Jimmy said something a bit off the wall which gave me pause. He said, "I enjoy getting lost in the changes. I think I play at my best when I'm lost."

Lost in the Changes

WEEKS HAD PASSED SINCE MY Louisville appearance and as promised, Jimmy sent me several scores of his jazz guitar quintet compositions. He was as fine a composer and arranger as he was a player. Good players typically make good writers. Along with the scores, he included several short stories he wrote in the style of S.J. Perelman, the American humorist, who was a staple of *The New Yorker* magazine for decades. Jimmy was also an acquaintance and admirer of James Thurber, another great American humorist. Jimmy's stories were every bit the high and dry quality of those he admired, and they revealed a side to the man only a handful of people knew first hand.

In December, we were making plans for me to come to Louisville to stay with him and hang out and play. When I called Jimmy to finalize the plan, his line was busy. For the next two days, I called every few hours, each time greeted with Ma Bell's torturous, yowling oscillator busy signal. I feared something was very wrong.

Late on a Sunday evening, Jimmy's girlfriend answered the phone and sounded quite upset. She was out of town over the weekend and came back to discover that one of Jimmy's many cats had knocked the phone off the hook. She knew it was a risk leaving Jimmy for a few days and to trust him to self-administer his disulfiram, which helped him control his acute alcoholism. Jimmy took his medicine, along with another pill to help relieve some of his inner ear symptoms. Unfortunately, he chose to chase the pills with two quarts of gin. The onslaught of the poisons competing for his brain's attention was too much for his lower brain stem to handle. He suffered a massive stroke, leaving him in a non-responsive, waking coma. I immediately called Attila to break the news.

The fast spreading news was a crushing blow to everyone who knew and loved the man and his music. Few were surprised that this is how he would meet his end. In August of 1994, the Louisville Jazz Society, with the help of Jamey Aebersold, put on a tribute concert for Jimmy on his 67th birthday. Attila and I flew in to join Jeff Sherman and Scott Henderson to perform in Jimmy's memory.

The next day, I was flying back to Boston. On my way to the airport, Jeff took Attila and me to see Jimmy at an extended care facility. We walked into his semi-private room, and there lay one of the 20th century's most important jazz guitar innovators, a musical progeny from the first generation to emerge out of the breast of Charlie Christian and Charlie Parker.

Jimmy's gray, oily matted hair framed a week of beard stubble. His knees were folded part-way to his chest, with his beautifully sculpted fingers, always destined to hold the guitar, poised slightly over his waist. They curled and atrophied in a way resembling the talons of a raptor about to pounce on its prey. His eyes were half-opened and his mouth slackened with his lips entwined over his teeth, his every breath causing his lower jaw to convulse with metronomic steadiness.

I stood quietly while Attila wiped away tears. He bent forward, in a bow of reverence, and gave his old and broken friend a kiss on his cheek and a hug around his neck, followed by a quiet phrase uttered in his native language. The nurse said Jimmy was conscious and aware, but unable to respond. It was pointless to speculate on what Jimmy was experiencing on the other side of his eyes and ears. I said my silent goodbye and thank you and headed to the airport. Attila stayed, refusing to leave his friend's side.

Jeff called the next day and told me of a miraculous turn of events. Attila went back to say a final goodbye before returning to New York City. Wanting a few moments with Jimmy, he entered the room alone. Jeff heard a commotion and when he rushed in, he saw Jimmy attempting to sit up and communicate with Attila. Jimmy's guttural sounds and thrashing sent Attila rushing from the room, fearing that his friend was dying, convinced that the sight of him walking into the room was the catalyst. The nurse calmed Attila and assured him Jimmy was experiencing a surge of emotion that was so strong, he summoned every trace of energy his brain could spare to reach out and make some kind of verbal and physical contact.

Jimmy Raney drew his last breath on May 9th, 1995. I recalled a conversation we had that night at Jeff's house. Our talk with Jimmy turned to life and death. He was an unapologetic, card-carrying atheist, and a fatalist about life in general. His entire life was about music, much to the neglect of other responsibilities he created. One of the last things he said, as he handed me a copy of the last album he ever recorded was, "I certainly don't want to live forever. I have a hard enough time finding something to do on a Saturday afternoon."

For a year and a half, Jimmy exercised a deep, mysterious will to live, especially in such a dreadful and prolonged state in medias res—imprisoned in a coffin of flesh with a brain no longer able to serve his every command.

I believe for nearly 500 days, he was hearing the final perfection of the music he worked all of his life to create. Any other reality is too sad and painful to contemplate. I hoped that he found himself lost in changes he never imagined, and maybe, when he made his way back, having left no line to be wrung, crowning a life of unvarnished musical brilliance, he did what every good musician will ultimately be summoned to do: he straddled the fermata and quietly waited in anticipation of the next downbeat.

Attila's Crucible

JOHN LAPORTA TOLD ME THE story about how he met and played with Attila. The year was 1959. John was a clinician at a jazz camp in Lenox, Massachusetts. Attila, full of Hungarian gypsy piss and vinegar, approached John and introduced himself. Attila barely escaped the 1948 Communist takeover of Hungary, surviving a snowy, three-day trek through the Western Carpathian Mountains. Vienna was his ultimate destination with only three possessions to his name: his guitar, three pairs of socks, and an inextinguishable will to live.

The first question out of Attila's mouth was, "Where's the beaches?"

LaPorta was a bit flummoxed with such a random question and answered, "You have to go east." Before the conversation went any further, it was time for them to take the stage to play a duet. LaPorta called a B flat blues.

After a few choruses, LaPorta wanted to play some polytonal shit, so he shifted to the key of E, expecting Attila to stay in B flat. Unbeknownst to John, Attila had perfect pitch, so Attila naturally went chasing the key changes. John went back to B flat and of course, Attila followed. For many choruses, they played this tritone cat and mouse game. Eventually John yelled at him to stay put. After the performance, Attila again asked, "So, heh mehn, where's the beaches?"

LaPorta said, "I told you, you have to go east."

Attila figured out John's confusion and said, "No, no, not the beaches. Where's the cheeks?"

Attila's multi-faceted personality was legendary. He also had a reputation for possessing an extravagant talent for his nightly hang-time in the jazz joints of New York. Attila Zoller was the absolute and undisputed hang-king of the five boroughs. He took no prisoners and left many wretched souls in his wake. Mine was no exception.

About a year after Jimmy died, Charles Carlini, a promoter from New York City, called me about his idea to organize a 75th birthday tribute concert for Tal. Charles got the JVC/Newport Jazz Festival machinery involved in the promotion and production, and the concert was set for Monday, June 24, 1996 at Merkin Hall. This was an unprecedented event, because it was the first time such a gathering of multiple generations of many of the world's foremost jazz guitarists would gather to celebrate Tal's birthday.

The promoter paired Attila with his protégé, a gifted, young Russian guitarist named Andrei Ryabov, and me. I arrived two days early to check into my hotel at the Park Central. To my surprise, the hotel was undergoing spot renovations, which were not mentioned in their advertisement. This would later become a huge problem for me.

The next morning, I took a train to Queens to meet Andre at Attila's apartment. A quick run-through of his tune was all we had planned. The rest of the day and evening left us open to hang. A sound check at two o'clock the next afternoon was the only thing on my agenda. The impact of the next several hours would remain with me for more years than I care to admit or calculate.

We began drinking during the run-through. It amounted to nothing more than a few beers between the three of us. Attila then rummaged through his cabinet and found a half-bottle of gin and cognac. We hadn't eaten much, so Attila ran out for some greasy Chinese carryout. The conviviality that started with beer deepened with each of the many toasts initiated by our gracious host.

Between laughter and discussions about how these two immigrants felt about their love for, and the uniqueness of their adopted homeland, we did a lot of listening. The time was getting on to five o'clock and Andre needed to get to Midtown to do his solo gig. We killed all of the alcohol, so Attila broke out a clump of hashish. Once our heads clouded and the air cleared, Attila offered to drive Andrei to the gig and off we went.

By the age of 42, I had logged some serious miles up and down many chemically-induced fog-bound highways. However, my excitement from being involved in this historic performance, in a city that held me spellbound since I was a child, added to the risky combinations of liquor within the cannabis buzz to create a euphoria in a class by itself—a sense of fearless freedom. I felt like a chess grandmaster who saw a thousand moves ahead, with endless combinations while playing a hundred simultaneous games blindfolded. I was experiencing the ultimate awareness—multi-synchronous transitional interfaces tangential to the Spiral. Or, maybe I was nothing more than very fucking drunk.

We dropped off Andrei and Attila decided he wanted to hear his first set. Andre was a fine young player who successfully translated a lot of Bill Evans' harmonic signature to the guitar—beautiful, lyrical, transparent textures with exquisite voice leading. During his set, Attila and I downed three more beers apiece.

Our next destination was West 42nd Street to hear Gene Bertoncini play his regular solo gig. The moment we walked into the place, the bartender immediately poured us a double single malt scotch, neat. This was my apex of the night. If I had the good sense to call it then and there, I'd have gone back to my room and collapsed with a reasonable expectation of sleeping it off. The greasy Chinese food from earlier in the day was long gone. Too many moments took on a larger-than-life reality, but I was bound and determined to hang in there with this gypsy madman, brain damage or not.

We said our goodbyes and headed downtown to the West Village to another jazz joint. We each downed four beers during the short set. By some miracle of the cooperation of unseen benevolent forces of nature, we got out of there and drove to one final spot Attila wanted to hit before closing: Bradley's.

By now it was well after midnight. Attila ordered each of us a very large vessel of tequila with a Heineken chaser. A quick inventory of my senses revealed I was fucked-up beyond recognition. I turned my head and sputtered, "Attila, I can't do this anymore!" He never turned his head in my direction. He sat staring straight ahead with the beer bottle slowly coming to his lips, greeted by a malevolent, guttural laugh in his native Hungarian. How the fuck can someone laugh in a foreign language? Whew!

I turned to step off the barstool, and that's when the entire helix collapsed at my feet, as if God threw his lariat from across eternity, and just missed His mark. Time and Space saluted me a fond farewell. I stood firm against the outside wall of Bradley's, attempting to figure out if I still represented a generic living embodiment of who, what, when, where, and especially why. The absolutely random shit that goes through one's mind in such a stupefied state of spifflication is quite remarkable, and not a little scary.

Attila came barging out of the door with a huge slam against the outside wall. He was part walking, part running, part stumbling, and listing forward while laughing his ass off. He fell headfirst into the driver's seat as I slithered into the passenger seat. From 14th Street, for the 43 blocks to 57th Street, he drove 60 miles an hour without stopping because he caught an unending cycle of green lights. Park Avenue was transformed into Zollerstrasse for the Attila Zollercoaster. He put in a cassette tape at full volume with his interview by Terry Gross, featuring his music and life story for her regular spot on National Public Radio. The interview was nearly impossible to hear because his constant laughter reached a fevered maniacal pitch. I believed Attila Zoller finally lost his mind.

Welcome To The Gig, Jun-ya

THE FINAL SCENE OF THIS preposterous evening played out as the car came to a screeching, fishtailing halt in front of the Park Central doorway. I forced my hands to open the door and I spilled out onto the curb. After I was clear of the door, he sped off down 7th Avenue with the forward thrust forcing my door to slam closed. The elevator arrived, and upon entering my room, I fell forward and collapsed across the bed and died.

I awoke unaware of time, space, or location. The television was on from the day before, tuned to a 24-hour news station. All evidence pointed to the fact that it was still 1996, and the date was Monday, June 24th, the day of the concert. I was so dehydrated my contact lenses bonded to my corneas, which meant any attempt to remove them would have resulted in spending the rest of my days with a white cane and a German Shepherd. As the blur began to clear, the details of the previous night replayed in painful detail.

Then, the Great Liver Rebellion began. I crawled to the toilet and began a bilious five-minute ritual of medieval retching. There was nothing inside me to satisfy the sacrificial offering demanded by the porcelain god, Commodious. I attempted to take a shower. Warm rushing water usually helped me get straight after a night of self-inflicted torture. The very sound of running water sent me back to dry heaves. I returned to the bathroom floor to assume the position of supplicant to this importunate, although obscure Roman deity, and I better come up with something for him. The best I could do was to go deep and re-gurgitate my ankle bone.

I made several complete circuits between the bed, the toilet, the shower, the toilet, and back to the bed. No relief was in sight. I was suffering from al-cohol poisoning. Panic set in because there was no way I could do this concert.

The opportunity to play the most important and high-profile gig of my life, in honor of my friend, was about to vanish like a cheap magic trick. I called Tal nearly in tears to explain what happened. His dramatically drawn out drawled response was, "Ohhh nooo, don't cross swords with Attila." His advice came 24 hours too late. I told him I wouldn't be able to do the gig. He said to get some food and water and suggested saltines and tomato juice. The sound check was at two and the show started at eight. If I could just get through the sound check, I would have several hours to continue my detox.

My fears about the spot renovations came true. The sound of hammers on cold chisels came from the bathroom next to mine. Once the anvilation stopped, there was a brief interlude. I took advantage of the silence to apologize to Malleus, Incus, and Stapes, which had taken refuge deep in my otic pit.

The torture continued with toxic fumes of industrial strength contact cement drifting and gliding under my door. Placing wet bath towels against the threshold did little to stem the pervasive waft. It was the same shit we used to sniff on the streets of Kentland for a cheap, drunken high. I had to get to the street level to find a minimum of two parts per billion of oxygen. That may have been too much to hope for in New York City's rush hour. It was nine in the morning and the heat on the street already reached 80 degrees. The smog was thick and the inverted air mass hadn't budged for days. I never before felt so much welcome relief.

And So Shows The Go

I WASN'T GOING TO ALLOW alcohol poisoning to keep me from playing the gig. The saltines and tomato juice helped me feel nearly sub-human, so I could dress and get a taxi to a few blocks north of Lincoln Center. As I waited for Attila and Andrei to arrive, an enormous thirst came over me. What an odd combination of sensations: freezing my ass off in an overly air conditioned theater and the desiccation of every cell in my body. I was now in the same freeze-dried existence as a jar of Taster's Choice coffee.

Attila came barging in the main door the same way he came out of Bradley's the night before, only this time, he was cold sober—a loud, boisterous laugh along with an un-tentative forward motion upright on the downslope of the floor. He could see how I was still at a level five hangover and he offered no comment. He got home with no problem, slept for three hours, got up and ran five miles, and then swam—impressive for someone who turned 69 a few weeks earlier. I was in no shape to carry on a conversation with anyone with any amount of energy and coherency. Tal made sure I was feeling well enough to play, and by the time we took the stage, which was early in the program, I was reasonably detoxed.

The jazz royalty who showed up to not only perform, but also to listen was quite spectacular. Johnny Smith—the legendary guitarist who composed "Walk, Don't Run!"—flew in from his quiet, retired life in Colorado Springs. He delivered a speech at intermission which was a funny and loving tribute to his dear old friend. Phil Schapp, the premier New York City jazz disc jockey and master jazz historian, took care of master of ceremonies. It was heartening to see many of Tal's friends, guitar notables such as Don Arnone, Billy Bauer, and Tony Mottola, reunited backstage with Tal among many hugs of affection and kisses on the cheek. The show was sold out, including the national press.

The magnitude and gravity of this night began to blanket me. I could feel the remaining effects of the toxins morph and settle into hunger, with exhaustion tinged by intermittent rushes of adrenaline. I stayed in the shadows until it was our turn to take the stage. The less I said and interacted with those waiting to play, the more I could save my physical and mental energies for the performance.

The moment we stepped out into the lights to the applause of approval and expectation, a strange sensation of calm came over me. I believed that every person in those seats wanted what I wanted: for every player to be successful in their highest possible level of performance. I think stage fright is one of the most irrational fears, unless one can otherwise prove that the paying public desires failure on the part of the performer.

The performance went fine, and then exit stage left we went. As much as I enjoyed the moment, the whole evening for me started to take on a feeling of letdown. I was as emotionally and physically drained as I can ever recall.

Johnny Smith's testimonial was an unforgettable highlight. After several minutes of singing Tal's praises as an innovative jazz guitarist, and an old and loyal friend, he finished with a story about the first time he ever heard Tal:

Johnny had invited his friend Art Carney to join him to hear this new guitarist everyone in New York was raving about. Tal had a week-long engagement in some new venue, which was essentially a restaurant. The man who owned the club was from another country and unfamiliar with American customs of public decorum. Unfortunately, he owned a violin and proudly brought it to the club every night; never a good sign. The man would impose himself and his violin on whatever unsuspecting musician happened to be in the middle of a song.

With Tal holding court on center stage, the owner struck like a cheap monster from a 1950s horror movie. Tal had complete command of the room and it was too much for this pathetic little man to bear. From the shadows of the stage, he charged at Tal, flailing his arms while screaming at the top of his lungs, in his broken accented English, "Stop! Stoppa da bip bop! No more uh da bippity bop!" He then proceeded to saw away with unbridled abuse on this poor classical instrument.

The rude interruption of Tal, followed by such screeching gibberish assaulting every auditory canal in the room, was too much for Art Carney to take, and the fact that the actor had consumed a lot of liquor didn't help matters. Johnny Smith stood by and watched this comic legend proceed to charge the stage to take apart this emperor wannabe. One thing led to another, and a minor scuffle ensued. The room cleared, except for Mr. Carney, who was beyond apoplectic.

THIS UNPRECEDENTED NIGHT OF TAL'S celebration went on for over three hours. Historically, Tal wasn't always as technically consistent a player as others of his generation, but for this evening, he was as brilliant and on top of his game at the age of 75 as he was 40 years earlier. In its silence, the renegade cell in Tal's esophagus was growing ever stronger with each passing month.

After the hall cleared out, everyone was going to the Iridium to hang out and continue the party, with Les Paul holding down his regular Monday night gig. I feared the combination of cigarette smoke and free flowing booze would send me right back to throwing up my one remaining ankle. I begged off and began hailing a cab back to the hotel when suddenly, an arm locked around my elbow. I turned to see a small, attractive woman in her early seventies gazing up with a huge smile as she said, "Come on honey, you can take me to the Iridium." I didn't recognize her as someone I ever formally met. There was a vague familiarity to her face, like she was someone I remembered seeing in a photo, or as a performer on an old television show. Maybe she was a legendary chanteuse who was fading into the sunset of a career that graced the finest New York clubs and cabarets. Maybe she was Blossom Dearie.

I thanked her for her interest and politely refused. I was too depleted to sustain any normal regenerative process on the most basic cellular level. In short, I was still sick as a motherfucker. With the help of Lou Levy and Wayne Wright, I aimed for the Carnegie Deli for their mile-high corned beef and pastrami sandwich, and half of a Black Forest cake, and then retired to my room. If I was going to throw up this time, at least I would have given my body something to celebrate.

Vic Juris and his wife happened to be approaching and saw this scene unfolding between this delightfully elegant, but insistent lady, and me. They glanced back and after a quick exchange of words, Vic offered, "Come on Blossom, you can go with us." She released my arm and walked to the waiting couple.

The next morning at checkout, I went on a three-minute tirade about the multiple sensory assaults I endured with the renovation next to my room. If I knew in advance the hotel was undergoing the facelift, I would have stayed elsewhere. They knocked $50 off of the bill and invited me to come again. I barely made it to Penn Station in time for the train back to Boston.

Homage for Talmage

Far too many years had passed since Tal Farlow made an appearance in the Boston area. On April 25th, 1997, the Talmage drought ended with one very special night at Ryle's Jazz Club, a small and storied venue nestled between Harvard and MIT. One of the major celestial events of the 20th century—the beginning of the post-perihelion phase of the Great Comet of 1997, better known as Comet Hale-Bopp—illuminated the poetic beauty of this special evening. For the time being, the spelling changed to Hail Bop.

Talmage packed his car with a small suitcase, his favorite guitar, his famous launching pad footstool and amp, and an unwavering smile of joy and gratitude, to make an appearance that would put a meager $500 in his pocket for the entire enterprise. He set off alone from Sea Bright, New Jersey, and drove nearly five hours to our home in Brookline.

The next day we headed to WHRB for an interview. Tal didn't enjoy talking about himself. He tolerated the intrusive questions for the sake of business. He was also from a generation of jazz musicians who rejected the codified academic sterility of a place like Berklee to spell out the language of the idiom.

His generation's musical and artistic development relied on the necessity of learning the popular repertoire as the pliant foundation for expressing their improvisational prowess. They all learned on the bandstand; high-risk and seat-of-the-pants. Tal and his peers held the formal academics of the jazz education industry in varying degrees of contempt. They expressed their constant criticisms with comments such as, "These college kids don't know any tunes," or "They always sound like they're playing scales when they solo." These were accurate and fair generalizations on both accounts. Attila could be brutal with such assessments. Tal was a gentleman about such matters. Jimmy Raney, as the most academically minded of the three, was objectively somewhere in between.

I assembled one of the best rhythm sections in Boston for this event. Joe Hunt, who got his start in Stan Getz's early 1960s group, took the drum chair and John Repucci occupied the bass chair. Ryle's was completely sold out for Tal, with many disappointed people turned away at the door. Local jazz radio programmers and jazz reviewers for the *Boston Globe* and *Boston Herald* were equally enthusiastic and gave it the respect and attention it deserved—a rare event never again duplicated. This was Tal's night. No one understood its importance better than I.

I took the stage to introduce the band and to say a few words about him I hoped hadn't already been said. I reminded everyone that directly outside of the enormous plate glass windows was the Hail Bop Comet in all of its visible glory. Tal greeted the introduction with his customary smile as he waited off-stage. He assumed his center spot on his launching pad, with the loping grace of Roald Dahl's big, friendly giant, clutching his blond Gibson. The way he held his instrument reminded me of Paul Bunyan, wielding his axe as he cut a huge swath through any chord changes standing in his way. Tal kicked us off with a bright tempo blues, and his show was underway. After the first number, I vacated the stage for Tal to take over the set. The history this man contained in the deepest marrow of his bones was nothing short of marvelous.

By this night, Tal had worked professionally for over 50 years. The gigs always came to him. He never had to knock on a door for work. All he did was answer, if he chose to do so, otherwise, he would paint someone a sign to pay his bills, and finish his day content in his living room with his beloved wife, Tina, always nearby. He played his heart out for her, for himself, and the knotty pine walls surrounding them in their small blue cottage on the bank of the Navesink river, a block from the Atlantic Ocean, on the planet Earth, in a solar system at the distant edge of the Milky Way galaxy—one of 200 billion in the universe, as one of untold numbers in the multiverse.

Hail Bop continued to leave behind its perihelion point, blazing a path, inviting Tal to follow, but only when he finished what he had to say. He carved beautiful lines from changes, the chords having no choice but to surrender willingly, with their undying gratitude to this master. He painted sonic landscapes with the songs he always loved, using the same chromatic palette he always used, but with a different outcome each time. The crowd sat in total silence as they held onto his every note.

Before I retook my corner on the stage to finish out the first set, Tal took time to lay before us a solo rendition of the Harold Arlen classic, "Last Night When We Were Young." I now understood the tears Jimmy Raney poured one long ago night in Louisville.

During our final set, Tal launched into "I've Got The World On A String." He finished his solo and to my great surprise turned to me offstage, and over the rhythm section, yelled for me to join him, to "Come on and get some of this." I took this as one more display of the enormous generosity in this man's heart.

During his several choruses, he filled me a plate of perfect al dente jazz, and, like a father inviting a hungry child to the table, he let me have my say as a response to all of the love he served. His accompaniment for me as I soloed, his response to my response to him, was some of the most secure and loving musical embrace I ever experienced in my professional life.

Tal Farlow's musical progeny are too numerous to mention over his more than half-century of occupying a first-row throne in the Chambers of Jazz Guitar. On this night in celebration of two rare celestial appearances, both of equal magnitude, Talmage Farlow was the father of everyone who ever picked up the instrument. After the show ended, he stayed for more than an hour to greet fans and erstwhile acquaintances. The man loved people and always signed an album or a guitar.

As I got behind the wheel to drive us back to Brookline, I glanced skyward toward the increasingly unnoticeable post-peak position of Hail Bop. The astronomers and astrophysicists already calculated that the comet would still be observable with telescopes up until the year 2020, as it neared 30th magnitude. Afterward, it would fade into the background of all the other space dust and debris of eternity. Hail Bop wouldn't reappear to the inhabitants of Earth until the year 4385. The deadly renegade cells in the system of the Meteor-man sitting next to me were now well-established and completely unstoppable.

Extoller for Zoller

ATTILA DIDN'T CARRY THE SAME historical weight and cache as Tal, but he was a loved and respected presence in the world of jazz guitar, and he enjoyed his legion of friends and fans. After Tal's appearance at Ryle's, I offered the same opportunity to Attila. He accepted the invitation, especially because he didn't have to travel far from his Vermont getaway to get to Boston. Joe Hunt was once again on drums and the bassist was Dave Clark. Both of them had history with Attila and were as solid a rhythm section as you'd find anywhere in the world.

The differences in the personalities between Attila and Tal existed on many levels. Tal carried himself with a towering, gentle grace, and a slight forward curve in his upper back; Attila moved forward with a jubilant, barrel-chested prance, as his eyes scanned the periphery for signs of mischief. Neither man suffered fools, but one became quiet with an air of indifference, while the other would verbally disassemble an adversary for about 15 seconds, at a temperature that rivaled the melting point of carborundum, and then would return with a gentle landing. Tal didn't drink. He came to terms with his alcoholism in the early 1980s. Attila never came to terms with his and wore his capacities as a badge of honor.

Attila and the band were tearing up the airwaves. Mitch Seidman, a former student and friend of Attila's and a Berklee colleague, showed up and joined us on Attila's blues tribute to Kenny Burrell. Gray Sargent, Tony Bennett's guitarist, also took time to stop in and catch the last set. The evening turned out to be looser than Tal's show, but united with the common bond of love and respect in all jazz musicians. It was the love of the music and the never-ending dynamics of the constantly moving, ephemeral mind of the improviser. It's a rarefied world. If every non-musician could undergo what the jazz musician experiences from the inside out, the discernment and sanctity for life in every human soul would lift to unimaginable heights. The improviser's tale envisions the deepest realities in proliferating freedom and love—where the barrier between the one who hears what there is to tell, no longer divides the one who can tell there's something to hear. There is no mystery, no enigma, and no riddle. There is simply truth in four dimensions.

Not long after the Ryle's show, colon cancer came calling on Attila's dance card. His operation was successful for only the short term. In the truest spirit of this indomitable musician, he was back on the bandstand, against all doctor's orders, for a three-night engagement at Birdland with his old friends Lee Konitz and Don Friedman. He was still drinking and smoking and living every last moment the way he chose to live: with all the windows down and blazing through an extended cycle of green lights at 60 miles an hour.

Attila became too sick to be alone in his Queens apartment. He took refuge in Townsend, Vermont among friends, where he slipped further into the end of his life. On January 25th, 1998, Mitch Seidman and I played a duo gig. The interaction between us was particularly strong, in light of the fact this was our first time playing together. Maybe our energy stemmed from the fact that our friend lay dying not two hours away. This moment was an unspoken homage to Attila.

Attila Zoller drew his last breath on that same day, in his 71st year. At his time of death, Mitch and I were in the middle of our second set, playing the old standard, "I'm Getting Sentimental Over You." If Attila could have been there, he would have situated himself between us with guitar in hand, a smirk and a glint and a quick glance from side to side, and said, "Okay, now let's play some sheet, mehn."

A Song That Will Not Die

TAL WAS BECOMING INCREASINGLY UNWELL with each passing month. He had a desire to record a solo album, the one format in which he never recorded. I was planning all of the technical arrangements to record him in his Sea Bright living room. It was a place of familiar surroundings and great comfort that he loved for 40 years. He became much too sick to make this a reality; an immeasurable loss to the jazz guitar world as the one final piece of Tal's entire recorded legacy.

The severity of his illness was a well-guarded secret from the public. He left his Sea Bright home to live out his days in their condo near Lincoln Center. Tal and his second wife Michele were hopeful for a radical new treatment developed in Israel, based on a drug developed around some kind of photosynthetic concept requiring Tal to avoid direct sunlight for a period of about six months. One of the strange side effects was a slight change in his pigmentation; he described it as a light, greenish hue. Michele and her mother gave him round-the-clock attention, with close access to Sloan-Kettering when the time came for palliative care.

Here was this gentle soul, who never chose for his musical brilliance to cast shadows, living his last days with shades drawn in filtered darkness, until the welcome sight of sunset, where the artificial illumination of incandescence provided some relief until the next sunrise. Tal waited with hope to fulfill a one-in-10 chance success story. For many, this is irony at its most sadistic and a desecration of justice as justness; for Talmage, this was simply life.

We visited by phone as often as he was up for talking. I asked him one question: how was he doing with all of this? He heard the meaning behind my words implying the question of how he was doing facing his imminent death.

He answered without hesitation, "I'm fine with it." There was no easy reply I could give to his answer. That was all he had to say about it. It was all I needed to hear. We both knew once our conversation was over, we would never again speak to one another.

I stayed on the phone in silence for a long time. Through my tears, all I could say was, "Thank you for everything. I love you." With a strained and weakened voice, he replied in kind.

On the kitchen counter was a piece of formal notepaper left by Laurie with a painful combination of one noun, one verb: "Tal died." This was news I was expecting, but no amount of expectation could soften the loss. I reached out to Michele. There was a sense of calmness and relief that beset her feeling of profound loss. I asked her how he handled his last days and hours. She said from even the earliest days of his diagnosis, he never once complained about anything. His pain in the last week became unbearable. When it was time to summon an ambulance to transport him to Sloan-Kettering, everyone knew he would never return.

As the paramedics wheeled him from the bedroom through the living room, he requested they stop next to Michele's mother. Tal took her by the hand and drew her closer so he could look her in the eyes and whispered, "I want to thank you for everything you have done for me." He released her hand and the journey from the living room continued down the hall to the ambulance waiting at the door.

Talmage Holt Farlow died on July 25th, 1998, early in his 77th year, and much too early in a life well-lived and well-loved. He left a deep and indelible impact on everyone who knew him and his music and his humanity.

When I first sought him out, after so many years hearing only his name, I was hoping, at most, for some brief guidance to set me steady of the tracks of the jazz train. Instead, his music and his life opened me to invaluable, vital lessons of how best to live and how best to die. For me, this was Tal's legacy: If you live well, you will die well. When I often think of my friend, I'm always reminded of a section of the lyric to "Stardust." "You wander down the lane and far away, leaving me a song that will not die…"

(12!)

THE FALL OF 2001 SEMESTER started my 17th year at Berklee. I awoke to the radio set to the local news channel. What made this morning different from all the other Tuesdays was the war starting on the soil of our homeland, under and against the clearest, deepest Marian blue skies.

It was a vicious and unprovoked sneak attack brought on by an enemy mired in the values of a seventh century religious tribal mentality refusing to make its way in the tenants of 21st century civilization—an Enemy from the Stone Age, attacking their Enemy from the Byte Age representing the inarguable ideal that mankind can survive in this world, but only if allowed to live as free individuals to make choices as our volitional nature demands; free to err, lapse, blunder, and fumble; free to succeed, triumph, flourish and thrive; first for the self and then for others.

There was no room in the mind of this enemy to understand that beyond the desire and choice to raise a family, the truly free individual aspires to owing nothing to anyone, and no one owing anything to them outside of clearly defined limitations of a mutually beneficial relationship. This attack was the baby boom generation's Pearl Harbor and nearly 3,000 fellow Americans died in three separate locations in a brief two hours. The world as we knew it had changed forever. The world as we would come to know it would unfold as a miasma of distress, against which the traditional barriers of defense operating under the old rules of Cold War geopolitics wouldn't apply.

The hyper-driven evolution of communication technology bringing changes to the state-of-the-art shifted from a multi-year timeline to one of multi-weeks, adding a layer of weaponry the Enemy from the Stone Age would learn to use only selectively, and with no concern for preserving anyone's right to freedom and privacy. In response to the shrouded and non-transparent nature of asymmetrical warfare, we, the Enemy from the Byte Age, strapped ourselves in ethical and moral irons, struggling to find the perfect balance between protecting the rights of the individual and the political ergonomics to preserve our creed.

We turned inward fearing not only these vicious throwbacks, but also fearing ourselves. The participation trophy, among the more serious deflections from reality called "no judgment, no value, or otherwise," eventually became America's post-9/11 mollifier for our children: a fatuous cultural hollow, complete with badges of unearned self-esteem and a viral sense of entitlement, wrapped in the trappings of "feel first, think later, or better yet, don't think at all, because thinking leads to judgement." After the last and final trophy has been handed out, the only decision left to make is who gets the entropy.

Any vestiges of the values I embraced through my drug-fueled indoctrination at the Village, especially moral equivalence, fell with those people, buildings, and planes. I knew the world my children would have to live in from that moment on would never be the same. My hope was they would understand why, by standing behind the ideals of their inherited birthright; the aspirational reach to something above and beyond the basest impulses of a human's nature to dominate their fellow man. My fear was of some officially sanctioned indoctrination to convince them this attack was a deserved and just punishment on us. Only time would tell.

The following day, I boarded the D train for Berklee. The shock and anger of the events from the day before was in need of balance and relief. I sat on the nearly empty train when my sorrow heard the call, and took its rightful place in the middle of my soul. All of those people going to work to make their living for themselves and their families; all of those first responders who would never again answer the call. I couldn't help but think of Ronnie and all of the years he put his life on the line to save people he didn't know, and rarely ever saw unless he was stumbling over the dead in the dark of a burned-out room. My cousin was also in the thick of the Pentagon attack, functioning in the role of a field commander. He had no idea if a second attack was coming that would wipe out him and everyone else on both sides of those historical and once-invincible walls.

As I sat on the train in tears, an unusual movement caught my attention. I looked down and there she was—an unexpected and welcome appearance from a very old friend: the ladybug whose life I saved at the edge of the backyard pool 25 years before. It was unmistakably her because when I put my left index under her legs, she crawled from the first joint of the finger, and left the same mark and imprint from the first time I encountered her—(12!).

She continued crawling down my finger. Without stopping, she traced the entire outline of my hand. When she reached the left pinky, I transferred the ladybug to my left thumb and she completed the circuit; her version of the Spiral. From there, I joined the two thumbs and she made her way across the Pollex Bridge, and continued to repeat the same tracing outline of my right hand. Astonishment washed over me as I felt my mood change from exceptional sadness to one of drowsy calm and quiet. The only sound I was aware of was the train in contact with the rails.

Her timing was such so that the moment she paused on my right thumb, the D pulled into the station. She was in complete control of my central nervous system. I made my way up the stairs to the landing before the street level. She turned her back to me and raised her wings, exactly like she did at the swimming pool. I took my time bringing her up to eye level. Her wings spread and the network of membranes I remembered appeared and began to fluctuate like the images inside a kaleidoscope. The chambers continued to divide into smaller partials, until I could see all 479,001,600 reflecting chambers.

As the image intensified, I felt the sensation of slight levitation. From the softest whisper, the sound of the Chord emanated from the rapid beating of her wings. Instead of coming at me head-on, the harmony seemed to start from inside the center of my brain, and like a pebble dropped into a pond, the music spread outward in every possible direction across Time and Space. The timbre of the sound was breathtaking and possibly of another world; a sound like no man-made instrument ever created.

The terminal point of all harmonic possibilities sounded like a new beginning. The chord expressed a resonant beauty so deep, for one brief moment of relief, I was able to experience my existence as if none of the pain I held so long and so deep in my soul ever happened. I was free from all of the memories of fear, hate, anger, and abuse. The ladybug's healing touch was her show of gratitude for having saved her life.

After she accomplished what she set out to do, she flew into the subway tunnel. "Ladybug, ladybug, fly away alone…" I glanced down at my right thumb. On the tip, where the lady brought me back to life without the dark, the same image as before appeared again— (12!)—then it slowly faded. Instead of disappearing, the image became a dark red rivulet streaming its way to gather and pool on the top of the web of my right hand, and absorbed by my original tattoo from 1967. The transformation was more than a reminder. Her secret was now my secret.

Satin Ceilings and Mirrored Floors

THE SPIRAL NEVER DISAPPOINTS WITH the endless opportunities to glance downward and backward to moments and events that anticipate many life-changing occurrences. Not every moment has equal value to another in such long-term foretelling. Some things just sit there, indifferent to what came before and after it. However, everything has a purpose to enable transitions from one convergence to the next, where I enjoy the outcome as repetition through contrast.

Of all the incalculable nodes in my Penrose pinwheel, I often reflect down on the original from-out-of-nowhere appearance of Larry Miller. I believe if Larry had lived long enough, he would have innovated a psycho-interior decoration concept of satin ceilings and mirrored floors. With mirrored floors, even when you are looking down, you are still looking up. With satin ceilings, once you go crashing into your upper limits, the luxury of a soft hit awaits. He likely would have included a high-quality turndown drug to make settling into the satin cocoon a little more delightful. Larry was a brilliant artistic conceptual thinker, but he was never satisfied with his natural skills, because he lived in constant denial of his true self.

The long-standing mystery of how, in 1972, Larry walked into a Washington, D.C. ghetto apartment with my beat-down Gretsch and returned an hour later with a marvelous new Telecaster was finally solved. I was told he offered up his bisexual hooker skills and traded a sexual favor in exchange for my exchange, for no reason other than to solve a problem which was entirely mine. His secret was now mine to tell. He disappeared from my life much the same way he appeared…poof! I was never able to say goodbye to Larry. I will never forget him.

Surround and Drown

Separation anxiety has been an unshakable constant for me. By now, that reality has been well documented. It's embedded to my core. I can't pin down when I first experienced it. The affliction may be an imprint from my mother, for whom the general condition of anxiety was more of a conceptual work-around than a problem. If my father suffered it, he attempted to bury it alive with gambling and whisky. My emotional sclerosis likely started long ago in Greenbelt, when my father caught my mother in bed with Willie, and I watched Dad beat her half to death. Someway, somehow, it always comes back to trust.

My lack of confidence in my parents permeated the air and cast a pall over everything during our early home life. The night my father went to jail for holding up the loan company may have been the moment awakening this lifelong, emotionally crippling condition. Mom's hateful and oft-stated buzz-words of imminent abandonment contributed their invisible power of fear and persuasion—she simply wasn't trustworthy. Mom presented her values as a desperate woman and mother with no reasonable expectation to succeed in both responsibilities. This undermined any moral standing in persuading me to follow in her furrows. She made navigating through the challenges of life far more difficult than life itself.

My need to be in the company of a validating female grew with high intensity through my adolescent years, and into my twenties. My outlook on interpersonal relationships was always informed by so many convoluted signals. I likened my state of mind to what happens to a glass of water when a child cleans a watercolor brush over and over until the initial cleaning and the beautiful red or blue from the first swish has disappeared, and a sludgy sewage brown tint is looking out at you.

The anxiety was less intense in my twenties because I was so rarely without the company of people, but it was more than the mere physical presence of friends and acquaintances. If I grew an attachment to a woman with an inadequate attempt at commitment, a prolonged separation would trigger lonely desperation to the point of obsession. I never felt it with men.

Time spent on the road was tantamount to a kid being given an all-day pass with unlimited access to all of the rides and concessions, but the barkers still lurked to make sure I measured the minimum height to get on certain rides. "Sorry kid, you have to be this tall to strap in."

The strains of my emotional shortcomings, wrapped in empty bravura, sent a signal to the mile-high antenna of any emotionally grounded woman in range. Holding only one ticket to punch, she wasn't going to waste it on me. I made the choice to leave the road, and the two years I spent with Lisa was the consummation of my first 30, doomed to not end well, because making choices to layer confusion on top of fear on top of confusion never does.

When Anna and Alex were born, I was living an emotional duality. On one hand, there is the incomparable joy that comes with the birth of your children. It brought me an ironic anti-stability as happiness wrapped in hyper-vigilance, with my pan-seared disposition for the 2,000-yard stare. I was as much a nervous a parent as I was a loving father, and added to that the intensity of my anxiety, which was at its most palpable when I was out of town or worse, out of the country. My fear of distance from those closest to me was distracting to the point of stasis.

Laurie and I worked hard to give our children the best of what we brought to the marriage. We worked equally hard to avoid opening the baggage of accumulated shit we all grind and extrude through our well-intended lives. My problem was in the long-held belief that I could achieve resolution and elimination of all the shit without opening the box. All I accomplished was imposing a Houdini solution on Schrodinger that was destined to fail before I could start. Toward the end, my marriage resembled a stopped clock—right for only two out of 1,444 minutes in the day.

There are many parallels between the nature of so many failed relationships with the women in my life and my relationship with Laurie. However, the one difference that made my relationship with her singularly unique was the perfect convergence of a basic shared value: our children. We loved one another enough to establish a reasonable foundation for starting a family. As time wore on, our expectations to sustain the more tender side of being in love, and our worldview in general, grew further apart. Disappointment overtook our remaining affections for one another.

To live with trust in my life, it would have to be of my own creation. I would have to bring it forth from within, with a very idealized goal of honorable-beyond-reproach to everyone in my life, from those closest to me to the other extreme with the strangers who inadvertently brush against me.

It's unrealistic to believe that the heart can survive on trust alone. Trust is only a means to an end. Trust relies on fixed values, but it's not a one-dimensional fixed state of mind. It's a dynamic and ever-shifting multi-faceted organism that works to preserve and protect the deepest reaches of one's moral and ethical sense of life. Trust is born of the best attributes of the mind and heart, and like a spider's web, possesses resilient strength containing many times its own weight, but also a delicate, translucent fragility able to withstand only so much negative force before it's torn to shreds and hopelessly abandoned.

Alone and relaxed in front of my open living room window in Brookline, during perfect weather in the gloaming of the day, accompanied by the seductive, susurrant choir of leaves from two old European beech trees, punctuated by the sound of a squirrel dropping the husks of half-eaten beechnuts on the driveway, the spells of intense melancholy increased—the same haunting sensations from when I walked along the Greenbelt pathways of my childhood, all of those lifetimes ago.

The mysterious warm flush in my chest, radiating throughout the rest of my body, was an intoxicant denigrating all other intoxicants. I felt transported to another place and time; maybe a place and time from long ago, or maybe a place and time yet to be? The ache of yearning always brought me to the brink of immobility, and nothing felt lonelier, or more futile, than this invisible force powerful enough to take on a life of its own—a place I found equally difficult to be and difficult to leave.

A failed marriage is never easy on children, especially young kids. I was an undisputed expert in that field; Laurie knew it only in theory. She grew up in the quintessential middle class suburban world of 'til death do they part. Death takes many forms and it impacts every aspect of existence.

In the end, Laurie and I stayed true to our absolute belief that above all else, she was the mother of my children and I was the father of her children, and anything short of a respectful and amicable dissolution of the marriage, for the good of all, was unacceptable. And then…

The Setting May Break, But...

...I AWOKE ALONE IN A strange double bed that folded into a small beige-colored couch. I was in a strange room, in the back part of a strange building; an old two-story house divided into several studio apartments. The heat of August of 2006 was brutal. I was living at the end a drippy air conditioner, exactly like the ones I recall from the days in the tenements—the ones hanging there for dear life by the precarious opposing side pressure caused by the ancient casements. The longer I lay there and focused on the mechanized sound, the less abstract it became. The vacuum in my mind played unmercifully on my depleted emotional state of being.

I began to envision the window unit as one of countless imprisoned alien robots from a moon near one of Saturn's rings. We brought them here to do our bidding because of their unique skill of processing and exchanging hot air for cold. What we didn't know was how much pain and distress was caused when the small, square mechanical creatures used their extra-terrestrial skill outside of their natural environment. The sound of keeping us cool was actually their sustained and anguished cries—the dripping water outside was what we call tears. If I continued such insane thinking for one more minute, I'd have blown my fucking brains out. It was way past time for me to get vertical from endless days of depression-flooded squirmy sleep. This rental was now my new home, for the time being.

Myr, who took away my life in 1962, seeped back into my daily conscience and topped my obsessions. It wasn't the typical flashbacks reliving every detail. Those memories were random and uncontrollable. I had to be patient and wait for such events to pass. I was dwelling on it during idle time, which seemed to be every minute I wasn't working.

The guilt I wore for never bringing him to justice increased when I considered the very real possibility that he was a serial pedophile. I feared I may have contributed to untold numbers of kids suffering the same fate as me, or worse. The pressure of this shame, coupled with severe adjustment depression stemming from the break-up of my marriage and family, was becoming too much to bear.

Then came the day of reckoning. I sat at my office desk and made the decision to track down my killer and take justice into my own hands. It was the only way I could achieve liberation from the knowledge he was still out there destroying untold lives. Killing him wouldn't erase my memories, but his removal from this world would be a good start to my healing process. I figured out a plan to accomplish my goal, and it would start with contacting the sexual crimes unit of the Prince George's County Police. The officer in charge took the information to track him down: name, approximate age (which in 2007 would have been around 65), where the assaults occurred, and all of my personal information. Before we ended the conversation, he assured me with a trace of emotional tremolo in his voice that he would find him.

When I returned to my desk, the phone rang and it was the investigator. He said, "I have good news and I have bad news. The good news is I found him; the bad news is that he's six feet under." I felt like I had the wind knocked out me. He allowed me a few moments to regain my composure, and then he continued, "He died in a car accident in 1988. According to my records, he had a wife and daughter."

I asked what would have been my recourse if they had arrested him and brought him dragging and squirming on his hands and knees to face charges. The officer said because of the era in which the crime occurred, he would face the penalty as it would have existed in 1962—a maximum of one year and one day. The irony was too much to take.

I was about to put into action a plan that would have forever removed a husband and a father from the lives of two innocent people. In the end, his death saved me from forcing myself to make the choice of going against every moral and ethical value I held dear to the sanctity of life. His fate may have saved him from a long, painful, and inglorious end.

...The Stone Remains Intact

I REMAINED FOR A LONG time in a state of confusion, with reason and feelings besting for the main stage of my own interior dime museum. For some reason, I reconnected with Candace Carpenter—distant, but familiar and safe. More than 25 years came and went since our time entangled in the lower reaches of the Spiral, which had started in D.C. and ended at Berklee.

The first thing I told her was how her brother Jay showed up at my gig at the Jazz Café at The Smithsonian Museum in Washington, in February of 2003. Instead of approaching me head-on with a "long time, no see" embrace, he ambushed me from behind whispering, "Mom always wished it was you who married Candy." Her response was a combination of nervous laughter and a dismissal of the teasing from an older brother at both of our expenses.

However, teasing was not restricted to Jay's well-intended greeting. Candace was still teasing and poking at her caged devils as I continued spending precious resources to house and feed mine. Our injured state of being in the early days had far more in common than we were aware, or were too scared to admit, which made us unsuited to ever enjoy a solid long-term romantic relationship. Candace chose to return to the land of her outer space and under-water pioneering father and paternal ancestors, to live a quiet life as a mountain woman in Northern Colorado, playing her instrument and teaching privately. I was living alone in a yak-less urban yurt in Brookline. The noise in our minds was mighty tremendous.

November rolled around and I gave online dating one more turn of the wheel. I was a bit more at ease and working things out. A woman appeared on the site who caught my immediate attention. Her photo was quite fetching, with no pretense of "I'm-actually-10-years-older-than-this-picture." There was a soul-soothing look in her eyes and a quality in her face that brought to mind the ancient appeal of the proportional beauty found in nature's golden ratio.

Kathleen was her name and she was only three years younger than me. This was the woman I would marry in six short years. In no time, I could tell she was the most well-rounded woman I ever met. Her father's goal was to raise his children with the confidence to function well in any social situation—from years of season tickets to the Boston Symphony, to season tickets for most of the Boston professional sports teams, and everything in between.

If Kathy had lived in 1888, I believe she would hold no fear of any man at the saloon card table, and if further evidence of her fearlessness among the cowboy rabble needed proof, she would not hesitate to drink whisky from a boot before departing with her winnings.

Kathy was, in many respects, the opposite of my mother, but she shouldered the same challenges of divorce and single motherhood. She helped me put to rest the old cliché that men attach themselves to women who share the same traits as their mothers. With few exceptions, I lived with that error in judgment for too many years. By the age of 54, I wanted to sober up and focus my standards with greater objectivity. Here was one more fighting chance to discover whether true and lasting love was going to be a reality for me, in whatever time I had remaining to negotiate the twists, turns, overlaps, and echoes in my life. I worked to avoid the traps and pitfalls of the redundancies of pleonastic tautologies within the Spiral. After all, as time tightens, it decreases to fill the space allotted for one's conclusions.

After our first year together, I gave up the yak-less yurt and relocated to the edge of the Earth. The spot we found on the east bank of the South River was nearly perfect. Kathy taught me the joys of paddling around a constantly dynamic tidal river, amidst getting lost in all of the sea grass labyrinths and tide pools collecting at their terminal points. I never imagined serenity as having a liquid surface that rises and falls under the power of the moon. This was the perfect location to feel the change from here to there to here and back again.

The Spiral Is A Fickle Prick

KATHY AND I WENT TO Statesville, North Carolina to visit Carol and Dad for a few days so that she could meet them and begin to get acquainted. She was an instant hit with both, despite Dad's continued slide into permanent oblivion with alcohol, his chosen tool of self-destruction.

Two remarkable events occurred, one of which was the perfect summation of Dad's fortunes in life, and parabolic of his own trials and travails in the Spiral. He wanted to explain to me why he left the working world, from a profession known as a tin man—a seller of aluminum siding and storm windows. His territory was throughout the Mid-Atlantic region. His earlier attempts to sell for a living, starting with life insurance during the Greenbelt years, wasn't something he was ready to embrace. He had to mature into it, whereby all of his other attempts at making a living, both legal and not so legal, got him where he landed.

The end of his working life began with a huge lead his boss threw him for a siding and window job. Unlike a typical cold call, this customer was waiting for the final turn of the screw. Dad's boss told him travel time required going to a very remote location on Maryland's Eastern Shore. After getting lost for the better part of the day, he made it to his destination by sunset, many hours after his expected arrival. This was already a strike against him because the client was pissed off and reluctantly agreed to give up his supper time to see this through.

Hungry and tired, Dad dragged in all of the heavy metal and glass samples needed to close this sale. The client was in no mood to be hospitable, but Dad kept his professional demeanor and went through his formal introduction. The man, who was much older than Dad, extended his hand for a reluctant handshake and gave Dad an odd look when he heard the name Stan Rochinski. It was as if he knew him from the distant past.

The evening wore on and Dad's blood sugar was dropping to dangerous levels. The old man was growing weary of the stranger in his living room. An hour passed with Dad doing his best to close the deal and was visibly sweating. The client seemed primed and ready to sign the contract and turn over a sizable deposit. A moment before he took the pen from Dad's hand, the client excused himself from the room for several minutes. This made Dad nervous—he didn't know if this guy had gone to bed and fallen asleep, or had gone to the toilet and fallen asleep, or worse, died on the throne. The old man returned holding a loaded revolver. The first words out of the man's mouth were, "It was you. It was you, you lousy son of a bitch."

My father sat there stunned, paralyzed with fear waiting for the hammer to drop. He was able to squeak out an airless, high-pitched squeal of a question. "Mister, I don't know what the fuck you're talking about, but who do you think I am?"

His reply was quick and concise. "You're the dirty bastard who held up my little girl when you robbed that Lenders Loan Company in Langley Park back in 1959. I always knew that someday I would see you again. Now, I'm going to do what I always said I would do."

Before he could squeeze off a shot, Dad figured the only way he could hope to get out of this alive was to fake a coronary. He let out a blood-draining scream and grabbed his left arm. The old man jolted back to his senses for a moment and he dropped the revolver. That's when Dad keeled over and landed on the coffee table, which shattered into several large pieces.

He didn't move. He even tried rolling his eyes in the back of his head when the wife kneeled down to check his pulse. The old man sat there cussing and wondering out loud if he should go ahead and shoot him anyway—put this poor bastard out of everyone's misery. His wife called an ambulance and was told to keep him warm until they could arrive. The old detective explained to his wife that Dad was the one who held up their daughter all those years ago. Dad's name sounded familiar, and he made the distant connection in his age-addled memory.

When the old man had left the room, he called his daughter to verify the name, which she never forgot. He told her the skinny, blond kid who robbed her was now a fat, sweaty, middle-aged diabetic sitting in his living room trying to sell him aluminum and storm windows worth thousands of dollars.

Other than Dad pissing himself, along with a bruised shoulder, the only thing he left behind and forever on that killing floor was his pride and ego. For someone who always put the odds at winning a bet on the long shot hooked to a sure thing, he saw this as a sure sign it was time to stop and spend his remaining days golfing before spinal stenosis and sepsis would have the final word.

On our last night of the visit, after one of Carol's memorable Southern dinners, Dad and I sat at the kitchen table indulging in some alcohol-infused stream-of-conscious bullshitting. I told him the story of my first encounter with the ladybug I saved at the edge of the pool in 1977. My ladybug encounter didn't impress him, until I told him the second part, when she returned to me more than two decades later during the train ride into work the morning after 9/11.

I could see through his spifflicated eyes he found the connection to be a remarkable coincidence, none the more. Without dropping a beat, in perfect segue fashion, there was a small disturbance in the lampshade hanging over the table. I stood up and gently reached up to retrieve the ladybug caught in the spell of the light. She settled on my right thumb, near the web, and the (12!) insignia slowly appeared and took on the translucent reddish-orange hue of carnelian. The combined look of fear, confusion, and wonderment in his eyes was like nothing I've ever seen. He got up without saying another word, and staggered into bed.

———

AT THE END OF SEPTEMBER, 2011, Carol summoned Kathy, Anna, Alex, and me to Statesville to see Dad for one last time. On the trip down, I reflected on his life and the choices he made, the chances he squandered, and what motivated him to keep on living the way he did, but most importantly, that he allowed himself to seek some level of redemption as a father. This part of his character always stood in stark contrast to Mom's. She would die believing she was always right and the rest of the world, and especially those closest to her, were always wrong.

I believe Dad wanted only the best for Karen and me. He proved that when given the choice to let Karen live or die at the time of her birth. The gamble he took in making that decision was a losing bet. Karen's demons, both pathological and emotional, would be her downfall and would lead to the most painful experience in Dad's life: she disowned him, never to hear one another's voice again.

His pain cut the deepest when Karen died in November of 2009 as a ward of the state, with her son and daughter as the only ones at her side when the doctor pulled the plug. Karen always had someone in the family at the ready to assist her to turn around her life, but it always had to be on her terms, and that was unacceptable to those at the ready. Mom was the one person she should have always avoided, and yet, she was the one to whom Karen always gravitated.

My sister never knew what she wanted in this world, and was always trapped in the terrible midst of things. She was living proof of how chasing the seductive mirage of the infinite distance between the inseparable boundary of the opposite-facing mirrors of here and there, will, in the end, leave you with neither.

After Karen died, Dad suffered one personal loss after another. Little did he know that the one who stayed by his side since 1964 was suffering a major emotional and physical toll in caring for a man who had nothing left to live for: Carol's cancer was slowly making a comeback in many other forms, but she never let on.

We arrived at the final nursing facility to give Dad a bed. This one was lower rent, and it came with all of the attendant smells and look of imminent death. Carol made his tiny, single room as comfortable and homey as possible. She posted a copy of a picture of Alex and me with Dad in the middle—three of countless generations of Rochinski men, two with a story to tell and one with many stories to come. One detail about that picture I never brought to his attention was that Alex was the same age as he when I was born.

Eventually, Dad and I were the only ones in the room. After a long silence, he turned his head to me and clearly whispered, without stammer or hesitation, what would be the last three words he would ever say to his only son. "It's a motherfucker." Plain in its brevity, simple in its structure, direct in its truth, and timeless in its verifying power of hindsight. If I had my way, I would have included his three little words on his gravestone.

On the evening of October 3rd, 2011, at seven o'clock, I got the call from Carol. Dad closed his eyes, made the Quarter Turn, let out his final breath, and went his separate way.

ANNA AND ALEX LOVED THEIR granddaddy, and their loss was poignant—it was Anna's first time ever seeing a human corpse, laid out in the traditional overcompensating fashion of the undertaker's art. Alex, along with me, was conscripted as a pallbearer because they were short on young, able-bodied men to handle the gravity of Dad's casket. As we turned to leave the graveside, I turned to my son, pulled him in close, looked him in the eyes, and said, "You and I have now moved one step closer to our own mortality."

To my father, I was his child-man, becoming a man-child, becoming a father, becoming a man. I allowed him to express his love for me, as the cost of whatever happiness he received for any goodness I brought to his life. He accepted my forgiveness with unspoken gratitude; to relieve at least some of his pain from a self-examined life filled with resignation, as the push back to any responsibility and willingness to change how he lived. After 80 times around the solar bubble, my father, Stanley James Rochinski Jr., Sonny to his mother, father, and friends, left a life imbued with regret and great self-loathing, where the only true forgiveness he ever knew came from me.

Transitional Interface

KATHY AND I CONTINUED TO live a semi-vagabond life moving from one spot on the river to the next. We married on January 19 of 2013, Kathy's 56th birthday and one day short of my 59th. Carol's presence at the wedding drew the most attention from me. Among the flashes of joy and pride through her smiles and bright-eyed tears, the complex of emotions in her lined and aging face brought to mind that I was the last connection she had to a life she started with Dad nearly 50 years before. She was also harboring a secret that would allow her only a few more years in the world. As anyone who has reached past the age of 50 knows, a year becomes nothing more than a slow-moving month in the perception of time's unremitting power as the solitary agent of change.

A Pleo-Blast From The Neo-Plast

THE RELATIONSHIP BETWEEN PLEONASM AND neoplasm is semantic perfection.
Both words convey the presence of excess. The former is a nuisance for an editor
and, unless you are a salamander seeking to replace a tail sacrificed to a curious
cat, the latter can result in spending a few bucks on wart remover, or it will just
plain kill you, especially when you're not looking.

For nearly 40 years, my race with rising and falling PSA numbers eventually ran its course. I conceded to my new primary care doctor that I would
schedule a prostate biopsy.

The pre-op release forms I signed included my understanding that I faced a
one-in-450 chance of contracting an infection. Out of over one million biopsies
performed each year, those odds, as my father would say, were not too good. I
knew the names of the bad actors lining up to put in their bids for hosting the
infection rager of the year, and the duke and duchess of Escherichia were at the
head of the line. I laid low and did what I was told.

On Sunday, September 22nd, 2013, I began a rapid process of dying and
leaving this world. Time was working against me. With each passing minute,
my vital signs continued seeking the threshold of no return. Maybe I'd be the
one to get God's rare call for a front seat in His crash tests in the afterlife after
all. At the very least, I could do the clean-up from the previous eternity's work.

I was in full-blown septic shock. My blood pressure dropped to a fatal
level. Despite my delirium, my recollection of the details of this moment seals
forever my awareness of being poised at the moment of pre-liminality. With the
skill and determination of the two surgeons attending to me, I could still turn
back and resume living to see another day. My fate was now in their hands, as
this death tango continued with time fast running out to save my life.

I moved to the critical ICU where I now faced an 80 percent chance of dying. No matter who I was, or who I thought I was, or who I thought I should be, I landed hard on the bottom of a physical underworld from which many never return. My life for the next five days was entirely in the hands of strangers trained to treat the sick and dying as the most important people in their world.

Against all of her doctor's orders about healing her recent surgical wounds, Kathy never left my side. She slept each night in what looked like a chair from Caligula's waiting room. Kathy asked Anna and Alex to stay put unless some drastic change occurred. Carol was kept entirely out of the loop to protect her from worry. Marked time owned the night.

———

THE VIVIDNESS OF THE WORLD beyond the unconscious was without equal. This was no ordinary dream-state. The electrical impulses in my brain must have blown out whatever organic function is comparable to a step-down transformer. Every sensation I ever processed through my five senses was now riding bare-back on a waveform of irrepressible energy: living, life-sized, three dimensional, beyond-dystopian dioramas appeared, colored in a narrow range of shades of gray. There was no quarter for me to take refuge. I had no power to repel what appeared before me, but only to stand and face each image on its own terms.

What looked like quarry rubble was strewn across a barren landscape with no horizon, in tightly packed, random and jagged clusters. Each collection looked like Picasso took a wrecking ball to a line of megaliths. In the center of each cluster was a small, rafted group of men and boys, diminished in size, resembling a drawing by an eight year old without lifting the pen from the paper. The only action they could perform was a slow, nearly motionless attempt to crawl among the formations.

I tried avoiding eye contact with the only one looking in my direction, but that was impossible. No matter how I positioned my head or body, closed my eyes, or covered my face, the image was always the same, as if it was generated internally, or as if I was looking at my face and into my own eyes without a mirror.

The others had their backs turned, or positioned in a side profile. It was always the same small group from one rubble cluster to the next. If I tried moving around an obstacle to gain a different vantage point of their faces, the image always remained the same. The feelings I intercepted from any single figure were always different, regardless of how many different places in which they appeared.

There was no door anywhere near me through which to escape. I was trapped at the center of the Deep Eldritch. The only exit was far ahead of me, where a horizon suddenly appeared. I feared I would have to face each individual in the clusters before I could get to the other end. I felt a strangely familiar, uncanny desire to press forward without hesitation—the same feeling I had long ago, as a four year old standing at the backdoor of the burned-out house in Greenbelt.

A moment of profound clarity came over me. What I faced in this unrivaled landscape was my penultimate point of arrival in the Spiral. I had to confront each of the male images as representing the Parts—the shards of my soul struggling to regain an identity in relation to the Whole from which they splintered.

I acknowledged them as the outcome of every deliberate act imposed against my will by another—everyone from those closest to me, all the way to the annihilators, and everyone in between. My challenge was to extricate and set aside every choice I ever made, in response to every action as the result of those decisions, and weighed against the entirety of my life.

Now ensnared in the web of some cellular, emotional manifestation of the Harmonic Series, I recalled that every Partial has the capacity to become a new Fundamental, which in turn, can generate new Partials. I had to separate and reabsorb only those deserving my focus. If I made the mistake of reabsorbing every Part, all of the Good would retreat to the dark shadows of the Evil where the differences to me would hold no distinction. My life would take a path of self-destruction from which I and everyone in my wake would never recover.

I had to reject and cast away the Inharmonics—to spin themselves through an extrinsic path that only I could determine, until they reached their maximum point of unattainability, with no other choice but to self-detonate out of existence.

I was becoming the Whole that was about to complete the perfect interaction with every choice I ever made, with only one good choice remaining—to do so now, before this waveform dissipated and forever took on new and unknown forms of energy. Whatever was left standing would take on a life of its own, where Evil becomes the Lesser Good and trust becomes a hyperinflated currency that can't be spent. Time was fast running out. Any further delay and I would never return. I would be forever imprisoned to intrinsically abide among these self-created images in a limited-range grey and interstitial world. I closed my dream eyes and began the process of Recombination— my last choice remaining to recover the true Timbre of my Soul.

The Real

I DON'T HOW MUCH TIME had passed. It may have been one extreme or the other. The image standing before me was the same spectacular and unimaginable vision I saw at the edge of the swimming pool in the summer of 1976, as my life interlaced with the life of the ladybug. This time, she stood the same height as an average adult woman. All of her coleopteran features were gone, except for one: she still possessed her fiery, moon-adorned elytra, but it was now fused, making flight impossible. Her elytra fit like a gown with a cape. Her face was a staggering combination of features taken from the most important women in my life over the last 65 years. She was the most beautiful woman I ever saw.

The unearthly hues were no longer confined to her wings. All of the colors from our first encounter were present. They emanated from her entire being, illuminating the space we shared. The colors passed through me and returned to pure, unfiltered white light of immeasurable candle power. As she reabsorbed the white light, it once again became the colors, only with each return, they grew more and more vivid. We were now caught in an ineffable, unending energy loop with a reverse prism effect. The intensity defied description.

I flashed back to my first encounter with her when I heard every pitch in the chromatic scale sounding in succession, but now, it took the form of a playback of every note I ever created; the unending stream of the sonic purity I always reach for, but never captured full in the moment. It had the logic and continuity I always reached for, but at the moment I fell short of what I wanted to hear. It carried the elusive minimum of eight measures of perfection of choice and continuity that all improvisers live and die for, and on rare occasions, are able to carve out of thin air and reach beyond the limits of eight. But now, the great lines came nonstop, spinning, and intoning from all directions.

The rare sensation of pneutralalia returned and washed over me—an incomparable feeling that could reduce sexual relief to the mundane—as nothing more than the finger of God reaching down and tickling me from the inside. It was the same arousal as when I launched into the Marian blue Greenbelt sky and the cocooning blanket waiting for my return, so many lifetimes ago.

Under normal circumstances, I would have by now awoken from this as a natural consequence of having nowhere left to go. My dream state persisted to push me beyond the Deep Eldritch and into the Real. I wasn't in the presence of a lost or dying ladybug. I was now face to face with the Oracle-poet Ladybird.

I stood there, sublimated in wonder and awe, and listened as she spoke. She knew every detail of every moment of my existence. She offered no explanations, no reasons, or apologies for the soul-draining actions imposed on me in my childhood. She never judged the choices I made in response to the choices of others.

I could feel the struggle between my subconscious wanting to remain indefinitely in her presence, and my conscious desire to awaken from this oneiric world. The Ladybird closed her eyes as she felt my struggle taking hold. She whispered with an unusual syntax; part poetic, part prosaic:

With your breath on my wings, it was I you saved from the cast
    back water—
From a far-off distance, I could hear the sounds you destined to hear
In the emerging surges of pulse to pitch stirring within and throughout you
Long before you were ready to bear the final formations sent to you
To shape the sonic matter so that what remained would lay bare all of
    life's proportions
Whispering and seeking justification in the Real—
Turbulent partials of your divided Fundamental gathered me to your
    destination
Steeped in oblivion beyond the edge of a Spiral Pool—
You wondered quite quietly if this was a moment of concurrence, or
If I was the Lone Ladybird on Earth, willing on that summer day

To surrender herself as a means to entice your consideration—

For my reason alone, I came to retrieve you, to recover you, to deliver you

But it was you who held out to save me, not as an act of ease or burden

But as an act of perfection—to honor that which mattered to you alone—

Without ever knowing that saving me would become your lifetime salvation

You chose to follow reason into your heart, as I knew you would

Reaching down and gently lifting us from a bound and early end—as
only you could

With your breath on my wings, my first offering of gratitude

Revealed the Source of what you, and all who hear the minor third
reciprocate,

Spending your lifetime receiving, and in turn, sending on and sending on

For the Love and Joy of the Synchronous Parts and their Whole

Not for the glory of vanity, but for the need of precision to feed your
captive soul

Without question, you heard it early and well—

So, my invitation of embrace beneath my Fiery Elytra

Was the one and only path for you to reach my Wings

Where the secrets of the (12!) were kept and told—

A Man of His Time

TIME UNDER THE ENERGY BEAM was short, yet the passing of time is irrelevant when you are staring into the waters of Lethe. Seven-hundred-and-twenty individual points of entry awaited the selective commands from unseen technicians inside the unseen control booth; just another multi-million-dollar video game. I knew some serious shit was about to begin when they lowered the lights to house-to-half Broadway theater dimness. It was time to start the show.

Once my eyes adjusted to the change of light, tiny and randomly placed hand-painted day-glow stars came into view on the ceiling, presumably for calming and distracting the patient. I distracted myself by imagining the six strings of my guitar running through this private little universe, as I looked for chord forms created by the grid to be sung silently in my head.

The energy from the linear accelerator penetrated and threaded its way into my body, with a focus of unimaginable precision and solitary purpose—to incinerate every goddamned renegade cell plotting inside their prostatic haven. The destruction of the malignancy would not come without a price: the ultimate destruction of the capsule that served as loyal and unfailing transportation for every drop of the human genome reaching back to the beginning of time, to do my willful bidding for every choice ever made in servitude to my libido. A very old and dear friend was about to go the gallows. I said a quiet goodbye, a thank you, and a fuck you with a tear.

A harsh lesson set me a long and lonely banquet table, with only a single one-legged stool with the mandatory footrests. A temporary chemically castrated existence was the only condition where I could partake in this revelatory feast with total objectivity and clarity. Libido took on a new and far broader meaning beyond sexual desire. Libido as a proper noun, the grandest sense of desire for all that makes life worth living, the nearly unpronounceable *zmysły życia*—the senses of life—as my paternal Polish ancestors would have described it.

I had no desire to do the one thing that has sustained me, that which has formed and held me for as far back as I can remember. The sad truth was I had no desire to do anything—neutered and neutralized, and left with only memories of seemingly endless sexual conquests. Living in medias res—neither here nor there—thrust into an epicene existence that took on the feel and weight of a living purgatory, with hell living next door as a very noisy nosey neighbor, and heaven as an absentee landlord living on a tiny, uncharted island.

Memories of sexual encounters going back through the decades brought me feelings of disgust, shame, and utter detestation. Any acknowledgement of an attractive woman went from the provocative richness and warmth of a multi-dimensional experience, to a cold, flat, one-dimensional image. This neutralized state of sexual being carried over to Kathy and that was a sad and painful reality I could not stand, with seemingly no end in sight.

The ties and shackles of two major transformative moments in my life left me in the lonely position to both ask and answer the questions, beginning with the sexual predators of my childhood lurking everywhere, existing in all shapes, ages, sizes, and stations in life; followed by conceits disguised as absolutes from the Headmen of the Village in the Woods—the champion apologists of the belief that every weakness exists to exploit for your own power and ego; that sex is the only true and lasting value and is the basis of all human interaction. The worst fiction promulgated by Aaron's enlightened cynicism was that there are only two kinds of females—the kind who like it and the kind who lie about it.

Every variation defined by the ever-fluid boundaries of those two transformative extremes played like badly composed counterpoint—weak and derivative themes, dominated by insufficient resolution of overwrought tension becoming an abstraction seeking its own identity, with no attribution to that which came before, or to that which will inevitably follow. Reductionism was the gold standard for all post-modern subjectivism in a world well beyond any capacity to recover and return.

Three years into my barren interior existence, the toll it took on Kathy was no small effect, but she always stayed committed. I thought to myself, *for the first time in my life, as I faced death head-on, I finally trusted someone without reservation.* She always remained true and never out of my mind and heart.

There were only two material desires for happiness on which Kathy stood: to live near the water, and to have a dog, either one or the other. We accomplished both.

Jacob, our Havanese, was a welcome and needed addition to our lives. I never before had a dog, and I made mistakes learning how to raise and train him. I found myself treating him like an over-protected toddler—a throwback to young and anxious fatherhood and a generous dose of projections of my overcompensating need for resolution. His calming presence and marvelous, loving character was a way for us to deflect our attention from ourselves to a smart and happy little creature, who needed us as much as we wanted him.

I never imagined that a dog would have such a salient and profound impact on my feelings and day-to-day life. For me and Jacob, it comes down to this: a dog existing and sharing in a human world is all this tiny and helpless creature will ever be. Any evolution of personal conceptual and emotional growth, as found in the best of people, would never be his reality.

His motivation for certain types of behavior and interaction in his adopted pack is in direct response to the sounds of our voices and the looks on our faces—no reasoning, no thinking, only the ancient responses to his most basic sensory instincts. In light of the choices I have made in a lifetime, I can relate to the meaning in what voices and eyes reveal behind the intentions. So, I will make his life a part of mine and as happy as possible while doing my best to train both of us about certain constraints and boundaries. The demands of the natural order of the wolf pack don't easily translate across the species, but we seem to find our way.

Kathy and I were equal partners to find the perfect spot to land our life after years of low-fuel circling over the edge of the Earth. This will likely be the last place I lay my head in life, knowing full well that in the end, we all will have to go our separate ways.

Now, I'm perched on my interior tangent of the Spiral that has been a haunting, constant unending looping presence in the deepest reaches of my life from the day I escaped my mother's impassive womb. For the time being I'm safe from the flood zone—full circle in three dimensions, where up and down are all around. I'm left with one final conclusion on the entirety of my life: *surviving the attacks does not guarantee surviving the recovery.*

As I await the return one day of the Oracle-poet Ladybird, the words that eluded me when I was in her presence have finally found their rightful place, in order and meaning. I hope that she will one day hear my words:

How I so much wanted to confess for those who ambushed my heart, body, and soul.
Not to cry, but with my instrument in hand,
To keep pressing on with the follow-through.
It all began so very long ago,
When I climbed down from the mass of another's life gone up in flames,
Where upon a time, I claimed a jewel crowning a world in ruin.
After all I've said and done, there's nothing left to run to or from.
As I listen in hard-won silence for the next song, I take great comfort that one day
I'll close my eyes a gentle man, knowing that I have loved.

Sitting with Kathy and Jake, on a perfectly warm August day, looking at the fish pond with all of the frogs making their way from here to there, under the calming rush of small, recirculating waterfalls, the idea to put all of this down on paper swirls and spirals throughout my mind and rests against my shuttered fontanel…yeah…maybe some other time.

About the Author

STEVE ROCHINSKI IS AN INDEPENDENT JAZZ musician, educator, recording artist, composer, arranger, and author. He is a Professor Emeritus of harmony at Berklee College of Music in Boston. Over his more than 35 years on Berklee's faculty, he has earned an international reputation for being pretty good at what he does. In 2014, Steve received the Berklee Distinguished Faculty Award. He currently resides with his wife, Kathy, and their dog, Jacob, near the edge of the earth in Southeastern Massachusetts.

Acknowledgments

I WISH TO EXPRESS MY unvarnished gratitude to Kris Stoever (Carpenter) and Matt Riley for their commitment to this book, as expressed by their objective insights and world-class professional skills in the early reading and draft editing stages Also, to Virtual Graphic Solutions for invaluable help in realizing the final design concept of the cover..

To all of the survivors-in-hiding: it's time to come out of the shadows, rise above victimhood, and reclaim what has always been yours—your life.